PLAIN
TEACHING

A Conversation with Colleagues

Dear Eddie,
My Good Brother,
Keep on inspiring our youth
(and keep on coaching
and singing!)

Agape,
Carl

08/13/92

Plain Teaching

A Conversation with Colleagues

Including
49 Lessons
On Becoming
A Positive Teacher

Carl R. Boyd

Westport Publishers, Inc.

Kansas City, Missouri

Cover Design: Noelle Kaplan, finedesign

ISBN 0-933701-56-X

Library of Congress Catalog #91-50136

The text of this book was transcribed from the author's
The Art of Positive Teaching *lectures.*

Printed in the United States of America

Dedication

To Gladys Frieson, one of my first students, who asked in 1965:

"Mr. Boyd, are you really going to write about us?"

Well, Gladys, it's only 26 years later. This book for teachers is to you, and, indeed, about you and millions of students—deserving of our love, and our best—like you.

Table of Contents

Teachers' Voluntary Oath
of Professionalism and Service

UNDERSTANDING the peculiar nature of the profession of teaching;

THAT IT IS NOT a field to be entered into lightly, nor an occupation compatible with ordinary personalities;

KNOWING that young minds and young hearts are immediately and lastingly affected by my actions in and out of the classroom.

THAT THOSE MINDS and hearts, and the personalities shaped around them, deserve the highest and greatest opportunity to learn what it takes, and how, to make this world more peaceful and purposefully productive in a learning atmosphere that is caring, competent, and consistent;

EXPECTING outstanding achievement from those I teach, and demanding outstanding effort from myself; and

BELIEVING that teaching is not an adversarial occupation but, rather, an "advocational" profession serving the educational needs of those under our charge and the social needs of a world longing for love,

I HEREBY voluntarily take this oath of professionalism, pledging to be the best teacher I know how to be, striving ever to be a better teacher than I've ever been, and putting the needs of my students—their learning, their social growth, their futures—as my first priority for as long as I am a teacher.

FINALLY, I pledge to continuously, honestly, evaluate my performance and attitude toward my work, and when I fall below my own standards of competence and care, I shall respectfully seek purposeful work elsewhere.

Date: _____ Signed:_____

This Oath of Professionalism is only as binding
as those who take it make it.

Acknowledgments

My wife, Wonderful Wanda, for being wonderful through my irregular dictation, lecturing, and writing schedule, and for unceasing support.

Terry Faulkner of Westport Publishers, Inc. for, first, accepting (even suggesting) the idea of a "conversation" in book form; and second, for patient assistance in seeing it through.

To Budgetyping for transcribing what must have sounded like one, endless, run-on sentence in places, and a series of unintelligible colloquialisms in other places.

Brenda Lyle-Gray for consistent, continuous encouragement, as a board member of The Art of Positive Teaching and as a friend.

Jawanza Kunjufu for lengthy conversations about format and quality.

Barb Friedmann and Cheri Brooks, who through the BASE project introduced me to Westport Publishers, Inc.

Ron Poplau whose invitation to Ottawa University launched this lecture series, and, Charles and Pat Jackard, who gave it national visibility.

Ruth Alderson, chairperson of The Art of Positive Teaching's first advisory board.

* * *   * * *

Thanks also to the following who have allowed me to present "Nobody Rises to Low Expectations" (sometimes more than once) for their school districts or organizations:

Jon Paden with the IDEA Fellows Institute;

Larry Ascough of Dallas, Texas;

Carrie Chevalier, Superintendent of Schools
    in Naples, Maine;

Jerry Thornsberry, Associate Superintendent of Schools in Grandview, Missouri;

Loyce Carruthers with McCREL;

JoAnne Evans with the Harvey, Illinois schools;

Mercedes Rubin in Cleveland, Ohio;

Jerry Jones In Topeka, Kansas;

Ray Richardson in Waterloo, Iowa;

Gloria Thompson of the Mississippi State Department of Education;

Lynn Jamot in Englewood, New Jersey;

Trevor Gardner at Eastern Michigan University;

Kathy Zecchino from Granger, Washington;

Adrianne Bills, senior high student and summer secretary for typing all of the final segment of this book;

Dr. Bob Brazil, my principal and mentor;

and the teachers from J.S. Chick, Faxon, and Kumpf elementary schools in Kansas City, Missouri who put singing into my lecture series;

and David L. Griffin, Sr., APT Board member and number one supporter of the Art of Positive Teaching.

Preface

$50,000 for 50 Good Reasons:—Why Teachers Should Be Compensated—For the Many Things They Do

I want to begin with a subject that I think is very serious, although it might appear that I'm being facetious.

Teachers entering the profession should receive by 1991 Kansas City standards, $50,000 a year starting pay. And there are 50 good reasons for arriving at this summary.

Reason #1: Because teachers are required to be arbitrators—labor relations managers, if you will. Just in the course of teaching school, teachers are required to resolve disputes, bring arguing factions together, make some sense out of the arguments that are presented and attempt to get both sides to see another's point of view. In fact, oftentimes when we are in the classroom talking to young people about arguments that they have, we insist that they be left alone until they can make friends with each other by saying something like "... and when you return to this classroom, I want you to return with a smile on your face, and I want you to be able to shake hands with each other, and to apologize to the class for disrupting their learning while you were arguing about something that was probably quite small."

Without any particular training in conflict resolution, a natural aspect of being a teacher is to be an arbitrator. When we go into the classroom we realize that one of the things that is absolutely critical in assisting young people in learning what they need to know is a classroom climate that prevents chaos and fosters harmony. This cannot be done if young people find petty things about which to argue: "He grabbed my pencil", "She looked at me in a strange way." Or, the young people who seem to come to school to find reasons to argue about different things such as: "She called me on the phone last night and said something unkind to my parents." A teacher not only resolves conflicts, but must do it expeditiously because he or she does not have as much time to concentrate on the subject at hand as he or she would like. Therefore, teachers do a good job of resolving conflict in non-violent ways and also do it quickly in order to get back to the work that they think is important.

Reason #2: Because teachers are CEOs—Chief Executive Officers. Teachers are responsible for maintaining some degree of rapport, not only teacher to student, but also in developing relationships, student to student, in order that they might work together so that all can learn and learn well.

Chief Executive Officers are people-movers. They delegate responsibility. They are the people who are responsible not only for the management of affairs, but also for setting the tone. They have leadership qualities that are to be emulated by those who follow them, and teachers are expert at doing those things just by virtue of the fact that they are the classroom head and responsible for the young people in the classroom doing what it is that they are supposed to do. As CEOs of the classrooms that they manage, teachers have to come up with creative approaches toward achieving particular goals. In doing that, they work well with young people with all kinds of personalities, particularly in public school settings. Teachers must work with personalities that come to them without having the opportunity to pick and choose who their students will be. Teachers must be Chief Executive Officers, who at the end of the school year will develop the desired product—the passing of students who have understood, comprehended, and shown comprehension of all kinds of subject matter through getting good grades.

Reason #3: Because teachers must be excellent consultants. Not only are they consultants to the students whom they teach, but they are consultants to the students' parents because really good teachers are able to assist parents in understanding the roles that the parents might assume in assisting their children to do well in a particular class. In addition to being consultants to the students and consultants to the students' parents, teachers are also consultants to colleagues without being compensated for being consultants, as an outside consultant, for instance, would be. There are teachers who are expert at teaching methodologies that are simply practiced by intuition, where there are many others who practice due to a particular theory that they have researched for years or who are expert because they have matriculated in a particular discipline for 6, 8, or 10 years. Many teachers are able to get into the minds of the children whom they teach and understand what motivates those young people. They then consult with colleagues as to how best to get to some young people that they don't know or don't know very well.

Good consultants research what they do and also practice, and after they practice and become good at what they do, they pass that information on. *A teacher who does not pass the information on is really not a very good teacher.* Truly effective teachers are also effective consultants.

Reason #4: Because teachers are almost automatically counselors; and excellent teachers are indeed automatically counselors. Look at the difference between being a consultant and a counselor. There are consultants who come up with different approaches and methodologies and in a clinical fashion teach those methodologies, have the client population try them out, evaluate whether or not the trying out worked, and then add to that whatever is necessary in order to enhance that practice that they have introduced to the client population, whether it be the students, their colleagues, the students' parents, or others involved in the school community. But as a counselor, they not only provide consultation, but become confidants, if you will. As counselors, they not only present to a group of young people, but they are available for the one or two young people who need particular help or advice. Not only do they represent what they are teaching in an academic sense, but they are available to get into the personal problems of young people who want to share their problems. They begin to counsel in a way that helps students address their personal problems, but also if they are excellent counselors, they help students feel good enough about the teacher to come to the teacher with their problems in the first place. Students do not feel comfortable going to just anyone with their problems. As a matter of fact, removing the "just anyone," many students do not feel comfortable going to their parents with personal problems. And certainly, their parents are not "just anyone." But with that particular, personal, close, fragile relationship that they have with parents, the student may find it very difficult to penetrate the situation when it comes to sensitive, personal issues.

Where then, do many young people go? Many go to that teacher in whom they have a great deal of trust and confidence. When young people come to a teacher with personal problems (and they come because they have that trust and confidence) the teacher steps out of the teacher role and becomes a counselor. Also, many teachers in their counselor role do the formal kinds of things that counselors must do. For instance, a teacher might advise young people as to the path that they might follow in order to enhance their options as it pertains to subsequent education and career choices, and they will research colleges and careers for that student. Therefore, this suggests that teachers as counselors in an informal sense assume that role simply by request of young people who trust and confide in them.

Reason #5: Because teachers are demographers and sociologists as a result of having to go into the classroom and meet the requirements of the particular local school. Now what do I mean by demographers and sociologists? While teaching in a public school, it is absolutely imperative that certain records be kept correctly. Among those records, for instance, would be the number of young people in a particular classroom who come from a certain ethnic background. This is particularly important in the areas where desegregation is taking place and a particular quota, if you will, has been required of each of the schools participating in desegregation in order to meet the needs of the local community engaged in desegregating the schools. The demographic data, being very important, requires teachers then, to keep very meticulous records. Also, as demographers and as sociologists, teachers need to develop a sensitivity, not only to the numbers as it pertains to the diverse population in terms of ethnicity, and of socioeconomic level, but also in terms of the different personalities and fears that young people have when they are in a setting to which they have not yet grown accustomed. From the sociological standpoint, the teacher needs to explain that those differences are indeed positive and can indeed foster a harmonious whole.

From the sociological standpoint, the teacher must exemplify the appreciation for what diverse cultures can do in enhancing the climate for the whole population. Demographically, actual funding allocations depend upon the degree to which teachers can keep proper records while understanding demographic terminology and what its implications are as it pertains to making sure that things are done to enhance the client population.

Reason #6: Because teachers are designers. Nobody asked teachers to become designers, but if we want our bulletin boards to look the way they should, if we want the window sills to look the way they should, if we want a classroom that is conducive to learning and promotes cheerfulness among young people, we have to become interior designers as soon as we face four barren walls at the beginning of the school year. Teachers are natural interior designers without having taken courses in it because you can see by students' actions (and just by the way you feel personally when you are in that classroom) that there needs to be more color in the classroom, plants in the windows, etc.

Teachers must change their bulletin boards either because it is a requirement of the school administration to do so every month, or, in keeping with professionalism as it pertains to the number of units required to teach over the year, the bulletin boards must be changed with each unit. But if a unit lasts for a particularly long time, additional segments in the unit require bulletin board changing. Not only that, students get bored easily. With certain kinds of plants in the windows the students might like to change the positioning of the plants. So you will have students and teachers moving furniture and plants, changing bulletin boards, putting signs up on the wall, etc. And as holidays come around, there is a change in the scenery, in the classroom, and in the hall.

Now, the interesting thing is that many teachers become so good at being interior designers that they forget that it is an extra function. It's just a natural thing that they do. If they already have an assignment and they know what classroom they are going to have, they will come in before anybody else and immediately begin to think of what they are going to do with this classroom in order to stimulate the students' thinking. Many teachers are motivated by the fact that there are certain things that can be done in the classroom that will really make students become curious about what the bulletin board suggests or what that figure hanging from the ceiling is, or what the students want to do to take part in developing bulletin boards and signs and mobiles, etc. In the process, teachers design and teach students to design as well.

Reason #7: Because teachers are editors. Think about it. Whenever students are given an assignment, teachers not only grade the assignment based on its accuracy versus its inaccuracy, but teachers will also make corrections. Some of the best kinds of examinations in order to determine whether or not students really understand the assignment they are given, are essay examinations. In grading the essay examinations, not only are we looking for the content of the examination, we are also looking for the grammar. How do students say what it is they are trying to say? How well do they say it? (Even in the case of students who say what they say extremely well.)

I would suspect that 87% to 95% of teachers will suggest to the excellent student that they might want to change a sentence, or to place a paragraph above another paragraph rather than below it, and that's even for the youngsters who write well. Now, think about the editing job the teacher must do for those students who did not understand the assignment or perhaps write poorly. Teachers are editors, not only from the standpoint of content as it pertains to accuracy, but also from the standpoint of enhancing the ideas that students are putting forth in order that the next time they do an assignment they can become more creative or more accurate. Students can communicate with more enthusiasm and with more flair based on a teacher's editing practice. And by the way, just like the interior designer-teacher, the editor-teacher does it naturally. These are things that teachers must do whether they have gone to school for journalism or not; they are natural editors on a day-to-day basis without even considering the fact that it is what they are doing.

Reason #8: Because teachers are equal opportunity compliance officials. A teacher who is truly effective must be one who sees to it that every young person in his or her class is a young person who receives an equal opportunity to express himself or herself in that classroom. As an equal opportunity compliance official, it is necessary that the teacher be the person in the classroom who is objective and fair. (Remember Reason #1: Teachers are required to be arbitrators.) The teacher is the one to whom all students can look to make sure that where there is a problem, this person will figure it out and make sure that the solution to the problem is one that is equitable and fair for all in the classroom—whomever they are, from wherever they happen to come, whatever their parents earn, whatever the color of their skin, or whatever their religion. For example, "In my subgroup, when you divided us into groups, this person in the group got all of the gravy assignments, and I'm the one who got all of the cleanup assignments." The teacher says, "That is not a cleanup assignment and his is not a gravy assignment because here is how you can make cleanup into gravy." Or, "We will insure that the next time assignments are given out, you are the one with the gravy assignment and somebody else will be the one with the cleanup assignment." Or, the teacher will make sure that the entire class recognizes that as we dole out assignments, it is imperative that everyone get an opportunity to do all kinds of different things because we are interested in the growth of the whole person, and if you are going to be a whole person, you get an opportunity to do all kinds of things. Again, the teacher is the equal opportunity compliance official in that classroom because as young people are rewarded for effort the teacher makes sure that everyone is compensated properly for doing the same kind of job. There is no student, for instance, to whom the teacher would issue an "A" because they received an 89 rather than a 90-100, while explaining the "A" was given based upon ability, not upon performance. And likewise, another student that gets an 89 would then receive a "B" because they are just "B" students.

As an equal opportunity compliance official, the teacher monitors that kind of situation rather than perpetrates, and therefore, is the one to whom we all look to do it right and to straighten out a situation where somebody is being treated unfairly. As the exemplar in the class of fairness, objectivity, and encouragement for every student in the class, the teacher becomes an advocate in favor of every student's opportunity to achieve greatness.

Reason #9: Because all teachers are file clerks. Now every teacher in the U.S. can identify directly with #9. You are going to be a record keeper for every student you teach. You are going to not only keep files, but these files must be kept so meticulously that if there is a case that involves young people going to court, the court ought to be able to secure the files from you, and based upon **your** recordkeeping actually enter those as exhibits in court. For instance, if you look at student attendance records and there is a case that suggests that students were involved in something outside of school at a particular time on a particular day, then those records can be used in court to say that this indicates students were, indeed, in school. When you look at a student's abilities as he or she goes through school, it may be that there are some young people who are not at all living up to their potential. You might want to look back at the records and find out when a student began to do poorly what he or she was previously accomplishing in satisfactory fashion.

Teachers must keep records not only on students' behavior and academic abilities, but also on students' and their families' mobility; moving from community to community, state to sate, or transferring from school to school. As was indicated in the role of teacher as demographer, some of the files that must be kept deal with the socioeconomic level of students because for some students, the only meal that they get is the school meal, based upon the fact that they are below the poverty level, and therefore, they are eligible for free meals at school. Teachers keep all kinds of files on students, and they maintain those files for the length of time that the student is in their classroom, and then those files are passed on to the next level teacher. The student's records will go askew if the current teacher does not keep accurate files. Thus, a teacher, by virtue of the fact that all students deserve an accurate record of their performance, where they have lived, what they have been doing from the time they entered school, must be not only file clerks, but excellent file clerks.

And what the teacher keeps as far as classroom records are concerned have a profound effect on the records that are also kept in the office. As classroom teachers, there have been many times when we have been engaged in some pleasant activity, and a messenger has come from the office with a note from a clerical staff person reminding us that the records that were supposed to have been sent to the office a week ago are now later than they were when they were asked for two days ago!

Reason #10: Because teachers are great insurance sales people. I suggest that teachers are great insurance sales people because insurance is what we are attempting to sell the young people with whom we work on a day-to-day basis. If you are going to be a teacher in the 1990s you have to be a magnificent sales person. The competition outside of school is so great that it is extremely difficult in many settings, perhaps in most settings, to convince young people that what they are learning in school is equally important as all of the other things that are competing to attract the minds of young people. Outside of school, TV is a formidable competitor to the ideas and subjects of the classroom. Sex and violence in movies, the drug culture on the street, the music that young people listen to, the immediate gratification to which modern young people have grown accustomed due to the fact that they have more than 100 TV channels that they can constantly switch and portable radios that they carry around with them, being able to become instantaneously entertained by all kinds of performers who seem to be catering more to the whimsical interests of young people, (as well as adults), than encouraging them to seek a higher development of their mind and spirit. All of these things compete, and compete well, with what we are attempting to say to them when they are in school. And, I'm just talking about **equally important**. To consider that we are attempting to sell them on the fact that what they are learning in school is more important than those things cited above require us to be master sales people.

Teachers don't even recognize the degree to which they are sales people on a day-to-day basis, not only as it pertains to the subject matter we are required to teach, but of the values that we attempt to instill in young people just in the course of one day—the appreciation and respect for other peoples' property, the need to operate on inclusion rather than exclusion, to attempt to help young people eliminate cliques and to keep people in the group instead of out of the group. There are a number of things that we attempt to sell as it pertains to an appreciation for long range goal setting, a concept that is extremely difficult to sell to young people because young people believe in immediate gratification.

We also attempt to sell young people the insurance that their subsequent lives will be productive, progressive, and peaceful, based upon a foundation that is laid for them during their school years. Most young people will attend 8 years of elementary (or some variation), four years of high school, four years of college (if they go into higher education), and perhaps 6 to 8 years beyond that in graduate school. Actually, at most, and this is of course not the average, but at most, someone might spend 24 years in school. Most young people, however, will spend between 12 to 16 years in school. Most Americans, as a matter of fact, do not graduate from college. That being the case, given the proper figure of 24 school years, if our average life span remains somewhere near 72 to 74 years as we approach the 21st century, then that means that at least 48 years will be spent outside of school. We want to be sure that the years they spend in school, which are years fewer (fewer than one-third the number of years) than those they will spend outside of school, will insure a productive life with great earning capacity. That is a tough selling job. But many teachers do it and do it well.

Reason #11: Because teachers are paramedics. To a lesser degree than the other 19 "occupations" that I mention, teachers serve as emergency medical technicians or paramedics. There are classroom or playground accidents. Often we are the first to get to the child in case of an accident. I am not suggesting for a moment that our role then is to administer any kind of medical first aid, but certainly spiritual first aid to the child. Not only that, in terms of being paramedics we also do a little bit of diagnosing. We can elicit, based on the confidence that the child has in us (because he or she knows us), how and where the child hurts. We can then size up based upon the child's hysteria, or lack thereof, whether or not it appears to be a very serious injury. We make the child feel comfortable, remove the crowd from the situation, send someone to the office to call for an ambulance (if that is necessary), or call for the gym teacher who has Bandaids if that is necessary). Certainly we never try to go beyond comforting and taking a cursory, but thorough, look at a medical emergency; but we do our best to help within the bounds of our function. Sometimes we call upon a fellow teacher. We then become "pair-a-medics."

Reason #12: Because teachers are asked to be surrogate parents. Some parents welcome this relationship with teachers and some parents frankly resent this kind of relationship. Sometimes, for those parents who welcome the relationship, we are asked to be surrogate parents by the parents themselves, either overtly by the parents saying, "My child really likes you, and you are like a mother (father) to that child and I really appreciate all that you are doing" or, covertly in terms of their actions as when the parents neglect some of their duties and the child naturally seeks that kind of relationship with you. As a teachers becomes a surrogate parent, not always willingly, he or she has to be very careful to maintain the professional relationship that is an equal opportunity compliance official making sure that all are treated fairly while attempting to avoid having "pets" or developing such a close relationship with some students that it causes other students to refrain from growing close to the teacher as they might. On the other hand, it is important to recognize the need in some students to have a close relationship, to not deprive them of the kind of counselor relationship a teacher can have as confidant, as noted earlier.

So you see, as teachers, not only do we make the determination as to whether or not this is a case in which we should become surrogate parents as it were, deciding that it is proper to offer this particular child or these particular children that kind of paternal/maternal relationship, we also must know how to do it in such a way as to not develop such a dependency syndrome in that child, so that when the child must leave it causes trauma. Many parents will come to school, it seems, when their child is enrolling in kindergarten and leave a sign at the office: *Please take care of my child for awhile. I will be back when he is eighteen.* In such a situation, then it would seem that the school just naturally takes on this parent-child relationship. But, in some cases, we have to make the determination as to when it is a bad idea to do that—when we must admonish the parents to, indeed, be parents. But what happens in situations where the parent is absolutely overwhelmed by virtue of the fact that it is a young parent who had a child at a young age, or is working three jobs in order to make ends meet, or happened to be abusing substances and does not have the capacity to serve in the way that parents ought to, or for some reason, the child does not have the necessary bonding with the parent, but has assumed that relationship with the teacher? We then make the determination that perhaps we can do a little more in order to help the child have this relationship perhaps temporarily in our presence.

We hear stories all the time about teachers who have maintained relationships with particular students through the years, to the point where some students who may have had teachers in fourth grade, are now social friends of those teachers by virtue of having kept up with them through letters and phone calls, or of teachers going to nonclassroom events, keeping up with the child's (and now adult's) development—and even becoming godparents of the children of some of the students whom they had when they were in their class. Teachers have a number of relationships and practice a number of professions, and parenting is certainly one.

Reason #13: Because teachers are plant breeders. I am very serious about these Agricultural Scientists. This may seem frivolous. However, we began to breed plants that we didn't know we could cultivate because of the lack of ability to do so in our own homes. Suddenly, plants are sprouting up all over the classroom. The students will come to you and ask if they may plant in the classroom because the classroom down the hall has some pretty plants and they want to put something in the window. And of course we say "Yes." And then, students come and say, "How far down should we put the seeds?" or, "How much water should we put in them every day, and how much sunlight do they need?" Thus, we begin to study those things and we begin to look at the little packages of instructions that are hung on the flowers that we get and suddenly we begin to breed plants and we enjoy it and we get more plants. And when students see that it is all right, they too begin to bring plants in the classroom. Of course, your classroom then takes on a certain climate. And if you plant for one year, you've got to do it every year, because students, parents, and the principal (who loves to bring visitors into your classroom so they can see what a magnificent, beautiful classroom you have) come to expect it.

Reason #14: Because teachers are required to be police officers in the classroom. As a matter of fact, in the classroom the teacher is the ultimate law enforcer. The teacher is the one who can go into the gymnasium and effect an arrest. Also, the teacher can break up a fight just by standing in front of some students who look up and say "Oh, oh. The teacher is here!" And the teacher not only effects an arrest but can mete out appropriate punishment such as causing youngsters to go to "jail" (i.e., the principal's office), based upon the behavior in the classroom.

Very strong teachers are oftentimes the ultimate police officer in the building. As a matter of fact, there are some teachers who are so tough students would rather be arrested by the real police than to have to face this particular teacher.

Reason #15: Because teachers are psychologists. It is absolutely amazing the amount of psychology a teacher practices in one school year. As a matter of fact, there are some people in psychology who would suggest that after studying psychology and even practicing many many years, they do not have the opportunity to use what they learned to the same degree that they would in one year of teaching, based upon interaction with a student of any age. It is important to note that teachers practice different levels of psychology, depending upon what grade they are teaching. If you should be asked to teach in a middle school one year and in the primary grades another year and then find yourself in a secondary school for three subsequent years, you will be a psychologist on several different levels based upon the level you are required to teach. The psychologist in the teacher finds us at some point putting fear in young people for some action that they have perpetrated, or inspiring young people to exercise their potential for greatness or quieting some young people in the midst of chaos, or exciting young people when they have no motivation at all. And oftentimes it is just a matter of using the right psychology to push that button that will cause a slow student to suddenly become fast, or a bored student to suddenly become motivated. Teachers are natural psychologists in the way that they go about their day-to-day business, and as a matter of fact, sometimes a teacher in one classroom will practice three or four levels of psychology in one day, based upon the various activities that are occurring simultaneously in school that day.

When I thought I was tough at Wendell Phillips Elementary School in the 1950s as a young boy, I wanted to hang out with guys who were just rough fellows in the neighborhood. Mr. James Collins, who was the gym instructor and supervisor of the safety patrol, asked me to become a patrol boy, and later made me patrol captain. My whole attitude about who I was and where I was going was changed by the psychology used by Mr. Collins. I still thought I was tough, but I became tough in a positive way because then I was the head of a new gang, the Safety Patrol. I think I was about 35 years old before I figured out that Mr. Collins had truly psyched me out. But the use of that particular kind of psychology was just a natural thing that was done when I was in school.

As a teacher beginning in 1964, I found myself using similar kinds of psychology; channeling a hyperactive student's energy into positive efforts, or putting a student who seemed to have captured the imaginations of the other students because he was so tough at the head of something to channel his energies in a positive manner as Mr. Collins had done for me.

Reason #16: Because teachers are secretaries. Teachers not only must keep files, but they also must record copious notes which allow them to interpret what is going on in their classroom. They must be able to report to the principal and administrators the minutes of activities that go on during classroom meetings. They must be able to read those minutes back to their students in order that the students can begin the lesson from where they left off. In order to insure academic continuity, teachers must be able, not only to take notes themselves, but to teach students how to take notes so that students can determine which facts are important to put down and which they can leave out, thereby avoiding the tendency to get bogged down with attempting to take down every word that a teacher says.

The teacher must be classroom secretary not only as a recording secretary to make sure that there is continuity in terms of the lesson plan development, but also as a corresponding secretary responding to notes that they receive from parents, while also initiating information to the parents in order that they know what is going on in the classroom and school. And many times a teacher must be a secretary to other school or department committees on which he or she serves.

Reason #17: Because teachers are social workers. You see, if indeed, teachers are demographers/sociologists (Reason #5), they must also follow up on some of the information gathered in order to assist parents and families of young people to develop a school community or school home relationship that again, enhances the learning climate for these youngsters. Let us suppose that there are young people who come to a classroom and are without suitable clothing. There are some teachers who actually go to their closets and get out old clothes. But if we attempted to do that for every child who needed them, we would soon deplete our own wardrobes, and that could become very cumbersome and very embarrassing to the child. So, rather than do that on an ongoing basis, we assume our social worker role and begin to tap the resources of the proper agencies who can insure that every child who attends school can attend in suitable clothing. The same thing holds true for children who are hungry.

Reason #18: Because teachers are stage directors. Not only are we stage directors, we are producers of some of the greatest acts that any entertainment industry mogul has ever seen. Just in the preparation for assembly programs, teachers make sure that young people are prepared to go on stage because "you are representing my class, and when you represent my class, you are going to go on that stage and you are going to really be ready for whatever it is that we are going to do." We

take young people down to the stage and see what their performance looks like and if they don't look right, we begin to block
and have this student stand over there, and we want all the tall
boys in the back, and we want the short people in the front, and
one ought to sit in a chair and one ought to stand to the side.

"Sherman—you are not speaking loudly enough."

"Elizabeth—your articulation is not what it ought to be.
When you sing the song, make sure that you are on key."

"Roy—maybe you shouldn't sing that solo. Maybe you
should be the one who narrates rather than sings."

There are some teachers, as a matter of fact, who go overboard in their stage directing, and not mentioning any names,
there was one teacher with whom I taught early in my career
who would have students prepare for assembly programs by
coming to school 40 minutes early, rehearsing through lunch
period, and staying after school 40 minutes in order that their
performance on stage be state-of-the-art. This scenario would
have the rest of the school talking about what a wonderful job
these poor, tired, hungry kids did because they had been kept in
for lunch and made to rehearse all kinds of hours in the morning
and evening in order to look good. Most do not go to this extent,
but we do assume the role often.

Reason #19: Because teachers are stock clerks. That's
right! Stock clerks. As materials are ordered, teachers must pick
up those materials, take them to the classroom, shelve them, and
make sure that at distribution time, everything is there that
ought to be there while finding its way to students. And, some
materials cannot belong to the students solely, so the students
must return the books at the end of the period. Or a student can
check out science equipment but cannot take the science equipment home. So a teacher must insure that the equipment is
properly stored. Teachers also make sure that that which is
marked on the box is consistent with what is inside of the package.

And, many times, while we like to look around and find the
larger boys in school to have them assist us with the movement
of the boxes—sometimes, not only are we stock clerks, but we
are heavy equipment movers. It is really a lonely feeling when

one is in the school because you decided to get there early to get a jump start on the coming year, and find that there are a number of heavy boxes downstairs waiting to be taken upstairs, and there is not one large boy to be found while your colleagues are busy taking care of whatever it is that they have to take care of. Sometimes there is no place for the material to go, which means that you have to create space in order to make sure that things are neatly put aside, because if you don't the Fire Marshall will come in and say that you are creating a fire hazard. But if you're careful to put the material out of the way, you might disrupt the area where the students are going to want to put their plants, or to improve the bulletin board. You can't stack them up where you can't see the students' bulletin boards because they have done such a great job creating them, so in being a stock clerk, you have to be a creative stock clerk.

Reason #20: Because teachers are also asked to be teachers. Surprise! Note that all of the things that are detailed in Reasons 1-19 are embodied in someone called a teacher. In addition to those auxiliary occupations that are automatically assembled by the classroom teacher, there is also the imparting of knowledge and student motivation. There is also keeping up with what is going on in education around us. The responsibilities of being a teacher are not responsibilities that simply come under the heading of one title.

The 19 reasons that were previously mentioned were not all of the occupations. Let me also suggest that I don't want to create a case for someone accusing me of being terribly naive. Obviously, classroom teachers as plant breeders have not studied and practiced to the degree that very respected agricultural scientists have. Obviously, as police officer, the teacher has not studied and practiced to the degree that official, municipal, and state police officers have. But, the roles that a teacher assumes certainly embark upon those professions that I have mentioned. And, in mentioning those, I have added up (based upon *The Occupational Outlook Handbook, 1988-89 Edition*, furnished by the U.S. Department of Labor, Bureau of Labor Statistics, April, 1988) the collective annual salaries of all those occupations. If teachers are indeed paid accordingly then our starting salaries should be $515,416 a year. Now, I am willing to suggest that it would be ludicrous to say that we are accomplished arbitrators from a labor relations manager's point of view or that indeed, the degree to which we function as editors approaches the kind of job that is being done on daily newspapers across the country. One of the salaries not included in my collection of salaries from Occupational Outlook Handbook was that of parent. It is very difficult for me to imagine how you would assign a salary to the job of rearing kids in this day and age, or for that matter any day and age. I am reminded of a song that was recorded by gospel singer Shirley Caesar in which her son came to her and wanted to be paid to go to the store, take out the garbage, or babysit his little sister. And, when he assigned a certain amount of money that ought to be attached to that and added to his allowance, Shirley sang to him the song with the title:

No Charge:

"No Charge for Carrying You for Nine Months."

"No Charge for being responsible for your development to this point in your life."

"No Charge for being there when you were ill and needed me."

"No Charge for attending the plays at school and taking you to church...."

"No Charge."

Parents do not assign a charge to their children for doing the monumental tasks that they must do, so in this collection of salaries for the various occupations, I simply put next to parents "No Charge."

Reason #21: Teachers should be compensated for being teachers. Now I am willing to concede the fact that, as it pertains to Chief Executive Officers, consultants, counselors, demographers, and others, teachers do not do all of the jobs cited in Reasons 1-20 full time. So if that is the case, I am willing to suggest that teachers should only get one-tenth compensation for not doing those jobs full time or not having studies to the degree that others have studied, in order to master those professions, and one-tenth of $515,000 is $51,000. (I'm only asking $50,000.)

Reason #22: Because teaching is a career rather than a job. I think that teachers should consider their occupation a career rather than a job. Reason #22 suggests that it be regarded a career rather than a job from the standpoint of longevity in the profession as well as attitude. I think that we should encourage young people who are attending our colleges today to go into teaching not as a stepping stone toward something else, but, indeed, to go into teaching as an opportunity to change a world, to look at a career wherein things that you do every day might possibly change a person's life—a person who is at a very young age but who will have a great deal of impact on his community, city, county, state, nation, and world.

Due to the influence that teachers indeed have over that child, I think that in terms of looking at the teaching profession as a career, young people should be encouraged to go in and make professional friends of those with whom they work every day, and meet at conferences and other gatherings. When you go into teaching, things will change not only on a day-to-day basis as it pertains to the personalities of the different children whom you confront, but teaching also changes as a profession in view of the fact that the world changes and history is recorded daily. Scientific discoveries are being made daily. Psychological phenomena that impact upon the behavior of not only children but adults are being discovered daily, and being in education ought to put one on the cutting edge of those things that are happening in the world.

As a matter of fact, unlike any other profession, the educator is responsible for interpreting human (as well as other) events around us. That being the case, it is an exciting profession. It is an interesting profession. It is an enlightening profession. I would want to, as a young person, go into it with the idea that I am going to become a part of a profession that can see a world change, but, indeed, can also **make** a world change, and to think in terms of being able to do that for the rest of my life because of the excitement, enlightenment, and human interaction.

Therefore, the benefits that ought to accompany this career ought to be such an incentive that I don't have to worry about "just making it." Certain things ought to be taken for granted in order for me to know that I can enjoy this career and be a part of something that will grow due to educational as well as world reform for the rest of my working life. And that working life can be a tremendous opportunity to experience personal growth as well as to observe the growth of those who come in contact with me because of that to which I expose them. The one thing that helps people to look at a position as a career is the financial incentive. That is not to suggest for a moment that the altruistic motives of most of us who are in education should be denied. I think, however, that because of how fragile young people are, the lives with which we must deal, and the import of that which we do on a day-to-day basis ought to dictate proper compensation.

Reason #23: Because a teacher's salary should inspire and demand professionalism. $50,000 per year ought to inspire professionalism and create a climate where those who are responsible for monitoring the behavior of teachers can demand professionalism. One can feel like a professional when one competes favorably salary-wise with others around him or her in other professions. Not only compete favorably, but in view of the fact that teaching is our most important profession, it would seem that teachers' salaries should reflect this.

If there is someone who can indicate a profession that is more important than teaching, my challenge would simply be to ask what if those who perform or practice that profession were poorly taught? The training that they get, the preparation that they get, and the inspiration that they get from someone who lines them up for that profession, whatever it might happen to be, is certainly as important as their undertaking that profession. It would seem to me that those who prepare others for whatever profession they go into certainly have the most important profession, and so I say that teaching is M.I.P., the **most important profession**. Now, given that brief and very simple argument, let me say that if indeed teaching is the most important profession, then it certainly ought to compete favorably with any other profession as it pertains to starting salary and proper financial compensation for the duties and responsibilities undertaken by those who are involved in that profession.

When I speak of inspiring professionalism, I am simply suggesting that when one is properly compensated, it helps one to feel good about who he is and what he does because he feels that in a capitalistic society where so much is measured by the dollar he is being respected by those who are responsible for seeing how he is paid for what he does. It will inspire professionalism because of the ability to use those dollars to live a lifestyle that is consistent with being a professional. And being a professional and being inspired toward professionalism has a very positive impact on the way one discharges one's function. Now if you are a very idealistic person and if you suggest that one ought to discharge his function professionally anyway, I do not disagree with you. However, being realistic as well as being idealistic, it just happens to be a human factor in the society in which we live that those who are paid well for what they do tend to be more enthusiastic about what they do. That's why they have so many incentives in sales. That's why they have such salaries in the professional athletics. That's why they have all kinds of programs and schemes coming to you through cable television and mail order catalogs for people to earn money so that they can live and feel a lifestyle that suggests that they are successful, that they are doing well. Certainly anyone who had been trained to train others for a myriad of professions and occupations and lifestyles ought to be considered a successful person.

In the U.S., success is often measured by how much one earns, and therefore, you can inspire professionalism by complementing the success of those that make all other professions by compensating them properly in terms of salary. I said "inspire professionalism" and "demand professionalism" because along with the territory comes one's being subjected to the demands of those who monitor teacher performance.

If you are getting paid to that degree, then you are to be held accountable for acting as though you are professional: mutual respect for students, contact with their parents, not going into the school year counting up the number of days that you can be absent based upon sick days and personal business days, the way that you dress, the kind of language that you use, honing up your skills as a professional person, being responsible for attending parent-teacher association meetings and school advisory council meetings and being a part of the community that you serve rather than looking upon the community as being accountable to you.

If you are not being properly compensated and one had the audacity to make demands upon you, it is very easy for you to say, "Well, with what I'm getting paid, it's just great that I'm getting here in the first place." In order to make sure that never occurs, then those in responsible positions ought to make sure from the beginning that you are going to be properly compensated.

Reason #24: Because a proper salary will provide for professional growth. This will provide for the professional growth of those who are being held accountable as professionals. If there are memberships to be taken out that will enhance professional growth and networking capabilities of those of us who are in the education profession, then it will be less difficult to become members of those professional organizations when the salaries that we receive do not make such memberships prohibitive. It also gives an opportunity to subscribe to periodicals that will help professional growth so that we don't have to depend upon looking at magazines in the teachers' lounge, but in fact, can have them delivered to our homes because we can afford to take out subscriptions in order to grow professionally. There are conferences, workshops, clinics, and classes. In order to participate in those professional development-type activities, it ought not to tax us economically to be able to become part of those things or to serve as facilitators ourselves.

Professional development ought to be demanded of educators but the capability to enjoy professional development without creating an economic hardship ought to be a part of the lifestyle of those who have come into this profession. Proper compensation can encourage and provide for professional growth for all of those who are part of the teaching profession.

Reason #25: Because the new base salary can create an immediate new image of teachers. When teachers are known to be getting a base salary of $50,000 (and that $50,000 again being measured by 1991 Kansas City, Missouri, standards so it might be a little more in Chicago, Los Angeles, or New York and a little less somewhere else) those who know that has occurred will see teachers in a new light. The respect that should be paid teachers is sometimes eroded by the fact that many who are asked to respect us are earning so much more than we do that they find it laughable that we would attempt to command respect and certainly laughable to demand respect.

Teachers will be held more accountable. It will cause people to begin to look at their children's relationships with teachers in a different way and begin to help their children demand from teachers the professionalism that is suggested by such a salary. It will cause people to see the teaching profession with a different degree of importance and begin to ask the question, "If, indeed, these kinds of salaries are available to teachers, then is this what we think about the teaching profession versus other professions or other areas of concern within our nation?" What does that say about the priorities in America?

Now, when you have a current president who suggests that he wants to be the education president, what does that now mean? It means that we are asking him to put our money where his mouth is. It suggests that there is a seriousness about the priorities of education in our nation and it is going to be reflected at every level and among those levels that reflect the seriousness is the level of teacher compensation for what teachers are required to do. It will create a new image in the minds of college students, not only from the standpoint of "Wow! Here's an opportunity to earn (what might be considered to some) a lot of money." I don't consider it to be a lot of money particularly as measured against some other professions that earn more, but it will cause college students to begin to think in terms of the fact that they can earn a comfortable salary but also that they must be going into something that is important because they don't put out that kind of money for something that is not important. It is good to create an image of an entire profession that says suddenly, "We have determined that this profession is important."

Reason #26: Because an education administration should be aggressive in pursuing educational priorities.
One way President Bush might become the education president is to become an educator himself by enlightening the entire na-

tion as to the implications of things that are going on in America and their impact upon what's happening worldwide. The reverse of that is what is happening worldwide and its impact upon America. He can release more information than any president before him, by holding more press conferences, for instance, than other presidents, by interpreting information for us more immediately than other presidents, by making plain what has been regarded as political jargon heretofore, and in plain language interpreting for us the events that are occurring around us.

So one way you can become an education president, Mr. Bush, is by educating the citizens of the U.S. as to what is going on, why it is going on, where we're going, and what caused us to go in the directions that we're going, and what you project for the future.

Another way that you can be an education president, Mr. Bush, would be by virtue of what you do with the field of education, either directly by yourself as an individual, or wielding your influence toward others who have something to say about the direction of education. And that is to say that if we can launch an 8 billion dollar war on drugs, then it ought to be worth 10 times that amount to launch a program that would prevent that problem in the first place. And certainly, one way to prevent the problems of abuses, not only drug abuse but other kinds of substance or human abuses, is to assist our children in growing in an educational atmosphere that is warm, comfortable, non-violent, nurturing, supportive, and uplifting. And the person who is responsible for setting the tone as it pertains to that kind of climate is, indeed, the frontline classroom teacher who is with children every day and helps them to appreciate that which is healthy, not only for the children as individuals and their families, but healthy for our society.

The President being the "tone setter" for the nation ought to understand that teachers are the "tone setters" for the community, and if that be so, teachers ought to be compensated in a similar fashion to the way that a president is compensated. It is unfortunate—well, I won't say unfortunate—it is ironic in the community in which we live that the President does not earn as much as some professional athletes and entertainers and Chief Executive Officers and good sales people. I think that there is some inconsistency there except that we live in a free enterprise system so I won't argue the merits or demerits of free enterprise as it pertains to presidential salaries vs. others who may not deserve (as we measure them on the scale of world influence) a salary that is greater than the President's. However, I think that a president can rest assured that he's not going to be concerned about making ends meet, paying the electric bill, making sure that he can pay the rent at the first of the month, or if it is necessary for him to be a part of an important session, conference or meeting wherever it occurs in the world—that he will not be able to be there because he cannot afford the plane ticket or the registration fee. I think that teachers ought to enjoy a similar comfort as it pertains to their ability to set a positive climate in the classroom based upon the fact that they are not overly concerned with simply making ends meet.

If this is going to be an administration that is an education administration, I think some bold statements need to be made. I think that there needs to be something that will capture the attention, not only of America's educators but the entire citizenry—something that is bold and serious enough that makes a statement in one fell swoop that we are serious about what we say. We are going to fully compensate teachers for the jobs that we demand that they do, and if indeed they do not do them, we will take measures to replace them.

Reason #27: Because we should show the world that America is serious. America has not been regarded lately, perhaps in the last couple of decades or so, as the major power that it was once seen as across the world. Oftentimes, if you look at how power is measured or how we see power, we talk about economic power and technological development. If you look around the world economically and technologically, the U.S. is slipping. There is another way power is regarded and that is as it pertains to the image or the philosophical or ideological image a nation has. And among the things that America can do to enhance its image is to show the world that America takes education seriously—so seriously that it is willing to place dollars where they count most.

Those who are responsible for delivering a new America are in the classrooms. They are the teachers who inspire the students as well as teach the students. They are the teachers who direct and guide as well as inform. They are the teachers who are motivators as well as educators. And that being the case, the world needs to understand in no uncertain terms that while America may have slipped economically and technologically, and may have slipped even in terms of putting forth its ideology, that America is once again on the rise. Not just on the rise as it pertains to our ability to create new weaponry but as it pertains to our ability to get into the hearts and minds of children who represent what America's future is going to be. And if America's future is to be solid, that means that the emphasis must be placed on America's children, not on America's soldiers. That means that its emphasis must be placed on America's classrooms, not on America's war rooms.

It is imperative that the world understands that we are in this for the long haul, and if we're in it for the long haul, we are not emphasizing the new machinery that might indeed wipe out a country. We are interested in the machinery of the mind that will transform a country, and thus, the world. We must allow the world to know that we are serious from the standpoint that our endeavors to create an educational system that sees our nation progress are not selfish, but that we want to inspire an entire world to become enlightened in order that people all over can be self-governing. You cannot be self-governing if you are not enlightened. You cannot lead if you are not educated and do not understand the implications of history in order that you can prepare for the future. Education, then, becomes more important than economics. It becomes more important than defense. It becomes more important than the political ramifications of world relations because all of those suffer for a lack of a proper and excellent educational foundation.

If we want people across the world to be enlightened enough to make decisions for themselves, then we have to show them that we are serious about what we are doing to enlighten Americans through our own educational systems.

Reason #28: Because we are approaching the turn of the century. While it may sound a bit frivolous to suggest that a bold step needs to be taken in education simply because we are approaching the turn of the century, it just happens to be a historical fact that major events occur as centuries turn, and if indeed something major should occur where the U.S. is concerned, I would suspect that turn needs to take place in education. One of the ways that the 1990s can project what is likely to happen at the turn of the century is for something to occur that makes it very clear that this is where our priority is and where our emphasis is going to be placed. This is what will dictate the direction of the 21st century, a century of enlightenment.

As researchers, theorists, prognosticators, and others look to a 21st century that will bring about a technological revolution and see the spread of democracy across the world, we look forward to a 21st century that might bring about peculiar gadgetry and an emphasis on physical health and medical breakthroughs that will see us living much longer and will increase the number of ecologically efficient housing developments. I think that America should do something as revolutionary (and yet simple) as insuring that everyone gets an excellent education.

I think that one of the ways this can come about is to be able to recruit into the education profession by the year 2000 the brightest, the best, the most dedicated and the most serious. Among the incentives for attracting those who are indeed the best and brightest is simply to pay salaries that are competitive.

Reason #29: Because we can help foster collegial support and cooperation. I think that the degree to which those who function well on the same team is often dictated by the perception of the members of that team feeling like they are winners. If I may use an athletic analogy—observe the degree to which teams that win championships seem to be very happy with each other. Teams that do well on a consistent basis, for the most part, seem to have members on that team who get along with each other, who assist each other in the finer points of the sport, and who seem to enjoy interaction with each other because they are part of a winning team.

To foster collegial support and cooperation among teachers, we might help them feel like they are winners and that they are on a winning team. And when indeed they begin to feel like they are properly compensated because they are somebody special, they will begin to treat each other in a special manner. I think that it is very important that teachers feel comfortable around each other, feel good about what their colleagues are doing, and feel comfortable with being able to challenge their colleagues based upon the fact that we're all no longer in a position to complain about our compensation as it pertains to our salaries, and therefore, we ought to work harder with each other in order to continue to be the winners that we must certainly be if this is the kind of money that they are agreeing voluntarily to pay us for the job that we do.

The climate of feeling good about who you are and what you do and who you do it with will help to develop cooperation and mutual support. Teachers then will create a climate in the local school wherein students and others around those teachers will feel like winners also because they just feel like they are on a team that is going somewhere and doing great things.

Climate and cooperation are important, and a comfortable salary for all promotes a professional climate.

Reason #30: Because we must command student respect. I think that the most important relationship in a school is the relationship between teacher and student. You may have an association, you may have a relationship, but you do not have school without a teacher and a student. That relationship is of the utmost importance. Oftentimes teachers labor hard to attain student respect based upon their professionalism—knowledge, personality, consistency and how the teacher is regarded by administration and colleagues in front of students.

Students will begin to gain respect and display respect as determined by the way teachers carry themselves while interacting with students to carry out their function as those who are responsible for helping young people learn.

Students respond, in kind, with whatever attitude we project, and proper compensation will help us project a confident, "respected" attitude. Also, being like adults, students will respect us for our new, more appropriate, earnings.

Reason #31: Because teachers are required to offer drug education. It does not matter what area, what discipline, what subject has been studied in college and it does not matter what one is currently teaching: at some point because of the unfortunate high incidence of drug distribution in the U.S., particularly among young people, teachers are being asked now to assist young people in learning the hazards of being involved with the drug culture. Therefore, a subject area for which we are not prepared as educators has become one of the major subjects that we must address in order to diminish a growing social ill.

In the case of drugs in America, it can no longer be regarded as a fad or passing fancy, nor does it simply affect a particular segment of the population based upon race, socioeconomic level, lifestyle, or lineage, but, indeed, the drug culture has infiltrated the smallest rural communities and certainly the largest urban communities. Since children are so infected by this growing epidemic, certainly those who come into contact with children on a daily basis—teachers—are asked to assist (sometimes even more than their own parents) in an ongoing effort to reduce the degree to which people become involved with drugs. Again, teachers must be compensated for the extra work they do even if it is not the discipline that they chose to study while in college.

Reason #32: Because teachers are asked to teach sex education. There are two ways in which educators are asked to teach sex education when it is a part of curriculum offerings—from the science department as a part of the study of the reproductive system or from the health and physical education department when it is part of understanding the need for psychological and social health as well as physical health. In family life and sex education, in understanding the human body, and understanding social conditions, teachers are asked to teach sex education as a part of a formal curriculum offering. In that regard, that would only call upon a few teachers who are charged with responsibility of either developing or following a particular curriculum.

Where all teachers are involved is the second way in which we are asked to teach sex education. And that is by example. All of us are asked to teach sex education as we encounter the peculiar habits (or peculiar to us at any rate) of young people walking down the hall holding hands and having to intercede in that situation to indicate why such behavior is indeed inappropriate in a school building which is an institution for learning and not an institution for dating. It is an institution where an appreciation for what is proper in different settings must be instilled within young people. Teachers who, when seeing behaviors in school that are improper, refuse to seize the moment to teach, are not doing their jobs, but those who are doing their jobs are just exemplifying another reason for being properly compensated for having to teach things that deal with the social climate of an entire society in addition to that for which they have been hired to teach specifically in whatever area they have been chosen to perform.

Therefore, if there are social ills or social consideration, we are asked to be teachers to help youngsters develop an appreciation for what is proper when, where, how, and with whom.

Reason #33: Because teachers must master the use of new technology. They must master not only new physical technology but new psychological technology. I guess the most immediate example of physical technological devices would be computers. Teachers must enhance their own capacity to deliver on teaching particular subjects, but also so they can help young people become proficient at the use of new technologies as they are entering a world where what has been novel and new to us in the latter part of the 20th century will be commonplace in the 21st century.

In terms of psychological technology we must think faster in order to keep up with developments that are in front of us on an ongoing basis from the microwave oven to cable channels on television, to uplinking and downlinking in satellite technology. And our response time to events that occur in front of us on an ongoing basis has to be a lot faster than it had to be just a couple of decades ago.

Therefore, even if we are not instructors of science and technology, higher math, or the use of developing machinery, we must be on top of it enough to be able to interpret what young people will be encountering now for the rest of their lives, and certainly for all of their children's and their children's children's lives.

If teachers are going to be on the cutting edge of those things that are occurring worldwide, that means that we must be two or three steps ahead of our students, even if the subject that we are teaching is music. I guess that I shouldn't even say "even if" in the case of music because there are new technologies being developed in the field of music all the time. As a matter of fact, our knowledge of new technologies is essential to assisting young people in the primary grades as their mastery of machinery technology must be born out of a firm foundation to which they have been introduced at a very young age. We teach technology through our use as well as through our concern for youth.

Reason #34: Because teachers are instructors and advocates of multi-culturalism and multi-ethnicity. Teachers must be not only instructors of multi-culturalism and multi-ethnicity, but also the multi-economics in terms of equal opportunity for all children whatever their economic level, whatever their racial background, and/or whatever their creed. A teacher may not have studied specifically the teaching of an appreciation for the democracy in which we live but certainly the learning of it has been a part of all our college experiences. Even if we disagree, teachers must choose professionalism over prejudices.

I also believe that when the question comes up as to whether or not teachers have pets, and whether or not teachers like one student more than another student, we feel an obligation to suggest that we certainly do not like one student over another student, and we like all students the same, and consequently because we like all students the same, we treat all the students the same. I think that there is a fallacy there in the answer and in the "logical" consequence of the answer. That is to say that if it is a fallacy, and I think it is, that I do like everybody the same, then I think that the logic, the conclusion that is drawn on the logic that follows would be equally fallacious. I like everybody the same, therefore I treat everybody the same. The fact of the matter is, the human condition does not allow us to like everybody the same. Therefore, if that is faulty, then the reason for treating everybody the same is faulty. I think that treating everybody the same has more to do with professionalism than it has to do with liking everybody the same. As an instructor I know that there are some students who have been problems and have not been particularly likeable. This does not, however, excuse unfair or "different" treatment. This is something that I would find extremely unprofessional and unacceptable.

Teachers must become advocates of multi-culturalism, multi-ethnicity and multi-economics because of its practicality and because of their professionalism. This happens to be a shrinking world. The fact that very different people make up this world is something that is not going to go away but, in fact, their interactions between different kinds of people is going to increase. Because that increase is going to shape a very different society in America and a very different world, teachers must develop a very early appreciation for differences in people, and when I say an appreciation for, I mean that in two ways: (1) an appreciation for the fact that people are so different, and (2) an appreciation for people because of their differences—not in spite of their differences.

We want to create a dynamic world. We can create that world based upon the fact that people are different and therefore have a great deal to bring that will help all of us in their own personal development. If we could sit 20 people around a table and all 20 of them came in with the same thoughts, with the same ideas, personal backgrounds, education, family roots, and philosophy of life, it is doubtful that any of the 20 would grow. Now that to me just seems to be a matter of pure logic. We are not going to grow much with a number of people who are just alike sitting around a table agreeing with each other. But the dynamic comes in when there is someone from an Asian culture who can come in and discuss how that culture has contributed to their personal growth based upon what happens in their family and what happens in the smaller community. And he may sit next to someone from an African culture who can discuss the similarities between the Asian and African cultures and then the differences that cause each of them to begin to compare and extract the positives from each culture that would enhance the growth of both. And if we take it to an even more micro-degree and not from the continental viewpoint but begin to talk about nations and countries, we look at people from Italy sitting with people from Ireland who are sitting with people from Poland who are sitting with people from Nicaragua who are sitting with people from Israel who are sitting with people from Germany who are sitting with people—you get the point.

If indeed the collective wisdom of people from different backgrounds can create a whole society, that would be ideal. If anybody ought to be able to recognize that, it should be professional educators. And if they can teach it, if they can use that model and spread it throughout the world among other educators, then perhaps we will have a different world based upon creating an harmonious "whole" in the sense that among people from different cultures who are willing to share what they know about their own culture and learn what they don't know about other cultures will appreciate that we all have some cultural similarities and use them to create a more dynamic culture worldwide. Teachers, by virtue of their profession, are advocates of bringing differences together and creating harmony out of chaos.

The classroom is a microcosm of the community—the city—the state—the nation—the world. We must make things work in the classroom the way they should/must work in the world. Teachers must appreciate multi-ethnicity and function singularly ethically.

Reason #35: Because if teachers are properly compensated, they can then engage in continued study. We must not only study on our own time, but we must be required to continue study not only in that discipline we are hired to teach, but also across curricula. We ought to be studying our field in order to make sure that we are not only teaching what is basic within the context of the subject area we have been hired to teach but what is state-of-the-art, what is current, and what is futuristic. In order to do that, teachers ought to be required to continue studying on an ongoing basis. Well, not only an "incentive" but also a "provider" for the possibility of that continued study would be proper compensation in the terms of the salaries that teachers earn.

Reason #36: Because we should upgrade college requirements and standards of education students in college. Requirements can be made that would upgrade teacher qualifications coming out of college.

I think that upon the declaration that indeed young people want to be teachers (ordinarily made at least by the college sophomore), students ought to begin student teaching and student teach every year thereafter. I think that student teaching ought to include a variety of settings—rural, suburban, urban, elementary, secondary, large school/small school, etc.

In terms of the classes that they are required to take and in view of the fact that indeed they are going to enter a profession that will cause them to have to teach some things for which they were not previously prepared, I think that colleges should offer as many experiences as possible and include in curricula offerings many of the things that come about because of societal occurrences rather than strictly educational developments.

I think that the attitude that has a student or some students make a statement similar to, "If I'm not successful elsewhere, I can always teach" can certainly be changed when the School of Education is seen as the most demanding. I suspect that it is possible that one of the reasons we as a society do not feel that we must be more demanding in Schools of Education and Teachers' Colleges is because we recognize that once students have completed their courses of study, they are not going to be earning a great deal, not only when they enter the profession of teaching but even if they spend 30 years in the profession. But, believe me, society will demand, once starting salaries go up, that Schools of Education produce the kind of teachers not only in terms of course completion but even character development in order to deserve such a salary.

Reason #37: Because teachers should spend two years on probation with no raise in pay. If salaries are upgraded, teachers should spend two years on probation with no raise in pay. Teachers would be evaluated over the two year period, and at the end of that probationary period they would then become eligible for certification and tenure.

For the two-year probationary period, I think that I would be working hard to be competent and to earn not only that amount and more later on, but also to earn the respect of my colleagues, my administrators, the community I serve, the students, the students' parents, in addition to my self-respect for recognizing that I have entered a profession that is serious about making me the best I can be.

Reason #38: Because we can initiate a 4-1 plan. This would be a plan wherein teachers would teach for four straight years and then be excused for one year or have a one-year paid sabbatical to upgrade their professionalism, and then come back, teach for four years with another one-year paid sabbatical continuing the cycle for three times.

(1) We tend to go through our educational lives with a four-year cycle (at least after middle school)—four years of high school and four years of college, and that's not as strong an argument as other arguments.

(2) I think that a year's sabbatical can keep us sharper because it gives an opportunity to again study what is state-of-the-art in the area that we are in. It gives us an opportunity to travel about, seeing what other people are doing in other areas. It gives us an opportunity to fraternize with others in the profession, and gives an opportunity to write, study, develop papers, study the papers of others, go to conferences—to stretch out as it were. I think that the 4-1 plan also would prevent, for lack of a better term, "staleness," coming back rejuvenated after that one year and going away without having grown bored or boring in order to be able to take that four-year cycle with some degree of enthusiasm and some degree of energy and at the peak of that energy, taking it into a year of paid study and professional development and coming back as enthusiastic as when we left having chosen that particular career. Also included would be a review of how I interact with the community that I serve, how I work as a

team member with my colleagues, how I am prepared when I come to school, how I choose to use the summer vacation in order to be psychologically and physically and mentally prepared at the start of the school year.

I would suspect that after 15 years the one-year sabbatical would not be necessary as it was when we first came in but there would also be, because of the experiences during the sabbatical periods in the 4-1 cycle-three-times plan, the desire in all of us to continue our professional growth based upon those experiences. Also, there might be the opportunity to become teachers' facilitators who offer during the newer teachers' one-year sabbaticals, workshops and conferences and help with their papers, advanced study and travel.

But, at any rate, I think that the $50,000 salary would be an inducement towards that kind of further study and travel at no cost to the school, school board, state or federal government, based upon being able to command a proper salary.

Reason #39: Because the proper salary could eliminate moonlighting. I believe that the proper salary could not only discourage, but totally eliminate, moonlighting. I think that there would be no reason to moonlight unless teachers particularly enjoy pumping gas at the local gas station or being security guards from 11 until 7 in the morning. One of the sociological facts of life that demographers point out is (1) there are more female classroom teachers than males in the U.S. and, as it pertains to millions of lifestyles, (2) more single-parent homes are headed by females. In some cases those females are classroom teachers who are working more than one job. And it is also true that even if it is not a single-parent household headed by someone who is a classroom teacher, it is difficult for two-parent households where the principle breadwinner is a classroom teacher to make ends meet.

I am suggesting that not only can moonlighting be eliminated by upgrading the salary, I am suggesting that this kind of salary could demand that teachers not be allowed to take on any other job, and that if they are found to be working somewhere else, can be reprimanded even to the point of being excused from the profession.

Use the proper salary to make the demand, "You make this kind of money, don't take another job."

Reason #40: Because we can use the salary to negotiate no strike, creative collective bargaining approaches with those who bargain collectively for teachers. Inasmuch as teaching is a critical occupation, whenever teachers go on strike, those who are most affected are the students. The ripple effects of a strike are not only that students are affected and must stay home, but that in many cases families are affected by the need to care for the child while the child is at home, and therefore some parents are required to stay home in lieu of getting day care providers for their children due to cost. And all students who must make up school days at the end of the year during what would ordinarily be holidays because of a strike, feel that they are "paying" because of adult politics.

In some cases, the enthusiasm with which young people approach the subject matter at hand is diminished by what they consider to be extra days at the end of the year, even though mathematically they are not extra because they got that time off during the strike. For purposes of continuity, and preventing disruption in the family and in the community for reasons of feeling good about the profession one enters, teachers should not be engaged in strikes.

I think that there ought be some negotiation that says, "Where there are our problems, there ought to be some creative ways that we can collectively bargain without costing young people continuity in their education." I don't know what that creative bargaining might be, but I am suggesting, at least, if teachers feel compensated salarywise for the many jobs they are asked to do in the classroom (and outside of the classroom) that would be one less reason they would have to walk out of the schools that are so critical to the development of this nation.

Once this society puts the $50,000 check in the hands of teachers, society then says, "You are accepting this $50,000 base salary with the understanding that there will be no strikes and we can negotiate fairly those things that are important to you without stopping the flow of education." That would be the one item that is non-negotiable. This may be difficult because classic collective bargaining in the U.S. always includes the possibility of a walkout. I am saying that as we approach the 21st century, there ought to be some things that should not even be considered, and I think that that's one of them, but I think that if, indeed, that is to be non-negotiable, then the one thing that would make it non-negotiable would be teachers feeling that they are regarded highly enough to be properly compensated.

It is important to children as they learn that there will be consistency and continuity. That is essential in anything that is learned, whether it be a foreign language that you learn by practice, practice, practice, or whether it be mathematical concepts that you learn by repetition, repetition, repetition, and build upon that repetition until higher mathematics is suddenly something that you know and you wonder how you got that far when all you were doing were repeating the basics and embellishing upon them until you found yourself doing math that you never thought you would know when you were first introduced to the concepts whatever they might be. It is the repetition, consistency, and the continuity that allows us to learn to the point where it becomes a very natural offering in our everyday lives rather than something that we must run back to the book to look up because we haven't studied it in a long time.

I think also when you are talking about a $50,000 salary among teachers is the statement that we are willing in this society to spend the money to develop an excellent educational system. It also suggests that we are willing to make parallel kinds of increases in the delivery of those things needed to develop a climate in the classroom that is conducive towards learning among students. Teachers sometimes have problems simply getting materials, equipment, and supplies that have been ordered on time, and that can be a sore spot. When these delivery of services are taken care of in a timely and orderly manner, the incentive for teachers to strike is reduced or eliminated.

I am not an advocate of putting collective bargaining agencies out of business because I think that a part of the American work ethic is to be properly represented and to have someone who can state your case from your perspective on your behalf, and I think there will always be a function for those agencies.

But there must be some way to speak in one's behalf and to speak authoritatively without putting children on the street because of the inability of school boards and educators to come together on matters that perhaps should be taken for granted way before the school year begins.

Reason #41: Because we need to foster "on-line" peer-level relationships with business partners. Across America there are school-business partnerships and in many communities there is an "Adopt A School" nature to those partnerships.

There ought to be an on-line peer-mentor relationship where the partnership is concerned, where a business that is forming a partnership with the school sees themselves as getting as much out of the relationship as the school sees themselves getting. But if there is a Chief Executive Officer at a company who is earning perhaps seven times as much as I am earning, then I am almost automatically psychologically that person's underling, and am willing to accept whatever suggestion he makes in this business partner relationship, and will somehow speak with a weaker voice on things I know to be true. But if I feel as though I am a peer, and that is reflected in the way I'm paid, then the suggestions I would make would be with as authoritative a voice as those who enter into partnerships with my school.

If you want a more pure partnership rather than an "Adopt A School" relationship, then those who are working at the school level ought to be regarded as equally important, knowledgeable, professional, and "in charge" as those who bring the partnership to them, so that when we come to our meetings it is not so much "Here's what we're offering you and here's how you can take advantage of it, and you can have your young people come and conduct field trips in our plants and we'll show them what the workday world is all about and we'll have them meet some of our people" but, "May we have our people come and tour the school and see how you operate, and how we can use this to enhance the growth of our business?"

Reason #42: Because we need to stimulate the economy. It would seem to me that if I have money to spend, the chances are I would spend it. If I feel that I must pinch each penny in order to make ends meet, then it's going to be very difficult for me to be a participant in the stimulation of the economy because I don't feel that I can afford to do anything that might be a little extra or that might be risk-taking. But if I am enjoying a proper kind of salary, then I think I would be able, first, as an individual, to participate more freely in the economic system that has been a part of what America is about for so long, and, as a teacher, to invest in the credit union and to take advantage of annuities and to begin to purchase some real estate in order that I might be able to live comfortably.

Just to be able to be a part of a thriving economy is important to me and I can do that better and more vigorously with a proper salary. In terms of making investments, there are times when you don't hear a great deal about teachers making investments because, again, we don't feel that we have anything extra that would allow us to take any risks. I think that with more expendable income we could be a greater part of stimulating the economy locally and beyond.

Reason #43: Because we can initiate "Teacher-Reacher" efforts. There could be more efforts where teachers can reach out into the community and become more of an integral part of that community where they teach.

There are professional athletes who conduct clinics within their particular sport. Arthur Ashe does tennis clinics, Tom Watson golf clinics, and Magic Johnson does basketball clinics. I think that it would be great to be able to conduct teacher clinics from two standpoints. One kind of teacher clinic would be within the tradition of athletics and that is to have youngsters gain an appreciation for our profession as we take them to a setting that is conducive for them to learn what the profession is about and begin to "clinic" them in the finer points of helping others learn. This is something that young people would be able to use as peer tutors and would also be a recruitment effort that would help them want to aspire towards becoming future teachers.

The other kind of teacher clinic would be wherein we would have youngsters learn the finer points of how to learn—not only how to teach—but how do you develop good study habits early in life and continue those good study habits? How do you develop the kind of personality and character that helps you become a friend to the teacher so that your reputation helps you to encourage teachers to give you the help that you need? How do you develop a good school-community relationship and what does it mean to be a good student? Is a good student one who has all As? Is a good student one who has a well-rounded character? Is it some combination of the two, and what should the relationship be between the teacher and the parent versus, or in concert with, the relationship between the teacher and the student?

Other "Teacher-Reachers" efforts might be for teachers in a local community to decide that they're just going to take youngsters on an annual family picnic, that is solely sponsored by, and financed by, this particular group of teachers, whoever they happen to be, as an event that makes the statement to students: This is the opportunity to really enjoy the "Last Fling" before you get into the business of really studying because you will be coming back to school. We can see each other as human beings and enjoy each other and then prepare for the serious business of school.

Teachers are among the most creative people in our society and have to be because of the many ways they are required to get across subject matter, and I'm sure that in that creative bent they can come up with any number of "Teacher-Reacher" efforts based upon our enhanced capacity to feel comfortable within the community because we're not worried about our salary needing upgrading.

Reason #44: Because teachers can develop teacher-school partnerships. Since there are school-business partnerships, it might be interesting for teachers to develop school partnerships among themselves where, during that 4-1 plan sabbatical time, not only would professional development take place but it might also be a time where teachers could share the knowledge that they had gained either from the local school where they have taught for the past four years or nine years or whatever it might be, but also to share what they are learning during this sabbatical time at conferences and workshops, in collecting materials and books that they are reading, etc.

It might be interesting when a particular school sees another school doing something that is creative and that is really working, to enter into school-school partnerships as opposed to school-business partnerships. I suggest that again the increased capacity to become creative and act on it is enhanced by not having to worry about personal dollars spent in the pursuit and the study of particular phenomena situations or circumstances so that teachers could initiate school-school partnerships or teacher-school partnerships where they work with each other.

Teachers already spend the little money that they have. Teachers are not becoming rich on the salaries that they are earning, and yet, perhaps to a larger degree than most professions, teachers have out-of-pocket expenses on a regular basis.

When a particular child is in need of something that the school does not have access to, oftentimes teachers spend their own money. Where there are certain pieces of equipment and materials that are damaged, oftentimes it is teachers who come together, or a particular teacher who just spends money out-of-pocket. This is not something that is unusual for teachers. I am saying that we would probably do it with a lot more enthusiasm if we felt that taking that money out of our pocket does not cause us to miss paying a particular bill because of the low salary that we might be receiving. Being properly compensated makes that issue a lot easier to confront.

Reason #45: Because there should be economic alignment. This is to suggest lateral movement will be a lot easier if I know that the compensation I get in one region of the nation is consistent with the compensation I will get moving to another region of the nation.

If the salaries are fairly consistent across the board, and this has to be weighed within the context of not violating any price-fixing kinds of legality, I would think that I would feel a lot better if I had to make a move with my family, knowing that I would be evaluated on the merits of the ability to do the job. The lateral movement would be a lot easier if the compensation were to be fairly, if not perfectly, consistent.

Reason #46: Because administrators and others in the educational setting should be likewise compensated for

the jobs that they do. It would seem to me that if teachers' salaries were to go up, then certainly it would be impossible for administrators responsible for "leading" teachers to be earning less.

I am also suggesting that other salaries would go up as well—coaches, counselors, administrators, and others in the education setting—because what I'm saying here is that teaching is, indeed, the most important profession. If that is so, then those who impact upon the ability of teachers to deliver in that important profession, must be likewise compensated, particularly those who are in positions where they are responsible for monitoring what teachers do.

Among the responsibilities that could result from this upgrade would be that administrators would be required to teach at least three days a month in a classroom so that they are not only leading teachers by virtue of their knowledge and administrative capabilities, but leading by example, going into the classroom, teaching concepts that they discuss with teachers in in-service meetings and conferences, etc.

Reason #47: Because we can align criteria for school board members. It is very interesting that in many school districts there are boards of education who are responsible for determining the direction of schools within the jurisdiction of those boards, and yet do not have as a requirement of their position some background in education.

I think that local school boards ought to be elected. I think that there ought to be some basic criteria for those who would run for the board positions, and I think that within those criteria, there ought to be something in the background of the person running that suggests that they have first-hand knowledge of how schools are run, either by virtue of having worked in the schools themselves or having served in some capacity that caused them to have interaction on a regular basis within the schools. Perhaps one of those capacities would be, in fact, developing and participating in a school-business partnership, and other criteria that would be important to the constituents who would vote for them knowing that they are voting for people with the proper knowledge.

And then I think that members of the board of education ought to be paid, and ought to be held strictly accountable for setting direction of their local school district. I think that when there are people who are chosen by meaningful qualifications and paid for their services accordingly, they can be held accountable for what they do. And I think that if there are paid boards of education in one city and one state in terms of public schools, then I think that there ought to be paid boards of education in every city and state.

Also, I feel that school board members could be paid on an hourly rate for time spent at official board meetings and in carrying out official functions as board members. And again it might be possible to hold them strictly accountable with possibility of removal if, indeed, they fail to live up to whatever requirements are imposed upon their being elected to their seat.

Why do I say pay the members of the board of education as opposed to their simply being elected in a volunteer capacity? Well, I think that what we want to do is to make sure that if, indeed, we upgrade the salaries of teachers, that there be a number of ways to monitor the performance of teachers and to monitor the progress at the schools where they teach. I simply think that people who do not have to worry about the money that they are losing from their principal occupation or out-of-pocket expenses when they travel on school-related business will be able to function more confidently and enthusiastically.

If we are going to hold educators accountable, then those around them who are part of that accountability ought to be required to be professional and be regarded as professional, and that certainly includes board of education members. I think that there would probably be fluctuation in compensation because the amount of time spent in a large metropolitan area on the board of education to carry out one's functions would be different from the amount of time that is spent perhaps in a smaller community with fewer schools, students, and problems.

Reason #48: Because we need to upgrade the pay and qualifications for teachers' aides and clerical staff. There are certain schools across this nation where teachers' aides are functioning, as the principal teacher in the classroom. There are other places where a teacher's aide is a sophisticated baby-sitter.

I think that there may come a time when the job description of a teacher's aide in the future will be practically the same as the job description of a teacher in the present, and the parallel growth will be that the job description of a teacher in the future is going to be more sophisticated and more involved so that the responsibilities of teachers' aides would enjoy the same kind of growth, if you will, as the responsibilities for a teacher.

I think that every teacher needs some kind of clerical support. If we continue to develop paper work and technology at the rate that we have, then we are getting to the point where every teacher needs a personal secretary. But whether or not that ever comes to pass, certainly those who are functioning in the positions of support personnel, in order to enhance what the teacher does, ought to be compensated in similar fashion.

As the teacher rises in esteem, so do those who are around them and among these aides are certainly the correct clerical support staff. Upgrading teachers' salaries to $50,000 (in 1991) should represent a "movement" which includes appropriate others.

Reason #49: Because we can provide for more teacher-sponsored scholarships for future teachers. To provide incentives and assistance for others to follow in our footsteps, not out of a conceited assessment of the importance of who we are, but just out of the experience of knowing that it is a serious profession that requires a great deal of study, practice, preparation and character, teachers should provide scholarships.

The chances are teacher organizations will begin to come together on a more regular basis, with greater frequency, and provide teacher-named scholarships for those who are coming into this profession. It is difficult to do so on a salary that just gets you by. It is more possible and more likely on a salary that does not cause a great deal of concern for investing in the future of our profession.

Reason 50: Because we need to be able to lead the profession toward dignity. Obviously different individuals will handle money differently. There are some people whom you can pay $10,000 a year and because of their personality and character, they could run a four-person home and survive with dignity. There are some whom you may pay $100,000 a year and would run a two-family home into debt without dignity.

Simply suggesting that $50,000 will somehow elicit character development from all who receive it is certainly ludicrous. But I am suggesting that the nature of the profession that they are in causes teachers to develop a great deal of character, perhaps more quickly than in other professions, because the encounters are so varied and so sudden based upon the different kinds of people—students, parents, colleagues, administrators, etc.— they encounter on a daily basis.

Most teachers come into the profession because they feel that they can help shape a better world. As it presently stands, it would be very difficult to find someone who had gone into the field of education in order to become rich. It is not that kind of occupation.

If, indeed, they can set aside and/or invest what is necessary for them to have a dignified post-career life, that can only serve to continue to enhance the profession's image. It is devastating to a young adult to run into a former teacher whom they regarded so highly who is now just barely making ends meet.

And I think that if demands made upon teachers would be consistent with higher salaries in order to see them retire in a dignified setting would speak well of the whole education arena. U.S. Presidents continue to have security around them. They retire well, and as a result of that, can write books comfortably, travel the world comfortably, and in many cases continue to make their mark upon a society that they served and loved. It may seem peculiar to compare teachers with presidents and/or heads of state, though I don't think the comparison is that far off, but let's suppose that it is and go to another extreme and compare teachers with athletes. Certainly teachers ought to be able to retire in as dignified a manner as professional athletes and entertainers.

I think that a consistent proper salary would provide for the possibility for teachers to leave the profession with dignity and with people who pay tribute to them and send them off into retirement in great style with a cruise somewhere. And we don't have to worry that not only when the cruise is over, but life's cruise is over, we will feel that they have served us well and they are able to spend the twilight years of their lives fulfilling some distant dream that they have wanted. Not only that, in order to prepare for it, Reason #50 would include that they could enhance their current benefits, their ability to remain happy and look after the health of their families and to take care of unfortunate happenstances all during their career, and again the opportunity to do that reduces the psychological discomfort and increases the ability to enjoy carrying out professional goals with a significant degree of enthusiasm.

*   *   *   *   *   *

This preface was called "$50,000 for 50 Good Reasons," and I am suggesting that whether or not you agree with every reason, the chances are that there must be two or three with which you agree that would accept the case being stated. Teachers in the U.S. do not get paid enough. Unfortunately, sometimes because of the lack of competitiveness, the profession does not attract the best and the brightest and so the Catch 22 is "Because teachers are not so good, we won't pay them so much." But, of course, if you don't pay them adequately, you cannot attract those who are good, and because they're not so good, we can't afford to pay them much. You understand the cycle?

And I'm saying that one way to break that cycle immediately, is to have the powers that be, all of the commissions since the National Commission on Excellence in Education in 1983, and all of the task forces, and all of the "Czars", and those who are looking at the educational situation and making suggestions, come together sometime and say, "Here's what we're going to do. We are going to make a bold statement that we have become serious where education is concerned and we're going to put our tax payers' money where our mouths are, and we're going to start paying teachers and we're going to start developing technology, and we're going to start to properly train those who are going into the profession, and we're going to make some demands and those demands are going to be carried out or they're not going to remain in the profession." And one of those bold statements would be to pay teachers $50,000 for one or more of the previous 50 good reasons.

A recent *Kansas City Times* sport section detailed the kind of money that is being paid to professional athletes, and I thought that what I might do, inasmuch as I have twenty-six years in education (and much of it in the area of workshops and in-services), I might act like a professional athlete and declare myself a free agent teacher."

And I think that if I go "free agent" in 1991, I might be able to attract some school districts across the U.S. that might want to negotiate with my attorney a contract similar to the way they negotiate with athletes, and I think that I would have a great chance of obtaining a significant salary because it would be a "first." I wouldn't want much more than the salaries that I see the basketball, football, and hockey players getting, and in declaring myself a free agent, I might start the bidding at somewhat less than a few of those whose contracts are mentioned in sports sections daily.

The newspaper article cited that Larry Byrd will get more than $6 million in the 1990-1991 season from the Boston Celtics. Kareem Abdul-Jabbar, Magic Johnson, Patrick Ewing, and Michael Jordan all have broken the $3 million per season barrier. So far baseball players, Kirby Puckett, Rickey Henderson, Mark Langston, Mark Davis, Joe Carter, and Robin Yount have $3 million contracts. And in football, Warren Moon, quarterback for the Houston Oilers broke the $2 million barrier in the National Football League. Wayne Gretzky and Mario Lemieux led the National Hockey League's march toward the 21st century at a little more than $2 million a piece.

Now I, in declaring myself a free agent teacher, would not ask for $3 million a year. I wouldn't even ask for the $2 million that the hockey players are getting. I would settle probably for starting my negotiations at ten percent of that amount, say,

$250,000 a year, to become a local teacher out here in the free agent market, realizing that I am compromising a bit and yet, inasmuch as I'm establishing a precedent, the ability to sign such a contract might lead to lucrative television commercials and book contracts. But just in case that sounds unreasonable, let me just suggest to you that Sugar Ray Leonard who is a professional boxer made an estimated $30 million in 1989 from two fights, one against Thomas Hearns that earned him about $13 million and another against Roberto Durand that earned him $17 million. Now here's a guy who can earn $30 million for fighting and I cannot earn one-tenth that much for breaking up fights!

In the last decade the **average** salary in the National Football League has gone from $80,000 to $300,000. So if I go free agent and ask for $250,000 as a free agent teacher, I'm asking for $50,000 less than the average salary and I've been in my business for 26 years. The average salary in the National Basketball Association is at $750,000 a year. That's the average salary for basketball players. Some of the guys in basketball and football leagues leave college before they graduate and some perhaps never go back to college. I have not only earned a degree but I also have been in my profession for 26 years and I'm asking for less than half as much as the average for basketball players whom I might have taught in order for them to get to the point where they could read the contracts that they're signing.

I mean, consider that a guy signs a $3 million contract in the National Football League and does precisely what is expected of him. He has the opportunity to take a losing football team and turn it around and when he turns that football team around, it can become a winning franchise. I have the opportunity, if I do what I'm paid to do as a teacher, to turn around the life of a child, perhaps, many children. If a guy signs a contract with the American League he gets on a baseball field for $3 million, he performs and performs well. He might take that baseball team to the World Series, and if I do what I am supposed to do, I might be able to help a child make a world serious. If somebody in the NBA were to do what they are supposed to do to bring crowds into the arena to stimulate television revenues causing the owner to be richer than they ever imagined themselves to be— then the guy has done everything he was hired to do and has truly earned his $3 million. If I do what I am supposed to do, then I may create or motivate 300 all-stars, but not just all-stars that would go to the NBA finals, but all-stars who would go into our courtrooms and mete out justice; all-stars, who go into the operating rooms and perhaps find that which would exorcise a cancer, not only from a patient but from our society. If I do what I'm supposed to do, I might inspire a young person to travel the world over and learn to speak the languages of people who have had differences from the time that many of them were born, and because of the inspiration of a teacher, be able to settle some differences across the world in order that we might live in peace and comfort—all for $250,000 or less then 10 percent of what the sports figure earned.

If I have a good season, if you pick up my free agency contract and I do what I'm supposed to do, then I will not pass a football or basketball efficiently, but I might be able to pass the torch of patriotism and progress to someone who would not only take on the other duties necessary to transform a society and lead a world, but also become a torch-passer himself or herself.

I would like to declare myself a free agent and get just one-tenth of what those who are half my age, half my experience, are getting by virtue of the fact that they have the capacity to be agile and strong and forceful, God-given gifts that they drop out of college to flaunt. But I would take my God-given compassion and study, prepare, teach, learn, and teach some more and learn some more to the point where I feel good enough to step out in the free agent market and declare myself available. Just give me less than one-tenth of that $3 million and I will work a longer season, I will exercise harder, and perhaps earn more but accept less.

Well, if you feel that these remarks are made with tongue-in-cheek, you're absolutely right. What I say with seriousness is that $50,000 for 50 good reasons is not a joke. And I would hope that those who read this understand that along with my call for properly compensating professional educators is certainly a serious need to talk about preparing educators for that compensation. I am not talking about just giving up $50,000 to someone who has determined that I teach because I can't do anything else. Oh, no. I'm not talking about giving up $50,000 because of what you want somebody to do. I'm talking about compensating many for what they have already done. I'm not talking about just simply giving up $50,000 without establishing any qualifications or criteria that will hold them accountable to the professional level to which they would be catapulted if indeed this could happen and happen quickly. And, if indeed one of those levels is proper pay, then also one of those levels is proper accountability.

There may come a time in our history when we will look back and actually find it amusing that there was a time when someone who was able to dunk a basketball actually earned twenty times as much as someone who was able to unlock the mysteries of the mind and teach someone how to make sense out of symbols. We may look back upon these times as the "Dark Ages" when we regarded educators as second-class citizens, when, in fact, they were the people responsible for bringing light to this darkness. *Plain Teaching*, is a book based upon the fact that there is an art to teaching that transcends even Michael Jordan's ability to stay up in the air minutes before dunking a basketball, and that transcends Wayne Gretzky's ability to control a hockey stick like Monét controlled a paint brush. If we are to be taken seriously as a society of enlightenment, then we must take seriously those who enlighten us. And that's our classroom teachers.

As I offer this book as a collection of "conversations with colleagues," my attempt is to reflect the contents of presentations made at conferences, in-services and institutes—if not verbatim, certainly close to it.

Among the "conversations" is a lecture that I call (consistent with the motto of *The Art of Positive Teaching*), "Nobody Rises to Low Expectations." In this lecture there are four mini-lectures which embody the philosophy of my service. The titles for the mini-lectures are:

1. You may not be able to teach people to love, but love will certainly help you teach people;
2. Please use CARE when you discipline;

3. Please leave teaching. Please leave, now. Don't wait. Don't hesitate. Don't pass go. Don't collect $200. Leave, now, and succeed elsewhere; and

4. Someone has chosen you.

As you read these offerings—and, for that matter, the rest of the book—you are reading what I say when I converse with colleagues (as opposed to what I would write if I were corresponding or, indeed, trying to write a book). The mini-lectures introduce *The Art of Positive Teaching.*

* * *   * * *

1 You May Not Be Able to Teach People to Love, But Love Will Certainly Help You Teach People

The Art of Positive Teaching asserts that love as a practical classroom concept is viable. In this context, the word love is being used as the agape love referred to by the Reverend Dr. Martin Luther King, Jr., as he discussed our need as human beings to find the capacity within each other and ourselves, to appreciate each other because we are humans and because our plight as human beings is a common plight as we attempt to overcome hatred, discrimination, fear and other negative elements that cause us to set up an estrangement between people, whether it be male-female, old-young, racial, teacher-student, or any other separation that is superficial in nature based upon society and barriers that seem to be put up between different entities. This is the kind of love that one gives, not because one expects love back, but because God gives us the capacity to love. It is the kind of love one gives because one feels good about one's self, and in feeling good about one's self, one is able then to pass on that good feeling to others because, if we really feel good about ourselves, we want other people to feel good. Within the educational arena, not only is it a love for self or because one feels good about self, but is also the love we have for those whom we teach. Most of us go into the profession of teaching because of altruistic and not economic factors. If there are those who have gone into the teaching field because you plan to become rich, my suggestion is that you speak with your colleagues who have been around for a while so that they might be able to advise you as to the reality of those prospects. Upon having this conversation, you might be able to find that you still have time to change professions because our profession is not yet respected in the manner that it should be, and yet there are those who insist on becoming teachers because we love ourselves, love those who we will teach, and love the prospect of being able to make a positive difference in the world by impacting positively on young minds who are idealistic, optimistic and patriotic.

Even as the preface discusses a rationale for teachers' being paid a base salary by 1991 standards of $50,000, I recognize that it might take years for America to come to that. I hope that it doesn't take too long because I think our priorities ought to be such that those of us who are responsible for the reproduction system of American society, that being the educational system, will, indeed, be respected and protected economically as well as socially and philosophically.

The love that I am saying should occur in the classroom, did not occur to me until 1972 when I ran into a former student whose name is Johnetta Lott. She asked me a question based upon a class that she was taking and a conversation that she had held with former students. And Johnetta's question was, "Mr. Boyd, what was it that you did when we attended Douglas that caused us to respond to you and do whatever you wanted us to do without raising your voice?" I thought that it was an interesting question and I appreciated Johnetta asking it because the first thing that occurred to me was how endeared I was to Johnetta for letting me know that the students at Douglas had done everything that I wanted them to do. I didn't realize that until Johnetta told me. And as I reflect on it, I'm sure that they really didn't. But in her mind, the perception was that the young people had indeed done "everything I wanted them to do."

But I didn't quite understand the question and I said to her, "What do you mean, Johnetta?" And she said, well, she had been exposed in a class at a community college to psychic phenomena—matters of the mind. And she said, "Do you practice transcendental meditation?" And my response was, "No, I don't practice T.M. and I really have no idea what kind of a psychic phenomenon may have existed in the classroom." We were getting ready to part and as we walked away from each other, it dawned on me to turn around and call back to Johnetta and say,

"It was love." And when I suggested that it was love, she kind of shrugged her shoulders and said, "O.K., Mr. Boyd." She didn't seem particularly impressed. Nor had I really internalized the concept, but at least I had put the thought in my mind as to what it was that caused young people to respond to me when I was teaching.

In my own mind I was not such a dynamic teacher. I certainly was not a great teacher, and, as a matter of fact, I could at the time that she posed that question to me, right off the top of my head name 100 teachers whom I know personally who could teach circles around me. I mean, just absolutely out-teach me without really even trying too hard, and I thought of John Jones, Mrs. Graves, Vivian Besley and Othello Laws at Douglas Elementary and Elma Dunbar whom I had met at Parkside and Janelle Hall, Sara Price, and Claudia McClain.

At any rate, I have been the recipient of teaching awards, both from my peers and from the Citizens' Schools Committee in Chicago, Illinois, and some other organizations who saw fit to cite me for being a good teacher. And it occurred to me that when I was effective, not that I always was, but when I was, it was really because of classroom climate, not my teaching methodology or necessarily knowledge of subject matter. And after having given Johnetta that response, it occurred to me that, indeed, love played a very important part in creating a classroom climate that caused young people to respond. I suggest that you may not be able to teach people to love because it is not something that can be taught. The fact that it is projected might cause someone else to pass the love along which makes it even more valuable than giving it back to you. Khalil Gibran in *The Prophet* says something like "Love is not binding, it is not possessive." Later on Gibran talks about the fact that love is sufficient unto himself. If God gives me the capacity to love, and I can pass it on, that gives me a great deal and that's sufficient. If it is given back to me, that's wonderful, but if it is passed on, that makes the passing on of love that much greater.

I wish that I could tell teachers that all you need do next Monday morning is go into your class and announce to your students, "Students, your teacher loves you." And students would then respond by saying, "Teacher, we love you too." And after the teacher says, "Your teacher loves you," and students say, "Teacher, we love you too," there would never be another problem in that classroom and students would learn everything they need to know. Excellence would be on everyone's agenda because everyone feels so wonderful and at the end of the day, everyday, people would hug each other and that would be magnificent.

Those of us who have taught for a while know that it is not likely to happen. As a matter of fact, if it did, that would be another book altogether. It is not something that you teach and it is not something that we can suggest that the passing on simply by itself will make all the difference in the classroom. It is just that in the U.S. we have become very cynical about using the word "love" and about embracing the concept of love. We have become cynical because there came a point in American history where love was translated "sex". Sex was translated as being something that was undesirable, negative or dirty, and suddenly for a teacher to suggest love of student would constitute inappropriate behavior.

The interesting thing about the issue of loving students and even embracing students is the fact that those students most in need of love are often perceived to be students who should not be shown love because of the possibility that they might misinterpret that show of love as being suggestive rather than encouraging. If there are students, for instance, who are at-risk, and part of their being at-risk is the fact that they have been sexually and psychologically abused, we then would have to be very careful about the way that we would show our love for them, and yet, because of their being abused, they are almost certain to be in need of our love. In such cases, we must learn to project our love in ways that are non-threatening to these students. But in terms of making the assumption that these are students most in need of being shown love, and that the assumption somehow being interpreted that they are the only ones who need love, would be an erroneous assumption, and, in fact, the majority of our students today are not the at-risk, abused population, but, indeed, a population that is in need of love.

Indeed, most of us are in need of love because in order for us to function in a society of other people our very existence depends on the constant need for acceptance by those whom we hold in some esteem to give us approval and to show us that approval in kind, considerate, and compassionate ways. That love must manifest itself in ways such as how we carry ourselves, how we project our sense of humor, how we call students by their names, how we get physically close to students in order that they know we perceive them as being human beings and we don't mind entering their space in non-threatening ways. We need to compliment students often rather than seeking opportunities to reprimand them—rewarding them more for what they do right rather than looking for opportunities to reprimand them for what they do wrong; becoming friendly without becoming familiar. These are ways that love can manifest itself when set up in a climate where learning is comfortable and students can recognize their own "somebodiness." *The Art of Positive Teaching* asserts that the most important element in effective instruction is the human dynamic that exists or occurs between teacher and student, and the most important ingredient in that dynamic is, indeed, love.

2 Please Use CARE When You Discipline

The acronym CARE stands for "Credible Authority Related to Esteem."

I suggest that credible authority related to esteem is an important ingredient in disciplining young people. Young people respond to a teacher's need for young people to discipline themselves rather than young people responding to a teacher's disciplining them. When we discuss the term discipline we should discuss the need for young people to control themselves rather than the need for young people to be controlled by the teacher, principal, coach, parent, or some outside entity. It would seem to me that a purpose of education is to assist young people in being able to control and discipline themselves in various settings.

When I speak of credible authority I am talking about authority that is attained due to consistent behavior over time. When I talk about credible authority I am saying that the authority acquires credibility in the child's mind based upon the child's observing the teacher, in various settings, being in control of him or herself. A child accepts the authority of someone whom the child trusts and whom the child sees as being in control as opposed to simply being in control of a situation. Children will certainly respond to the authority of people who may not have credibility in that child's mind, but their response might be out of fear. When children perceive that person in authority to be credible, that is to say, when children feel that the person is serious, sincere, and cares about the child, then the child considers that person to be credible because they are unwavering in their ability to be in control. When I talk about credible authority I am suggesting that it is important for us to have that because our aim is not, indeed, to be able to control the children. Our aim is, as I said at the outset, to assist children in growing to the point of controlling themselves, and children learn more by example than by instruction.

Credible authority as it relates to esteem suggests that children will respond to those whom they hold in esteem because the child's feeling about that person is that the person has achieved a level of integrity, intelligence, proficiency and success, if you will, that is desirable to the child. The child wants to emulate that behavior sometime in their own future. If one is held in high esteem, then a student is likely to follow directions because they feel that this person has something credible to say, and their directions ought to be heeded because the student believes that this person is helping them to go in the right direction. I say, use CARE when you discipline because I feel that CARE must precede discipline. One does not attain credible authority by disciplining others. One is able to discipline others upon attaining credible authority and being regarded with esteem.

Growing up in Ida B. Wells Project in Chicago, Illinois, in the 1940s and 50s, I grew up in a community that was, by all sociological standards, an impoverished community. However, while economically we might have been regarded as being on the low end of the socioeconomic scale, we were certainly wealthy as it pertained to the richness of our social relationships. We lived in a community where, if a child was disrespectful or disobedient in the presence of any adult, then any adult in the community had the authority of the child's parent to reprimand that child. Why was it that, indeed, any adult, had that authority? They had that authority because they were an integral part of the community and an integral part of the child's upbringing. The children would respond to the reprimand of an adult outside of the home because outside of the home was still an extension of the home. How do you develop a community that way? Well, you don't develop it overnight. It is due to consistent behavior over time.

All of the adults in the community seemed to know each other. All of the adults in the community seemed to respect each other, and there were silent codes, if you will, among the adults in the community that suggested that there was a separation between the adults and the children. The kind of separation between the adults and the children suggested to us as we were growing up that some things are just "grown folks' business." Indeed, children should stay out of grown folks' business. Now what that meant was that, as a child, I regarded the adults with some degree of esteem just by virtue of the fact that there were adult things that they did that were apart from the childlike things that I did. To be an adult was to be someone special, for example, able to purchase things at a grocery that children could not purchase. I can recall, and I'm certainly glad that I did not become a smoker, but I remember when I was growing up that smoking was an adult thing. Children didn't do that. Children didn't mess in grown folks' business. I can recall that when I was a child, if there were certain kinds of forms at school that needed to be signed, they were not authenticated unless somebody grown (an adult) signed those forms. I remember that when I was a child, your report card could not be returned to school unless your parents (somebody grown) signed the report card and then sent it back to school. I can recall that if the children wanted to have a party or a picnic, a softball tournament, a basketball game, to go on an outing or take a trip out of the city, somebody who was an adult had to chaperone, sign the forms, and apply far ahead to help plan it. Therefore, adults got some degree of authority by virtue of the fact that they were old enough to do these grown folks-type things. That authority became credible authority when my parents said, "You are to mind Mr. McAdams just like you are to mind me." And the reason that we will, indeed, mind Mr. McAdams was because Luther McAdams was to mind our parents just like he was to mind Mr. and Mrs. McAdams. They knew each other. They understood each other's values. They knew that if another parent reprimanded their own child, it would not be an abusive reprimand.

They knew that if, indeed, another adult in the community saw fit to invite a child into their house, even to wash up, that they were adults who could be trusted, and the first thing an adult did when a child went into another house was to call the parents and say, "I just want you to know I've got Carl over here. He was playing in the mud and the dirt. He is filthy. He is washing up. I'm going to send him home as soon as I get through." The likely response from my parents would be, "That's all right. Keep him if you want to. You can send him home next week." But both of those adults understood that their responsibility to the children was to prepare us for an unkind world that had rules to which we must adhere and that they must take us in hand at an early age, to make sure that we understood there were certain things that we must do if we were going to grow and mature and be properly educated—not schooled, but educated.

When a society has a community with adults who have credible authority, young people are likely to respond to that credible authority because that entire community buys into that authority, because we all know each other and know that the authority will be projected in a proper manner. Credibility comes with consistent behavior over time and exposure of that consistent behavior to children and the handing of credible authority from one adult to the next to mete out the same kind of punishment to all of the children in that community. The esteem comes when adults in the presence of children say things about other adults such as, "The reason that I appreciate Mr. Zeno is because he doesn't send his children to church—he takes them to church." "The reason I have respect for Mrs. Carr is because she doesn't let her children go out of the house until they get through with their homework." "The reason I love to go to Mrs. Dixon's home is because it is always spotless, and she decorates her home herself and does a beautiful job. I wish she would come and decorate my house sometime." "The reason I appreciate Mr. Collins is because he is such a good role model for young boys in the community." Hearing that consistently implants in the minds of the children in that community that the adults around there are really something.

Esteem also comes into play when adults in the community are complementary toward their children. We assume in the community that all the children will do well, but if they fall the adults will be there to pick them up because that's our job. Children will hold adults in high esteem because, somehow, they're always around, and if they're always around, then the children are not going to get away with too much because if they know that all the adults are in agreement on the upbringing of the children the child cannot get away with doing something in front of one adult because that adult agrees with another adult from whom they are hiding. They might as well give it up and not try to do it in front of any of the adults because, not only do the adults agree, they're also always around. It is also important that the child can depend upon adults to be there when they need some advice. They can depend upon an adult to be there when, indeed, they need these papers signed or they need permission to do something, or when the children want to go on a picnic or have a party.

I suggest using credible authority related to esteem when we discipline because my belief is that corporal punishment is not necessary in school settings. As a matter of fact, as you know, several states have outlawed corporal punishment in their public schools. When children respond to adults whom they regard as having their welfare at heart, they respond to how they regard the adults rather than respond to the adults' treatment of them based upon how the adults regard the children. It is what's in the child's mind that's important in discipline. Children who perceive adults as wanting control only do not respond well to discipline. Children who feel that adults operating in their best interest and want the children to control themselves respond better to discipline, and I believe that the desired response is elicited more easily and effectively without physical striking than with physical striking.

When I first began to teach, I tried corporal punishment. As a matter of fact, I thought that I was pretty tough as a teacher. However, I wasn't really tough. I was really a bully, and the reason I say I was a bully was because, in fact, if I used the paddle on someone, that someone on whom I used the paddle could not hit me back. And if they did hit me back, they could not win the confrontation because I was the person in authority and therefore, I could expel the student, or I could suspend the student, or I could require the student to bring his or her parents to school. The student could not do the same to me. That being the case, and since I know that I was not 100% correct when I meted out punishment, that means then that I hit some students whom I should not have hit, and hit them pretty hard. Young people being who they are, and their parents allowing me to have the credible authority were forgiving and allowed me to, indeed, be a bully. But at that point in my teaching career, it was credible authority *outside* of esteem because the young people also knew when I was wrong. It is to the credit of our youth that so many of them do not respond in kind when they are bullied by those of us who are in positions of authority, credible or not.

Another reason I suggest that corporal punishment is not appropriate in the school setting is school is the place where we assist young people in learning how to "Do it right." In America, too often, we teach young people, either overtly or inadvertently, that the resolution to conflict must be violence. In movies, in television series, in idolizing hockey players who fight and boxers who are triumphant, in cheering on the football players who grimace at their victims of a hard tackle, we encourage young people in this society to be tough, to be mean, and to be violently triumphant. But, at the same time, all society discusses our quest for world peace. In school we should be assisting young people in understanding that conflicts can, indeed, should be, resolved non-violently.

If we want students who have problems with each other to learn how to come together with understanding and to resolve their conflicts peacefully, then we ought to model that in the way we handle conflicts with our students, not through the use of corporal punishment. Another reason that I think that corporal punishment should not be used in schools is because more and more we are asked as educators to be the surrogate parents of children who come to us. As we use corporal punishment, we are usurping that aspect of the child's discipline from the parents whose rightful place it is if the child is going to be punished physically, to, indeed, do so. I think that CARE, *teaching through love and understanding is far more effective than teaching* through intimidation and fear. If there is such a thing as a total environment of love and understanding and caring, it is likely that children will grow up to embrace love, understanding, and caring as a means toward approaching other people including their own children. Children should see school as a pleasant place to be where they can learn confidently and with joy.

CARE recognizes this need for consistency, not only in the continuity of behavior of a particular teacher, but based upon the uniformity of application of rules or the uniformity of application of consequences for violating rules by all members of a staff at a school. If there's one thing that is important about school discipline, it is the need for all those in authority to embrace and enforce school rules. A single person in authority, whether it be a teacher, administrator, or paraprofessional, can be the weak link that causes an entire chain in a school community to be irreparably damaged and cause young people to respond poorly to our need to have them be disciplined.

My reference to the community in which I grew up is made to suggest that, if schools are to enjoy the same kind of credible authority among teachers as was recognized in our neighborhood adults, schools must function as communities. Being a proponent of neighborhood schools (see Lesson 39), I believe the community-school can be achieved in that setting. Where there are not neighborhood schools, we need school communities.

3 Please Leave Teaching. Please Leave, Now. Don't Wait. Don't Hesitate. Don't Pass Go. Don't Collect $200.00. Leave, Now, And Succeed, Elsewhere!

Inasmusch as *The Art Of Positive Teaching*, as the name suggests, is a positive effort, I anticipate the question, "Why would something that seeks to project positiveness suggest something that is so negative?" Allow me to put this consideration in a positive perspective. Teaching is a peculiar profession. Everyone cannot do this. And, those who cannot should not feel badly about the fact that they cannot teach. They should only feel badly when they cannot teach, know that they cannot teach, but insist on teaching anyway. To be an ineffective teacher does not, necessarily, mean that one is an ineffective person. The greatest college or university academician can become a terrible classroom teacher. Perhaps the intelligence is there, but not the sensitivity. A fantastic television personality could be perfectly comfortable in front of a camera but just awful in front of a classroom full of fourth graders. Everyone can't do this stuff. It's hard, and getting harder as the world grows more complex.

Now, when I suggest that there are those who should "please leave" our profession, I am not talking about those who may have a bad year—or, perhaps, two bad years. Some of you have taught long enough to know what it means to get "that class." I'm talking about that class which is intent on proving how terrible they can be. That class that is attempting to live up to (or, "down to") the self-fulfilling prophecy, suggested unwittingly by several teachers, that no one can handle them. There was a classroom at one of the schools where I taught—Parkside Elementary in Chicago—that was so bad that, at the end of the school year, the principal, Mrs. Saxon, decided to "retire their room number." If we teach long enough, we are likely to run into "that" class.

When I request that some among us should leave our ranks, I'm talking about those who really don't want to be here anyway. Teaching is, by far, the most important profession there is, bar none. If you want to challenge me on that, I will accept your challenge with a simple question. You tell me the profession you believe to be more important than teaching and I'll ask you the question, "What if those who practice that profession were poorly taught?" If you think the guardians of our shores are more important than teachers, just consider what danger we would be in, in this high-tech world, if an ill-trained soldier pushed a wrong button or failed to follow instructions as he or she had been taught early in life. If you think that those who are the guardians of our liberties are more important than teachers, I ask you to consider the peril present if those "guardians" were taught by cynics or ill-informed historians. The reproductive system of our society is our educational system, and what becomes of us depends—not solely, but greatly—on elementary through high school teachers.

Whenever I address a group I always ask this question; but, I also ask that no one punch the person next to you, and point at someone in the room. The question is, inasmuch as we teach by subscription, not conscription, is it not odd to see someone who has chosen this profession come to school, everyday, angry? Upset before the day begins. Isn't it a little strange that someone would choose to work with children who obviously hates children? An unkind word uttered by a disgruntled teacher on a given day might turn off a child from school for the rest of the child's life.

I also ask you, teachers, "Would you want you to be your child's teacher?" If the answer is, "No," then you should not be anybody's child's teacher. Everybody is somebody's child, and that parent deserves from us the same things we expect from the teachers of our children.

Too often, in teaching, we are our own worst public relations representatives. Some who are good will be talked about by students, their parents and others in the community. But, it seems, all who are bad will be talked about. And, as we ourselves complain—even when complaints are justifiable—we need to take care where we speak, and to whom. Students are turned off by negative attitudes just as they can be turned on by positives. Media will sometimes probe into our complaints in search of an exposé-type story, and we won't even realize that the catalyst for the probe was something that we said in a moment of frustration.

Often, colleagues repeat, "I can make a lot more money somewhere else!" Well, please, go get the money. Do not take out your cynicism and bitterness on someone else's children, six hours a day, five days a week.

Consider this. Suppose you are the one who gets "that" class. And suppose you work harder than you've ever worked to turn them around. And, for some reason, they decide—near the end of the year; say, in March—to respond, positively, to your teaching. Only a couple of months left, but at least they've come around. In those last couple of months you work even harder, because now you're seeing results. This class will not soar to the top in your school, but they can do all right with the proper effort and encouragement. And, they're worth it, as are any other students. How do you feel when you know that, next year, they're going to get someone who does not care? How do you feel, knowing that they are going to get someone who will, in the first few days of the new school year, undo what it has taken you a year to do? Don't you want to say to your colleague—even if it's to a friend—"Please leave teaching!?"

Or, suppose you get "that" class which is on the other end of the behavioral and academic spectrum: I mean the class that is going to conquer the world; the class you've been waiting for. These students raise their hands when you ask questions—with answers. They do homework, on time, and initiate creative learning activities. You knew there were students like this, but you never expected them to all show up in the same classroom— yours. And, so you work with them. You challenge their minds.

Never any remediation; only enrichment. You guide them toward reaching beyond their grasp. They are sometimes hyperactive; sometimes over-enterprising. But, wouldn't they be? You help them temper unfocused enthusiasm with calm reflection. This is the class they trained you by in teachers' college—you remember; when you thought all classes were going to be like this. Now, here they are. And you only had to wait 23 years. How do you feel when you take them higher than they knew they could go; knowing that next year they are going to get a teacher who will not only be uninspired, but who also resents "smart alecks" like these? Don't you want to say to that person, ahead of time, before the students have to go to that class, "Please leave teaching!?"

Let me tell you a question I hate to hear but love to answer: "Carl, whatever happened to the good ol' 'dedicated teachers' like we used to have? You know the teachers like (and, then a list of names from when 'we' had)?" I don't like the question because it assumes that there are no dedicated teachers left. But, I enjoy answering the question because it gives me an opportunity to answer, "The dedicated teachers are where they've always been: in classrooms throughout the nation. In fact, in today's world teachers have to be—and, are—more dedicated than ever. As we are called upon, not only to address academic subject matter, but the social ills of the time: crime, addiction, pregnancy, sexually transmitted diseases, war, homelessness, "pre-puberty peer pressure," and more, to teach means to be dedicated or be ineffective. You see, when folks ask about teachers' dedication, they only ask part of the real question. Instead of simply asking, "Whatever happened to the ol' dedicated teachers?" those inquiring need to complete the question: "Whatever happened to the ol' dedicated teachers? And the ol' dedicated parents? And the ol' dedicated support systems which, at one time, gave teachers 'credible authority' simply by virtue of the fact that our children were their charges?"

We are functioning almost in isolation. The larger society seems to want to accuse us more than assist us. If we are not dedicated, we're in the wrong profession. This is some hard stuff. It's nothin' to play around with; or to use as a stepping stone to some other, unrelated, field. This is not for amateurs. We have young people coming to us burning with needs that they have not the sophistication to identify nor, if they could, the articulation to express. Considering all that we face in today's world (and should anticipate in the years to come), I'd like to paraphrase Harry Truman's great quote and suggest, "If you can't stand the kids, get out of teaching."

Well, I said I'd like to put this mini-lecture, though it might sound negative, in a positive light; first by indicating that everyone can't do it, and, now secondly, by saying that, as I ask those that should not be here to leave, I ask those who ought to to please keep teaching. We need the brightest and the best. We need the strong and the wise, the sensitive and the demanding. If you are loving; if you care before disciplining, if you understand that one bad year does not a poor teacher make; please keep teaching. Your students need you. Enhance who we are collectively by making an important individual decision: please keep teaching.

But, if you know that this is not the place for you, do not feel badly. Understand that you are not the only one affected by what you do, or fail to do. If you know deep in your heart that teaching is not in your heart—and you don't do it well—I ask you with no malice or prejudice, "Please leave teaching. Please leave, now. Don't wait. Don't hesitate...."

4 Someone Has Chosen You

On May 25, 1974, I heard Dr. Barbara Sizemore who was then the Superintendent of Schools in Washington D.C., lecture on future information and the technological age, and I think that Barbara Sizemore was right on target. In fact, that was before *Megatrends*. During her discussion, Dr. Sizemore hit on a number of things that are of extreme importance. The one thing, however, that I took away with me and has been with me now for 16 years was, "Someone has chosen you. You may believe that you exist in relative or absolute anonymity, but someone has chosen you as a role model." Dr. Sizemore's point seemed to be, and what I carried away with me was, that whoever you are, there is someone who is determined that they like the way you walk and the way you relate to people. And, for some reason, they like the way you relate to them in particular.

They have chosen you as a role model and if, indeed, that is the case, then we as educators ought to be very careful about the way we carry ourselves in front of anyone because someone has chosen each of us. And they have chosen each of us for the peculiar qualities that we bring to the profession—not because of our cheap imitation of someone else's qualities. The someone who has chosen us often is the someone whom we would least expect to have chosen us as their role model. In fact, there are many teachers who have taught long enough to know that those who come back to say "thank you" in later years, are those we would have thought to have had in their "job descriptions" the responsibility to drive us absolutely crazy when they were in our classrooms. These visitors are those who show up at our classroom doors as we duck behind the desk thinking that they might be returning or that they might have children. We did not realize at the time that the seeking of our attention was not to bother or irritate us, but to gain our attention because they had a need to identify with us because they had chosen us as a person to emulate.

Someone *has* chosen you, and when you consider that someone has chosen you, perhaps that will dictate to you that when you are in a solemn mood, you will not want to say the wrong thing based upon your emotions because that person may be watching, and in so watching, may have a negative feeling, not only about the person who said it, but also about teaching or about themselves in relationship to the person whom they have chosen. If we understand that, then we will also attempt to heighten our level of professionalism in that person's presence because we would want to encourage that person with positive examples with what it is to be a good person in order to stimulate that person toward a productive and positive lifestyle.

Now, inasmuch as I don't know who that person is, then what that suggests is that we ought to be careful in front of everyone. It is important for us at all times to recognize that it may not be a student who is the one who has chosen us. It may be an impressionable colleague, and that impressionable colleague does not necessarily have to be someone who is younger than we. It may, indeed, be someone who is older and perhaps, based on some negative experiences or the fact that young people have changed, has developed a negative attitude toward the profession and sees in our new blood some idealism, faith, optimism, or energy that they wished they had, and because, they wish they had it, they begin to imitate, even emulate, things that we do. And we are thinking that they are the ones who know everything about the profession because they have been in it for so long. We don't know who has chosen us, but whomever it is, they deserve to see our best. That doesn't mean that they deserve to see us in a phony light—that is, attempting to be something that we are not or attempting to be some peculiar definition of what being professional is, using words that are not common to our everyday vocabulary or dressing in an ostentatious fashion or being syrupy sweet when, indeed, our emotions would dictate that we are truly upset. It is important that those who are looking to us as role models see the real us, and in some cases, that would include being upset because one aspect that they will want to see in us is how we react to being upset, and what skills we might impart to them by our example as to how to cope with negative circumstances that might occur during the course of a day or a school year. The reason it is important to realize that we are "chosen" by someone because of our own character is because we might want to be like someone else. That doesn't work.

To give an example of what I'm talking about, when I came into teaching in September 1964, I wanted to be not only a "nice" person, but I also wanted to be a disciplinarian and didn't quite know how to manage the two. But I would suspect that at the time that I came into teaching, if I had to choose between the two, I would have wanted to have been a stern disciplinarian. As it turned out, I was less a disciplinarian than I was a "nice" person. But there was a disciplinarian after whom I wanted to pattern myself, and I just didn't have the wherewithal to do it.

A teacher who taught at Douglas Elementary School in Chicago epitomized what my perception of the professional teacher ought to be. In fact, it was a female teacher who had taught for several years by the time I became a first-year teacher at Douglas. Her name was Mrs. Vivian Besley. Mrs. Besley was part of the matriarchy of Douglas and she taught on the third floor with Mrs. Brown, Mrs. Major, Miss Laws, Miss Jackson, Mrs. Redd, Mrs. Bishop, and a number of other teachers who were recognized in that school as being strong, old-fashioned teachers who took no "stuff" from anybody, and, in fact, would make sure that all who came there must toe the mark. Douglas Elementary School at the time was K-8 and had an enrollment of 2,000 students. In that elementary school students might dare to run on the first floor, they might walk fast on the second floor, but nobody fooled around on the third floor. And if Mrs. Besley spotted someone on the third floor who was supposed to be on the first floor, she might say "What are you doing on the third floor when you know you belong on the first floor? I see no document in your hand giving you permission to be on the third floor, so I would suggest that you reach in your pocket and find something signed by someone in authority that gives you permission to be up here. I want you to take care of your business expeditiously, then beat a path back down to the first floor where you belong." And that's when she was talking to the principal! That's how tough Mrs. Besley was. She was one of those teachers who could just fold her arms and do it with her eyes. All she had to do was roll her eyes in your direction and you stood still. She wouldn't even turn her head. Just her eyes pointed in your direction would cause you to straighten up, stand at attention, answer whatever she asked, and get on about your business.

I wanted to be like Mrs. Besley. I remember a school year when I had four students whom other seventh grade teachers would not take. I taught on the second floor, and during that school year, a couple of these fellows were in the corner of the room boxing, and I decided that I was going to "Mrs. Besley" them. I stood with my arms folded and without moving my head, I gave those young brothers the eye. Then I gave them another eye. Pretty soon Barbara Brantley, sitting in front of me, said, "Mr. Boyd, is there something in your eye?" I mean, there was no way that I could be a Mrs. Besley, and yet somehow there was something that I learned to do. Something that was among the strengths that I have and was able to cultivate and that caused Johnetta Lott some years later to say to me, "Mr. Boyd, what was it that you used on us that caused us to respond to your teaching methodology?" I had to answer for Johnetta, in my case, I feel that it was love.

Everyone has something. Reverend Dr. C.A.W. Clark, an evangelistic minister, spoke at Palestine Missionary Baptist Church of Jesus Christ May 29, 1981 and made this statement: "God did not give anybody everything, but He gave everybody something." There is something that every teacher has that they can give that will help their colleagues share with each other and share well; that will help their administrators feel good about the fact that they have someone on their team who is a team player who understands the human dynamic that exists and occurs between teacher and student, and in that understanding, attempts every day to be THE role model that they ought to be, just in case someone has chosen them.

* * *　　* * *

The following 49 lessons are divided into 7 chapters. Chapter 1 simply entitled "Self". For each of the chapters, the first word will be "Self", based on the art of positive teaching philosophy, that, because we are the ones responsible for ourselves and for the classroom, what we do begins with "self".

SELF

Lesson 1
Love

A teacher instructs those who have learned to want as well as those who want to learn. In this case, love is a verb rather than a noun. It is an action word. In his book, *The Prophet*, Khalil Gibran suggests, "Love possesses not, nor would it be possessed, for love is sufficient unto love." When I talk about a teacher's love, I'm not talking about a love that requires, nor even love that desires, but a love that is borne out of an inward feeling of goodness about one's self, about one's situation, about those with whom one works, and about those whom we serve— meaning the students and the community. And I am suggesting that in the classroom love is as much a practical application as an altruistic orientation because feeling good about one's self really manifests itself in certain kinds of behaviors that are easily detectable by those who are acted upon by the teacher.

As a matter of fact, in a very simple, practical way, think about how you approach your family and friends, social and other situations when you feel good, when you have a feeling of lightness, a feeling of positive anticipation, a feeling of wanting to make others around you feel as good as you do because you have such a great feeling. If we listen to Khalil Gibran, it suggests to us that we do not want to require of others that they love us back just because we project this feeling of love, but because we want the best for those who are the recipients of this love which is sufficient unto itself and not something that would make it an obligation of those receiving it to return it. It is important that young people perceive not only that we feel good toward them in terms of the way we act toward them, but that we also feel good about them. The motto, if you will, of the art of positive teaching is: **No one rises to low expectations.** And so it is that we ought to, indeed, have high expectations for those with whom we work. This feeling of love rises because we're not so much talking about our high expectations for the abilities of those with whom we work, but we're talking about really wanting these young people to do well and to feel very good about who they are. We have such a good feeling about ourselves and about what we do and why we are doing it that anybody who encounters us knows that we are there because we love being there.

Why is this important? Well, I don't know whether we want to go back to Disraeli in *Sybil*, but Disraeli's quote is "We are all born for love. It is the principle of existence, and its only end." So often what we find in peculiar behavior is really the reaching out for acceptance. I go so far as to say, "reaching out for love." If that is true of those we teach, it is probably also true of us—perhaps to a greater or lesser degree in some people. All of us are in search of love and an acceptance that says, "Even with your faults, I feel good about you and want the best for you." If I am in search of that, then I ought to suspect that perhaps, at least, my students are also in search of that. So even if the students who come into contact with me receive a reprimand from me, even that reprimand can be couched within the context of love. If my students receive criticism, I must make sure that it is constructive criticism because of this very feeling of love. If my students have not earned a passing grade or have not earned the right to receive certain privileges, it is my responsibility to make sure that not only do they earn it, but that they understand why they should earn the privilege to go forward because I want a great deal from them based on this feeling of love.

If, indeed, we were teaching a very young child to cross the street, look both ways, observe traffic lights, listen for the traffic, we would not take the chance on their crossing the street alone if they have not learned the previous skills. We would be doing them an injustice to say "O.K.—you're ready to cross on your own now." We just don't do that with people whom we love because we know the dangers that exist in crossing that street and possibly losing their lives.

This is a lesson based on the attitude that "I love you too much to allow you to go by yourself without having earned the right and the privilege to do so."

In the classroom the practical application of having a love that is so profound that you will not allow students to go on unless they have earned the right and the privilege to do so ought to be a very pronounced aspect of loving young people in order that they will understand—that they have to earn the right to cross the educational, academic streets by themselves by learning the lessons that we present to them at a young age and building upon those lessons until they can, indeed, do this on their own. I am saying that the way we approach it is significantly impacted upon by how deeply we feel toward those whom we teach. If we do not care whether they learn or not, it may very well be that we will allow them to pass on based on their personalities or based upon their age or based upon local convenience because our love is not strong enough to insist on preventing them from going further when they are not prepared to do so. I am saying that "If I love you enough, I will want to make sure that you have all the tools to make it in life and that, until you do, I will not push you into a dangerous arena of performance that could adversely affect your progress because you are too important too me."

There is also the consideration of what love does to the classroom and school climate for the collective recipient of our attitudes toward what we do, meaning the entire classroom and/or student body. A feeling of love creates an atmosphere that makes learning comfortable. A feeling of love helps us send signals to students that are positive, caring, nurturing, and loving. Using care when you discipline is an acceptable kind of authority because it is couched within the context of a caring that is important to anyone who is to receive a reprimand. But even without the consideration of using care when you discipline, using love when you teach—which may be all positive—carries with it a significant psychological boost because the collective feeling as well as the individual feeling within that classroom and school, where love seems to abound helps everyone to feel ashamed of not knowing something because they know that the people around them want, so much, for them to learn.

This carries with it a significant psychological boost because it is a climate where the feeling is that people are there because they want to be there, not because they are required to be there. This carries with it a significant psychological boost because, in some form or other, I do believe Disraeli from the standpoint that we all seek some love if it is not, indeed, the ultimate quest, and receiving it, feeling it, seeing it around us on a day to day basis really helps us to do what we must do. And I am saying, in this instance, it helps us to teach and it helps young people to learn when they are learning from those who project this feeling of love.

Let me say here that I am not suggesting that this is a simple thing because the way things are going in our educational institutions today, particularly public schools from grades K-12, there are some educators who are finding it very difficult to allow this love that they do have to manifest itself overtly because many of the young people whom we encounter today not only seem unable to reciprocate that love, but even to reciprocate an appreciable degree of respect. We are working with young people today who seem to want what they want at the time they want it so that their real deep emphasis is on immediate gratification. They exist in a world that emphasizes material things rather than concepts or feelings. We also exist within a society today where young people are more assertive, less likely to accept simply because we, as the teacher, say that things are so and many of us can remember a teacher's "Do that because I said 'Do that' and I have no need to explain to you why. Just do it because I said so." Now young people today do not accept that —not only in many cases from figures of authority in the school, but sometimes they don't even accept it from figures of authority at home.

When we encounter young people who do not have what we would consider basic manners, respect, and courtesy that is learned at home, sometimes it is very difficult for us to project a feeling of love because our interpretation of projecting a feeling of love is to do things overtly that look like we want youngsters to like us and that we like them. Generally, love behaviors manifest themselves based on the way we were taught, not just on the way that we feel.

And so it is that if someone says that they love you, then that means they will be nice to you because that is something that we have learned. If someone says that they love you, that means that they will not give you a hard time because if you love someone, you really want to make them feel good and want to ease them into learning. We have been taught that if someone says that they love, they will give you what you want. We have been taught that when someone says that they love you, they will back you up in tight situation.

I believe that there are not as many young people who are disrespectful as we perceive there to be based upon media coverage of the disrespectful. But, even as we encounter, those who believe in immediate gratification, those who defy authority in large numbers, we must realize that they are in greater need of love than we were when we were their age because for them to live in a society absent of love, not only are they deprived of the feeling but they are also deprived of an opportunity to learn what is and how love behaves in social settings. Therefore, the practical application of love from a classroom teacher not only has to do with the development of a certain learning climate based upon that good feeling, but it also has a great deal to do with setting the kind of example that lets young people know what love is, how love acts and what it does in particular situations. Love also suggests that rather than being a sweet, syrupy "I will allow you to do whatever you want to do because I love you" kind of projection, love suggests that "I must prepare you for a very harsh world, and in preparing you for a very harsh world, I must be honest with you, I must criticize you when you deserve criticism, I must reprimand you when you have earned reprimand, and I must slow you down when you're going too fast and pick you up when you're going too slowly." The manifestation of love is not something that I see as simply being an unconditional acceptance of any behavior in any setting, but the manifestation of love is to assist young people in understanding, recognizing, and internalizing healthy social and psychological behavior toward themselves and then toward others. And we cannot assist young people in realizing that if we do not have love within ourselves.

Lesson 2
Dare to Fail

In consideration of educational reform in schools across America, there are those (even those who are not classroom practitioners) who are suggesting various ways to help schools succeed in their efforts to teach *all* children. With the various suggestions there is still a need to come up with the way to do it right. There are a number of methodologies and approaches being forwarded by theoreticians in universities, governors' commissions, and the business community interested in making sure that those who enter the work force are prepared to do quality work.

Because the future is so important, we are trying desperately to find ways to make sure all young people who are educated, learn and learn well. Everyone has the right as well as the responsibility to come up with what they think is a proper solution. And if those solutions are born out of significant research, either based on teaching experience and/or extensive reading on the matter of what makes for a successful school and/or attendance at conferences, workshops, universities, etc., it would seem proper to take note as to what those who are forwarding suggestions are saying. If we are to take serious note as to what is being said by those who are studying the issue of how to make schools work, then it only makes sense to me that among those who should be listened to first and most intently, should be classroom teachers.

It is peculiar then, that there are so many of us who are in the classroom on a day to day basis who are intimidated by others whose theories seem to be lofty and, in so being intimidated, do not attempt those things that perhaps intuitively make sense to us. We feel, because oftentimes we teach the way we were taught, that anything that we do must be grounded in empirical data based upon years of research, or must come from someone with the proper letters, credit, and number of books

behind them either having written them or having read and
analyzed them.

In informal conversation there are times when we say, "You
know, somebody ought to....", and then the end of that sentence
becomes nothing more that a mere suggestion, and sometimes it
doesn't even formulate into a suggestion; it is just kind of a
statement in passing.

One of the reasons that we are reluctant to suggest is because of "Evaluaphobia." Evaluaphobia is the fear that a classroom teacher holds for improperly implementing someone else's
good idea. I'd like to expand upon that definition of
Evaluaphobia now by saying that it is also a classroom teacher's
fear of improperly implementing *one's own good idea*. We are
reluctant because we are evaluated based upon results and if,
indeed, we try something that may not immediately yield observ-
able results, then it may very well be that we will be evaluated
poorly or we may evaluate ourselves poorly based upon something that, here again, was not grounded deeply in educational
theory or observed practice.

I am suggesting that we dare to fail. I am suggesting that if
our creative juices are flowing and it is born out of an earnest
desire to try something that might, indeed, get to the young
people whom we are teaching on a day to day basis, I am saying,
"Why not try it?" If, indeed, throughout the years, it appears
that no one had come up with THE definitive answer as to how
to teach all children and teach them well, and infuse within
them a spirit that would have them not only learn but want to
apply that learning to the progress and productivity of a nation
that they love, then why should one classroom teacher be afraid
or ashamed to assert their own ideas? Others have been wrong.
Others have failed, and based upon those failures, some good
ideas have come out because failure is one of the things that
helps us to learn how to do it right.

I am suggesting that if anyone has the right to dare to fail,
it is the classroom teacher because the teacher is the one who
suffers the brunt of whatever evaluation might come out of attempting to implement somebody else's idea, so certainly they
ought to be able to attempt some of their own ideas. And, in most

cases, I would suspect it would be a better idea than theorists come up with because we are there every day. A classroom teacher ought to dare to fail because young people observing the process of attempting something that may work, but then again, may not, will also learn from the process and from the teacher's reaction to his or her success or failure. If, indeed, we come up with something that makes sense to us and attempt it in the classroom, if we have colleagues observe our attempts in the classroom and critique it, if we have the young people whom we are attempting to teach participate in a particular experiment in the learning process and allow them not only to make suggestions but also to criticize it, it might be very interesting for all to observe not only the outcome but to critique the process so even the process itself may be a part of the development of something better should this particular effort fail.

Classroom teachers should be able to dare to fail because they ought to feel confident enough about themselves that they would share with those in authority "above them" what their ideas are and what they are going to attempt to do, and enlist support and assistance. Many good ideas die for lack of proper timing. We contemplate, we wait, we study, we discuss—sometimes discussing to the point of talking the idea away.

The number one reason for daring to fail is that we might come up with something that is important and significant in the learning process that will benefit all students. The second reason for suggesting that we dare to fail has to do with what will happen to us personally. Remember the title of this chapter is simply "Self" and remember that I am suggesting those things that occur within a classroom depend primarily on what happens within the psyche and the teacher's personality more than anything else in that classroom as an initiator of setting a climate and exemplifying what a good learner does. To dare to fail will give us the confidence that we are projecting what we'd like to see in students. We are fortified by our daring whether it results in success or failure. It is important in life that we must look around us at the number of failures that precede a significant success. If we would study the autobiographies of successful entertainers, business people, entrepreneurs and public figures, we will find in many instances, if not in most, that their lives have been filled with mishaps, obstacles, indeed, failures preceding whatever success they now enjoy. And even now, a great part of the success that they do enjoy carries some failure if they continue to be risk takers. It is those very failures that help us to learn, and as we learn through taking risks, our successes will become far more frequent and far more substantial than our failures.

This does not suggest by any means that anyone ought to seek failure or that which we try should be frivolous or without some significant thought. I am not suggesting that simply on a whim we ought to risk the educational lives of those who follow our lead in the classroom on a day-to-day basis. I am not suggesting that we be creative for creativity's sake, or that we need risk failure if we are succeeding in many ways in our classrooms in the first place. Certainly, those things that are working ought to be continued and repeated and embellished upon. But if we are to be exemplars of positive risk taking, then we ought to dare to fail and should that daring result in success continue, and should that daring result in failure, note it, critique it, understand it, and do it differently the next time. However, we will never find out if we do not dare to fail.

$$\boxed{\text{SELF}}$$

Lesson 3
Emphasize Your Strengths

Each of us brings something to the educational climate and, for that matter, each of us has something to bring to whatever situation we find ourselves in. And whatever it is, it is something that, if used properly, can enhance the situation we face. As it pertains to teachers in a learning situation, every teacher has something to bring that is probably unique or peculiar to that particular teacher. No two of us are the same, and no one of us has everything that is excellent in the teaching arena.

It is important for us to (a) Realize that each of us has something; (b) To recognize that that something is in ourselves as well as publicly recognize and reward that which is positively used by others, and in recognizing what it is that we have, learn how to use whatever strengths we have been given in positive and productive ways in the classroom, and then practice that to the point where it becomes natural and comfortable so that young people can benefit greatly from whatever strengths that we have. It is not a matter of positive humility to be shy about the strengths that we have and can use in the classroom It is not useful, and, to my way of thinking, it is not proper to hide one's talents in the interest of being humble. And the reason that I say it is not positive humility is because we owe it to the world and certainly as professional educators, we owe it to our students who depend upon us to do our very best, to show our best, and to use our best to achieve the desired result. And in the case of the classroom, that desired result is to create a climate wherein young people can learn to their greatest potential—whether that learning be rapid or slow, deep or shallow, enthusiastic or reluctant. Our responsibility as professionals is to use whatever strengths we have to make sure that we pull out the deepest potential in each of our students.

Emphasizing one's own strength is a matter of fairness. I believe that it is absolutely unfair to our students, to have a great talent in some area that can enhance the classroom climate and to use it only in social situations among personal friends or only to use it at home among family, or not to use it at all. We are given talents for a reason, and that reason is not simply to keep them to ourselves, but, indeed, to share with a world longing for whatever resources we can give to help us move toward peace and productivity.

It is good to recognize the talents of others, but if those talents are not ours, sometimes it is a waste of time to attempt to imitate those talents. In my own case, I think that I am long on creativity and short on administration. Therefore, I attempt to use my human skills in ways that enhance the learning climate while improving upon my administrative, academic, and technical skills. But if I recognize that my creativity is a greater strength than my technical output, it would not be fair to my students to be technically rigid while allowing my creative juices to flow only within the realms of my own imagination without ever taking a chance on letting my students see the humanness in me, the daring that I talked about in Lesson 2, and the creative romantic side of what I bring to the educational situation.

In a guest-teaching situation, for instance, I observed a classroom teacher teaching adolescents who were going over parts of speech. These adolescents were attending a senior high school, but they were doing work that was on a sixth grade level. Observing the situation, I noticed that the regular classroom teacher was very good on technique, understood how to introduce a lesson, to use the textbook, to delegate responsibility to the young people, to read and do the exercises that were at the end of the chapter, and to discuss the answers when asked about nouns, pronouns, verbs, adverbs, adjectives, etc. When allowed to take over this class, my interest was to achieve the same outcome desired by the regular classroom teacher which was, indeed, to enhance these adolescents' understanding of the parts of speech and their usage in everyday language as well as the written word. As you can well imagine, if they were in secondary school but were doing sixth grade work their abilities were not consistent with their peers. That being the case, along with other social and environmental factors and perhaps peer influence, the youngsters were not attacking their assignment with any degree of appreciable enthusiasm.

My approach, because of my own personality, and because I wanted to introduce myself to them as someone who understood their plight, was to begin to discuss something that was relevant to their lesson but not immediately recognized as pertinent to what was going on at the time. And since many of the students in the class were adolescent boys, I asked them about practicing basketball, and I opened the discussion by saying to them, "Who can play basketball?" Now, with a group of adolescent boys, whether they can play or not their response is going to be in the affirmative because, being in front of their peers, they don't want to say that they don't know anything about athletics, and oftentimes they will say it even though they don't. (Now I have some argument with that because I don't think that we should allow young people to feel ashamed because of a lack of athletic prowess. Whatever strengths a child might have should be complimented. And, I need, as an educator, to go back and offer other similar introductions in areas that might interest those who are not interested in athletics.) But at any rate, when I said, "Who can play basketball?", practically all of the fellows and a couple of girls said they could. And I said, "What do you do before going on the basketball court to play in a tournament with your team?" The answer from many was, "We practice." And I said, "Why do you practice?" and what was interesting in terms of this particular first response was that it was exactly what I wanted, almost as though the student had read my mind because, had this not come about, I would have tried to get it out of them and again, that might have been a longer conversation than I needed, but this student came forth with the answer immediately. He said, "When you practice, you practice the fundamentals." And I said, "Fundamentals meaning what?" And he said, "How to pass, how to dribble, how to shoot, how to run plays—these are fundamentals." Then I said, "Once you get the fundamentals down, then are you ready to play?" And they agreed that they were almost ready to play but they needed to then scrimmage, practice as a team, practice against other teams, and they could also be creative once the fundamentals were learned so well that it was just natural to them. And I said, "Well, if you look at what you're doing in your English textbooks, then I think that you might agree with me that these are the fundamentals." A couple of them said, "Yeah," and I said, "Well, once you learn the fundamentals, then you will be able to be creative in terms of your speech—whether it be in a drama club, in writing poetry, rap music, or in a conversation on the phone for endless hours. Once you master the fundamentals, then you are able to become creative. Now, how many of you prefer practicing basketball to playing in the game?" A couple raised their hands then lowered them, and then they all came to consensus that it's a lot more fun participating in the tournament games than it is preparing—doing the calisthenics, exercises, learning plays, running drills, over and over again. Then I said, "It's the same way in English. The fundamentals are not necessarily that much fun. I don't see any of you expressing any degree of enthusiasm about learning the parts of speech, but at least if you understand what they represent, that these are the fundamentals that you must get down well so that they are natural to you in order that you can go on and become more creative as you express yourselves. Perhaps you might attack this lesson with a greater degree of enthusiasm than I am seeing so far."

Now I give that example only to say that while technique is important to me, and, indeed, my introduction of the lesson represents a technique, and my technique leans toward the creative and conversational as opposed to the technical, step-by-step process that might be peculiar to someone else's method of teaching, I think that each of us has strengths that we bring and since that is the case not only should these strengths be used but they should be emphasized. It may be personality, technique, leadership quality, charisma or other strengths that may lie in the ability to motivate.

Another person's strength may be in discipline. One may be a firm disciplinarian and command respect and attention just by entering a room. There may be another person whose strength lies in the ability to speak softly and command the attention of an audience in an auditorium. It's just something about the way that they speak that causes you to look up even in the teachers' lounge. A person may have a tremendous strength in preparation, study, and interpretation. They may be able to take a lesson and know it inside out from a historical perspective as well as a technical presentation perspective. There may be someone whose strength is in variety of approach. They may have seven different ways to introduce a lesson and that being their strength, there's no telling what you might see when you see them introduce a lesson.

What is your strength? Is it in your technique? It is in your preparation? Is it in your personality? Is it in preparing a physical classroom that is conducive to learning so that when young people enter the classroom, they know that they are in a place where something exciting is going to occur? It is important to find your strength. We must identify what we find ourselves doing over and over again. We might be good story tellers but we never bother to look at that as a particular strength in introducing a science lesson. But if that's what we do comfortably and do well, using a story to introduce a science lesson is altogether appropriate. If we find that we really feel comfortable being at the board and having students come to the board and use it to draw diagrams, then we should do that from time to time. If we find that we happen to be that particular teacher down the hall to whom other teachers send students who have a problem with control, rather than looking at that as a bother that those other teachers ought to be able to take care of their own problems, maybe we ought to see that as a compliment and not only should we emphasize those strengths, but we might want to call a teacher's meeting or inservice, and attempt to impart to others why it is and how it is that we are successful in getting to students in the way we can so that they will be able to gain from our strengths even though they will not be able to imitate them directly or immediately.

Obviously, it is also important to point out that emphasizing one's strengths does not mean to repeat to the point of monotony or to become so involved in the emphasis of strengths that we do not learn any other approaches toward attaining the desired end. It is important that teachers use a variety of methods in order to keep students' interest. It is important also that professionally we attempt to learn different ways to gain greater strength by becoming strong in areas other than those in which we are naturally comfortable. Those things are, of course, important, but what I am suggesting is that where there are particular strengths, we should not hide them nor neglect them when they can be the key to creating a learning climate that can be enjoyed by all.

Please emphasize your strengths. Also, appreciate the strengths of others. And if you have colleagues whose strengths you notice but they seem not to notice them themselves, call it to their attention so that they might be able to do something that enhances the learning environment of all.

SELF

Lesson 4
Improve Your DEPTH

The "D" in DEPTH stands for diet. The "E" in DEPTH stands for exercise. The "P" stands for physique, the "T" for temperament, and the "H" for health. We need to improve our DEPTH (diet, exercise, physique, temperament, and overall health) because the demands of the occupation we have are often so intense, particularly in the times in which we teach, that it is absolutely imperative that we enjoy optimum health in order to face the day-to-day circumstances of this very intense profession.

When I talk about improving diet, I am not suggesting for a moment that I am a nutritionist. I am suggesting as a nutritional layman that I certainly know when I eat too much. I certainly know when I eat too late at night. I certainly know when I stop at fast food restaurants and observe that the fish sandwiches that I eat are prepared in the same way as some of the more "harmful" red meats that I avoid. Also, I have a tremendous sweet tooth and I know that it is important to avoid sweets in the abundance that I enjoy them, so it makes a great deal of sense, even if I have never read a book about diet, or studied or watched a TV program about diet and exercise, that I am both intuitive and intelligent enough to know that a complete volume on how to lose weight could be summed up in four words: Eat less, exercise more.

I would suggest that the first thing we ought to do as educators is convince ourselves that optimal health is a prerequisite to optimum results in our profession. It is certainly logical that whatever one's profession, one ought to take a great deal of care in how one feels physically and psychologically about his or her well-being as well as feeling good about the profession one is in.

I would also like to see my colleagues pay close attention to their own diets in order that I might be in a climate among fellow professionals who, by their example, would encourage me to be disciplined along those lines myself. I think that it is fairly easy to find books and programs that assist us in observing some simple rules.

Also, it is important for us to pay close attention to our DEPTH, if you will, in order that we might be exemplars for our students because if we are not conscientious about what and how we eat in order to enjoy maximum proficiency at what we do, then we should not be critical of those whom we teach in this fast food society in which we live when they come to us ill prepared, indeed, ill, based upon improper nutrition. Let me also suggest that while I'm talking about the diet issue, that my assumption is that even as we are not properly monetarily compensated for what we do, most of us in this profession can at least afford the luxury of making a determination as to what and how much we will eat. Often we teach young people who do not have that luxury and must eat that which comes before them or, in some cases, eat very little at all based upon the fact that nothing comes before them with any degree of frequency. If that is so, then just considering the issue of diet as a prerequisite to our proficiency ought to raise the level of our consciousness about those who are denied the privilege of a regular meal. If we are conscientious about our own need to be totally healthy, then we must also be conscientious about seeing to it that those whom we expect to fare well in our classrooms also eat well.

As is pertains to exercise, I think that the least we can do is seize upon opportunities to walk. We know intuitively when we adopt a sedentary lifestyle and simply being in the profession that we're in, we know what the implications of that sedentary lifestyle are. Therefore, even if we do not enjoy a membership at the local health club and cannot afford a companion physician to travel around with us and to tell us how much we should jog, walk, sit-up, pull-up, push-up, push-out, or whatever is necessary, I think that we can certainly appreciate the need to complement our food with a degree of exercise that helps us to simply feel better, and helps our heart function in a proper way.

I don't see any merit in being so exercise-conscious that we overdo it and hurt ourselves attempting to impress someone with how exercise-conscious we are. I think that there are some people who are jogging-oriented, do it well, know how to do it, and understand what it does to their bodies to help them function. I think that there are others who would do well in other kinds of exercise based upon their own physical attributes, or lack thereof, and even more so, based upon their commitment to the regimen they have chosen. Personally, I have found that I do not enjoy jogging enough to make it a part of a regular regimen. I do enjoy walking. Not only that, walking is easier for me. It's more relaxing. It's more comfortable. I think clearer. I can do it longer at a good pace, and I think, done right, it is as beneficial, if not more so, as jogging. There are some who have a more rigorous program that is probably monitored and might include certain kinds of machinery that they can afford either to "rent", as it were, at a local health club or even perhaps purchase. But whether it be rigorous or relaxed, it certainly needs to be regular because our obligation to our profession is to be in the greatest possible physical health.

Our physique ought to reveal a degree of health consciousness. Does that suggest that all of us ought to have the same measurements and the same weight, or that we ought to be able to go into a physician's office, and on the scale that says, "If you are this age and this height, you ought to weigh this much," and all of us fit that? I think that there are many people who have written about diet and exercise and physique who have suggested that, for different people, differing amounts of weight are appropriate based upon bone structure and lifestyle. So certainly I'm not among those who would say that thin is necessarily beautiful or handsome, or muscular is necessarily healthy. I am saying that for the most part, we can see how people move about and how they look and get some clue as to their physical health, and I believe that students are impressed when we look like we are healthy, especially when we are trying to impress upon them a need to be healthy, physically and intellectually.

So let me move on to the "T" in the acronym DEPTH—temperament. I believe that if we are in good physical shape, it will enhance our temperament inasmuch as we have to be psychologically flexible during a school day that will seldom be exactly as we have planned it. And if our temperament is complementary to our physique, our diet, and our exercise, then I am suggesting that there is a direct correlation between being in good shape and having a good attitude. Therefore, I am also suggesting that there is a direct correlation between being out of shape and having a bad attitude. Some people will argue with that because some people are out of shape and they laugh about it and they suggest that, "I'm going to die by something, so it might as well be by smoking these cigarettes or I keep my weight on because I know that women like fat men, and this is the woman's playground,"—pointing at a big belly. But sometimes poking fun at one's self is a defense mechanism that says, "I am lacking in the discipline to get myself together."

And if, indeed, that is the case, then one's temperament suffers because there is the constant realization that, "I have not yet gotten myself together, but after the weekend, or after the holidays, or at the beginning of the school year, or at the beginning of the calendar year, or as soon as I get my daughter through college, or as soon as I have my next visit with my doctor, I'm going to get started." And so often we never do, and if a particular aspect of one's existence suffers in this way, then it is possible, if not likely, that it has a negative impact on our ability to teach because we are not whole people. One aspect of our being affects our total being. All we need to do is get the smallest piece of hair in our eyes, and that can affect our entire bodies, and we are preoccupied with removing that small piece of hair from the eye until we are successful in getting it out of our way.

I think that it is unreasonable to think that we're going to do the best that we can by our students if our psyche is adversely impacted by a deteriorating body, not due to an illness we cannot prevent but simply due to lack of discipline and a failure to relate our health with our profession. So I am suggesting that we need to improve our diet, exercise, physique, temperament, and, indeed, our overall health because we are the tone setters in our classrooms, and a healthy person will create a healthy climate in that classroom.

Lesson 5
Show Enthusiasm

Overall health is not only to be adequately healthy, but to be so healthy in mind, body, and spirit that we bring with us to the classroom a degree of enthusiasm that becomes infectious to our students. As we recall our own personal experiences coming through elementary school, high school, and college, we can probably look back upon one, two, or several (if we were fortunate) very impressionable teachers whose enthusiasm caused us to enjoy their classes even though we did not particularly like the subject that they were teaching. We have a responsibility to understand our subject matter and to teach it as though the class "I teach" is the most important class there is in the school where I teach, in the country that I serve. We should come to class with such enthusiasm that our students see in us a need to impart this information as though this was our final day on earth. And if one cannot get these things across to the students in the 50 minutes that we have, we will have died having lived in vain based upon the fact that we were not able to get this important material across.

It is interesting that the two most common words used among students, particularly at this time, are 1) boring, and 2) unfair. But one of the things that we would sometimes like to have our young people realize is that if they think this subject matter bores them, they ought to feel how we feel about the subject matter because everything that we teach is not that exciting to us. I mentioned in "$50,000 for 50 Good Reasons" that this is one of the few, if not the only, professions in which one can matriculate in a particular subject area and be asked upon arriving at work the first day to teach something that is totally outside of the discipline for which we are prepared. This alone can cause one to lose enthusiasm not only for the subject matter at hand, but also for the profession itself.

I am a believer that lack of enthusiasm is noticed by young people who are often a lot more perceptive than we realize.

Sometimes a lack of enthusiasm is so obvious that students, colleagues, parents, and administrators are aware. Also, unfortunately, there are times when administrators excuse a lack of enthusiasm and apologize to a particular teacher, recognizing, "I know that this is not your field, but if you would just bear with us for this semester, this year, these two years, we will work on getting you in the position that we know you would like. But do the best that you can." Well, for a given child during a given semester, just doing "the best you can" absent of any degree of enthusiasm whatsoever is not good enough because if one intends to matriculate in a certain discipline in college, and does not get the foundation in elementary and senior high school based upon excused deficiency in enthusiasm, then we have done that student a tremendous disservice.

I think that certainly honesty in teaching is important, but it may be necessary to do a little acting if one is teaching outside of the desired discipline because we are asking students to act for us. We want students who, perhaps, had no desire to be at school, to sit up, pay attention, and return to us information that we give them, that we think, not *they*, but *we* think, is important, and we want them to give us that information in an enthusiastic way. But how can we ask that of students, indeed, demand that of students when we signal to them by our behavior that we're not that impressed ourselves with the subject matter at hand. I think that not only is the showing of enthusiasm important as it pertains to being infectious for the students, but I think showing enthusiasm for the subject matter that we are charged to teach might even infect us if we act toward what we teach as though it is, indeed, the most important subject area in the school, or if we are in self-contained elementary classes, the most important subject areas, the most important grade in the school. Pretty soon, we'll begin to believe our own enthusiasm. We'll begin to become creative, to do research, to talk to colleagues about better approaches toward getting across what it is that we want to get across. Our growing enthusiasm will be picked up by our students who then should return some of that enthusiasm to us and we will then feel that we are doing something important because our students are beginning to return something to us, and we will, as a result, become more legitimately enthusiastic about what we do.

The examples that we set are more important than the concepts we attempt to teach because young people learn a great deal more by example than by instruction. One of the things that occurs in projecting an enthusiastic attitude is that those around us want to capture some of that enthusiasm. "How do you do it?", "What do you have for breakfast?", "What is this that you're so high on, and how can I get some of that?"

One of the unfortunate aspects of growing up in America in the 1990s is having to deal with the drug culture, and as much as I do not like mentioning the drug culture, I will suggest that one of the reasons that those who compete with us for our children's minds and, indeed, their bodies seem to do a better job than we is because of their enthusiasm about what they're selling. They make young people feel like there is nothing on earth that can make you feel better and if you become a part of the culture of substances as well as addicted to the material itself, you are somehow a greater individual. You are more popular. This enhances your overall persona. If we are going to compete favorably with entertainers, athletes, and unfortunately, criminals, then the degree of our classroom enthusiasm has to be greater than their enthusiasm on the football field and basketball court and the street corners of urban, suburban, and rural America. But, indeed, if there were no drug culture, and if we did not have to compete with athletes and entertainers, the degree of our enthusiasm is still quite important because, in essence, we are attempting to sell something. And what we are attempting to sell goes beyond subject matter.

We are attempting to sell a lifelong learning style. Particularly at the elementary level, we are attempting to establish a foundation of a learning pattern that creates in young people good habits for living. In Og Mandino's book, *The Greatest Salesman in the World*, there is a statement that reads, "If you want to know one's potential for success, observe one's habits." And what we would like to do for young people at a very early age is instill within them lifestyle habits that include a thirst for finding out, for discovery, for applying research techniques. We want to instill within young people the kinds of lifestyle orientation that sees them looking not so much into subject matter, but looking into how to discover answers regardless of the area they are studying. And I am suggesting that there are so many things that young people do not learn in a formal sense, that they pick up in an informal sense based upon the environment in which they matriculate, whether it be in the classroom, in the home, or on the street. And the environment in our classrooms ought to ring with enthusiasm. And creating that environment is the responsibility of the classroom teacher. No one in the classroom has a greater responsibility for showing enthusiasm. Our young people are accustomed to having things given to them based upon their prior generation's needs to make sure that they can have more than those of us who came before them. These young people are part of an immediate gratification era, and they are simply not going to come to us enthusiastic just because they're in our classrooms. They have to pick up something from us, and one of the things that we can project that is not difficult to project is our enthusiasm about what we do. I would like to suggest that we wouldn't be in this profession if we were not enthusiastic about it. I want to think that we all have that enthusiasm but there are teachers who are no more automatically enthusiastic than the "immediate gratification" youngsters. We are charged with the responsibility to put 100% into what we do.

We are preparing young people to lead us into the 21st century. Our leadership is toward instilling virtue and value, and again helping young people to develop habits that are helpful, not only to their individual selves but to the local societies in which they live as well as society at large. And that being the case, we must be exemplars of enthusiasm as well as requesters for enthusiasm. One ought to go into the classroom with the attitude that we just don't have enough time to learn all there is to learn. We ought to go into the classroom with an attitude like, "We can't wait to begin," on whatever it is that we are going to teach that day, hour, or period.

And we need the attitude that we hate to see this particular unit come to an end because it has such great information and it is such a privilege to get an opportunity to interact with the students on this particular subject. If one pretends not to know what I'm talking about, just consider how you feel when you get to that unit that you truly enjoy teaching. Think about how you feel when you finally get to the discipline that you've always wanted to teach. Think about how you feel when you are asked to teach that grade that you wanted to teach.

You know that there are certain lessons that you enjoy more than other lessons. There are certain days obviously for all of us when we feel better than we feel on other days, and when everything seems to click, and you think that by some magic the students were just great today. Well, the students were not "just great", the young people were great in an atmosphere that produces greatness. It is within each of us to draw out of all of us the best that we have in us, and we can do that by projecting our best, by being prepared, and being in class early waiting for the students.

Now, a caution about the performance, if, indeed, we decide that we have so little enthusiasm that we will have to be perpetual actors. Young people are perceptive as well as impressionable. Being impressionable, much of our enthusiasm will rub off on them. Being perceptive, if we are phony, they will also pick up our phoniness. I am saying that we should perform to the degree that it helps us to become enthusiastic because part of the performance will be to research those aspects of a particular lesson, of a particular class, that we can truly get into it so that enthusiasm is a meaningful part of our teaching technique. One thing that we must realize is: our enthusiasm as teachers will not guarantee enthusiasm from students. But a lack of enthusiasm from us as teachers can almost certainly guarantee a lack of enthusiasm from most, if not all, students.

SELF

Lesson 6
Enjoy Sara's Hour

Sara Price is a teacher with whom I taught at Parkside Elementary School in Chicago, Illinois, from 1972 until 1975. In the community where Sara had taught some years before I arrived at Parkside, there were several large local youth gangs. One in particular was larger than the rest and many of the gang members seemed to make an impression on some of the students who attended Parkside. And while, out of respect for the faculty, the large local gang did not come in and riot at the school or have gang fights up and down the hall, certainly the influence of some of the gang members revealed itself in the behaviors of some of the young elementary students who wanted to imitate their older brothers and sisters or neighbors. That meant that there were discipline problems at Parkside. And, of course, certainly, there are discipline problems at every school you can name. By the time I arrived at Parkside, many of the problems confronted by the very professional staff there had been eliminated or significantly reduced in impact, and yet there were some vestiges of anti-social attitudes among the students in attendance during my tenure there.

One of the things I observed about Sara was her ability to get through each day, even though many of the problematic students would find themselves in Mrs. Price's presence because she was often called upon by others of us who knew her positive influence on young people to assist us in making a point to violators of school rules. And, her ability to do so and to get through the day psychologically unscathed caused me to ask her on a given day, "How is it that you manage to fare so well even under conditions sometimes bordering on chaos?" And when I say "chaos", I'm not saying that the school was in chaos, I am saying that there were some individual young people whose personal problems were such that it caused them to act out and be in need of some added attention from Sara. And what Sara told me was that she got up each morning at least one hour prior to her beginning to prepare physically for the school day. Now this certainly helped to prepare her psychologically for the day, but it was one hour prior to any need to get papers together or to develop particular lessons or simply to begin physically to dress for the day—those kinds of things. This was Sara's Hour. Being a religious person, as she is, Sara's Hour is spent in quiet meditation, reflection, and Bible study.

And upon learning that spending this time with one's self was a valuable part of Sara Price's day, I decided to begin to spend Sara's Hour with myself. When I began Sara's Hour (and having heard a bit about Eastern philosophy), I decided that I would get up an hour early and begin to meditate, even to the point of putting myself in the lotus position and chanting in order to get psychologically and spiritually prepared for what might otherwise be a chaotic day. And sitting in the lotus position and chanting, I practiced Sara's Hour every day for one day, half of that hour being the attempt to get myself out of the lotus position. My romantic thoughts about becoming attuned to the earth on which we live and the gods above as being my version of dealing with Sara's Hour, did not work quite so well because I was so involved in the romanticism of it that I didn't realize until after that first day, that for me Sara's Hour had to begin with fifteen minutes.

But as I continued with fifteen minutes of contemplation and then a few minutes of exercise, my "Hour" grew into what is now an hour—sometimes more—of morning exercise in order to prepare for the rest of my day. Arising in the morning fully an hour or two before my wife, going to a local health club and getting on the stationary cycle and then working on some machinery, and then, walking helps me not only physically but helps me psychologically. And I think that all of us can benefit from Sara's Hour whether it be fifteen minutes or two hours if one can afford that much time per day.

Now please understand that when I talk about Sara's Hour, I'm talking about your time for yourself. I'm not talking about taking out some extra time during a day to converse on the phone with a special friend which is not a bad idea itself, because we need support and we need opportunities to get away from concentrating on that which is required of us in the classroom. I'm not talking about spending an extra hour preparing lessons for the school day, taking advantage of extra time. I'm talking about spending extra time every day with one's self—not with a spouse, not with special friends, not with children, but with one's self. Not grappling with the lofty issues of world affairs or the parochial concerns of the school where we teach, but simply taking a moment to be spiritual, to thank God for being and for giving us the unique opportunity to impact upon the lives of those who will see us through our own earthly futures, to consider the miracle of existence and the magic of interaction with youthful minds and personal friends, family, and the wonder of having healthy minds, the appreciation for being as fit as we are, even if we are not as fit as we feel we need to be. I think that one's spiritual orientation can determine whether Sara's Hour as it is for Sara, and I pray as it is for myself, is spent contemplating a closer relationship with God, or one's physical orientation suggests that Sara's Hour is developing one's DEPTH as used in a previous lesson, or Sara's Hour is used "selfishly" just thinking about how good I am and how much better I'm going to be, not in any narcissistic way but just understanding that we have been given the capacity to grow beyond our immediate reach, and to be something special because we're already something unique on this Earth. If one has a need to find some humor in some personal reading or some romance or mystery in something that one reads that has nothing to do with preparing for the school day, other than spiritually or psychologically, let that be your Sara's Hour. If family responsibilities and professional time constraints dictate that you cannot devote more than five to ten minutes a day to your Sara's Hour, do it. Take the time. Understand that it really isn't being selfish when you spend some time developing your personal self in a way that will positively impact all around you because they recognize within you a peace of mind similar to that I found in the 1973-74 school year at Parkside Elementary School in Chicago, Illinois, in Sara Price.

Lesson 7
Be Patriotic

Two words that I think are extremely important in the United States of America that are met so often with cynicism and suspicion are the words "love" and "patriotism." "Love" is a word that I have already used and will probably continue to use throughout this book, and I need not repeat my definition or rationale for using the word "love" but I hope that throughout you will recognize that that's really what this book is based upon. But I would like to focus on the word "patriotism" and the suggestion that we as teachers ought to be patriotic. And when I talk about being patriotic, I am talking about showing an allegiance to the land in which we live, to the degree that we understand our purpose for teaching in America, for being American citizens and world citizens, and to the degree that our patriotism would suggest that part of truth in patriotism is seeking truth from those in positions of power in the nation to which we declare our patriotism.

I am suggesting that we be unashamedly patriotic inasmuch as we are the reproductive system of this nation. I am also declaring as an African-American citizen that patriotism does not contradict our efforts as minority citizens to insure equity and parity in our pursuits to enjoy the fruits of our historical labors in a land that has neglected to offer equal opportunities among its citizens of color and peculiar, if you will, surnames. I am suggesting that our young people have a distorted view of patriotism because those of us who are older are not certain of what we stand for collectively and individually.

Let me suggest to you that I believe that for the rest of my life, I will be a U.S. citizen. I don't know that to be true but I believe that is true, and I believe that being a U.S. citizen, I must work toward assisting the U.S. in becoming a nation that can lead a world toward peace, love, and prosperity. If I go into my classroom each day feeling that someone whom I teach, indeed, some ones whom I teach, may be singularly or collectively responsible in transforming this nation into a land of opportunity for all in its most literal and human sense, then I must instill within them by way of my own example, optimism about the possibilities for equal opportunities for everyone to develop to their optimal potential.

Now how does an African-American reconcile his patriotic bent with his realization that overall, this country has not seen fit and, currently, does not seem willing to seriously offer all of its citizens chances at enjoying the fruits of a very prosperous society? Well, I reconcile it in these ways. One, I believe that teaching truths is patriotic. Therefore, our students must be taught the kind of history and current events which reflect what the U.S. has done that makes her shameful. I believe that there is enough greatness in the U.S. to maintain a degree of leadership throughout the world, and I think there's enough shame in the U.S. to keep us busy for several lifetimes to make of this nation what it says but has not shown what it ought to be.

Truth in teaching then would include in all schools, ethnic studies. In the African-American community where there are young people who are not matriculating up to their potential, I am one who, like several others, believes that youngsters lacking in a knowledge of self are not likely to perform to a high degree of efficiency based not only upon ignorance about the accomplishments of those who created a glorious heritage, but also have little need to see themselves as any more than this society has taught them they are, which, all too often through various media, is to be comedic, athletic, and/or criminal, as opposed to being noble, intelligent, and successful. Teachers of other cultures, of other ethnic backgrounds cry out for methodologies in which to teach young Black Americans because they seem to be so different from the standards and norms that are perceived by many educators to be those to which we should all aspire.

And, if I feel qualified to make the case for African-American studies infused throughout the curriculum in terms of time and geographic span, then I would also state the case for others in need of self-realization preceding school realization. How can I realistically assert that we need to be patriotic? I can assert that we need to be patriotic because, being an educator, I have a position that has a purpose and professionalism. I can indeed pay the rent and eat and transport myself from place to place. I can "cavort," if you will, with people who are considered to be movers and shakers. I am called "mister." I can shop and move about in various places and talk about the lofty proposition of being patriotic not because of, but in spite of, my color.

I know that the patriotism I assert is based upon an expectation, not a present circumstance. It is my need to see the U.S. of the future, rather than be overly concerned about the U.S. of the present. It was Robert Kennedy who said, "Some see things as they are and ask 'Why?' I dream things that never were and ask, 'Why not?'" America is full of dreams, but America never was what America had and has the potential to become. If there are those responsible for making the U.S. what it could and ought to be, it is the classroom teacher. On one hand, I should not teach in the public schools and, being a teacher, teach against my country, if you will, to the point of creating young revolutionaries who will upset this nation and have nowhere to go after so revolting. On the other hand, I cannot be African-American without offering to young African-Americans the tools to be successful in a society that is negligent as it pertains to truth in teaching and the offering of equal opportunity. My patriotism, therefore, is based upon the possibility of an enlightened nation, the possibility of equal participation among all of its citizens and yet the realization that it will take all of us working at it every day, most of our day, to overcome the social ills that have caused us to lag behind emerging nations in their quest to become what the U.S. has pretended she already is.

I see patriotism, therefore, as a need to infuse what many term "multiculturalism" in curricula throughout school districts, not only for the domestic benefit of highly populated minority schools or school districts, but for the significant benefit of schools throughout—urban, suburban, and rural—where there may be no Native Americans in attendance whatsoever, but which teach the truth about the Native American experience on this soil. Where there may be no Asian American students in attendance, but where our understanding of these recent immigrants to our land will enhance our capacity to become world citizens. Where there may, indeed, be no African-Americans in attendance, whatsoever, but where truth in teaching dictates a need to understand the significant contributions of a people who immigrated not by choice but by force and yet have made significant contributions and have emerged in many quarters successful, but unfortunately, successful as exceptions rather than as the rule. And I am suggesting that the rule for success for all citizens has a great deal to do with what is taught and how it is taught in school classrooms every day.

Another way that I reconcile my patriotism is grounded in practicality. That is to say, that the opportunity for the realization of dreams is probably greater in the U.S. than in most places on Earth. I am certainly cautious about thinking and therefore teaching others that you can become anything you want to become in America based upon character, talent, and fortitude. The simple facts of the matter belie such idealism. But I would suggest that inasmuch as we can speak out, we can gain support from each other in particular ethnic groups as well as each other across cultural and ethnic lines, and in as much as at this point in our history the U.S. still finds a need to project itself across the world as a free and equitable society, it would seem to me that the time is now to take advantage of those freedoms we do enjoy, to assist each other and to teach each other how to work toward making this nation fully free and far more equitable than it has ever been. It is grounded in the practicality that massive efforts to secede and become, for instance, an African-American nation are not realistic and certainly not forthcoming in the near future.

Therefore, as a teacher, I have not only the responsibility but the opportunity to teach the practicality of all segments of the population working together in order to strengthen a nation seemingly destined to crumble from within based upon the selfish interest of many who seem more interested in power and the power to control than in empowering others and therefore remaining in control of our nation.

It is important that we learn about our ethnic selves, our history beyond that of American history, about our collective selves, that being the history of all who immigrated this way as well as those who were already here, about our individual selves and potentials based upon strengthening our self-concept after learning who we are and from whence we have come and where we can potentially go and then using that knowledge and enhanced self-image to strengthen a community that ought to be a model for the world. I think that in Afro-centric values we talk about the need for cooperativeness and interdependence because we recognize that we do not have the individual wherewithal to lift an entire people. Part of our charge is to reach over and pull someone else along in order that more of us can enjoy the benefits of our personal successes. That Afro-centric view holds true for all in a nation where a small percentage (almost a minute percentage) of the population controls a huge percentage of the nation's wealth and therefore political and social, as well as economic, power. If we are going to continue to attract the admiration as well as support of other nations in a shrinking world which can see immediately and thoroughly through the continuing technological advance of media which expose us all to each other, then we must be patriotic enough to insure that the homeless get housing, the hungry are fed, the disenfranchised are heard, and inasmuch as we are ushering in a new century, we must understand that our lofty goals will be realized not through the graduating classes of the 1990s, but those who will graduate and lead beyond the year 2000. And, their approach toward leading us out of the mire of selfishness and the impracticality of discrimination will depend, to a great degree, on how we offer them the intellectual tools of learning and the philosophical tools of appreciating the potential that this great nation has. As I continue to suggest that our students will learn more by example than by instruction, then part of the patriotism of which I speak must manifest itself in the removal of sexism, racism and other forms of discrimination not only in the subject matter that we teach, but also in the profile of what our schools and school districts look like. It is important that if we talk about equity and parity in our classrooms we must also make efforts to insure that those in positions of leadership, those who are role models in the classroom, and those to whom students look for examples of what we are attempting to teach must be reflective of that enlightenment, equity and parity that we say we desire. Therefore, we need more minority teachers in classrooms, certainly in places where there are more minority students, but it is also important that if we are going to exemplify what we say we are about, that there be more representation of our cultural and ethnic mix even where there seems to be a monolith of culture so that those young people matriculating in a local society seemingly hidden from the realities of a growing multiculture should not suffer from insulation. When I speak of patriotism as being truth in teaching I must be honest enough to assert that while much of my ethnic history has been neglected, that all of American history that has been taught is not false, and that all of my personal history is not necessarily virtuous. The young of all races, nationalities, creeds, religions, and origins need to be motivated through the legacies of their forefathers and warned against the mistakes of their forefathers.

Patriotism in teaching demands facing some ugly individual truths and project some dynamic collective potential. To teach the facts of what we are, and have been, does not preclude teaching the truth of what we can become.

I think that a significant part of patriotism in teaching is to teach with enthusiasm that part of our history, whether it be ethnic history or American history which includes the cultural mix that reveals virtue and goodness and success. I think that part of the truth in teaching includes patriotism for not only discussing the positive aspects of overall American history, but for each of us boasting about the positive contributions of others of us so that if I am a history teacher and part of my responsibility in teaching history is, and indeed it certainly should be, to discuss the plight of the Native American, I must certainly point out some of the atrocities they suffered, but also with enthusiasm talk about some of their great contributions and nobility that causes our history to be rich. I am not a Native American, but because I am putting the word American after Native and because, in my own case I put the word American after African, I can boast about their contributions to what should become a great land. I can boast about the contributions of Irish Americans, Italian Americans, Jewish Americans, and Polish Americans.

When I talk about Asian Americans and African Americans I talk about continent-Americans but then I can also talk about that hyphen which speaks more locally to the nation from which one comes rather than simply the continent from which one comes. Part of our growing exploration that helps to explain who we ultimately are is to continue to search so that the hyphenated culture that helps to define us becomes increasingly local as we continue to learn and teach about the various experiences that make America the unique culture that it is. And when we discuss the positives we ought to discuss them enthusiastically. And when we discuss the negatives we ought to discuss them hopefully in a solutions-oriented classroom climate that causes young people to think critically not only in that immediate and local classroom situation, but to spend their very lives contemplating how they can be a part of making the nation in which they live greater than it is and greater than it imagines. I think that we are the ones who must project a realistic patriotism which teaches us all that we cannot emerge productive and peaceful without the developing alliances among the various ethnic groups that make up this country.

If we look at all of the various immigrants to the U.S. and attempt to determine which among us will run the rest of us, the fact is that none among us by themselves are able to do that nor would it be desirable for any of us to do that if, indeed, one particular group was able because that sows the seeds of inevitable revolution. But when we realize the need for a universal acceptance of the Afro-centric "cooperative" mode of matriculating and act accordingly and teach and learn accordingly that we must work together in order to live together and part of being able to work together is being able to understand each other, based upon history as well as current habits, then our patriotism will be a great deal more than theoretic and our progress will be a great deal more than personal. These seven lessons are devoted to a discussion of how a teacher can directly impact upon positive responses from students.

A clear statement of the mission of American education—embodying inclusion of the contributions and successes of all peoples helping us to grow throughout curricula in every discipline; and expectations for where we can, collectively, rise through knowledge and effort—is needed in every school in the nation.

* * *   * * *

The next seven lessons, "Self—Students," are devoted to a discussion of how a teacher can impact directly upon positive responses from students.

SELF—STUDENTS

Lesson 8
Lift Every Voice and Sing

There are those who will recognize "Lift Every Voice and Sing" as being the title and first line of what is currently termed the Black National Anthem, written by James Weldon Johnson. In this context, "Lift Every Voice and Sing" speaks to the need for teachers to recognize every student in that teacher's classroom. Every student is important. Every student has some contribution they can make, and every student, even though they may appear to be totally self-sufficient or on the other hand totally noncaring, has a need to be recognized by their classroom teacher. "Lift Every Voice and Sing" suggests that we must consciously pay attention to each individual in our class and where we are in situations where students indeed pass from class to class, we must recognize every individual in our classes.

Do I suggest that it is easy? Not by any means. Do I suggest that it is imperative? By all means. Teaching is not an easy profession, but human beings—whether it be in the classroom, workplace, or in family settings—have individual needs that when neglected can sometimes, perhaps often, lead to personality defects (in some instances, severe personality defects result when the negligence is continuous and pronounced). Severe personality defects, I would suspect, can arise from even subtle negligence and not so severe personality defects could result from severe neglect. It depends upon the individual students, family member, or worker. Inasmuch as we are in the people profession, not just serving people, but indeed shaping character, we must be more sensitive than others at recognizing the need for individual attention and going beyond recognizing the need to offer that individual attention in ways that help young people grow. Offering individual attention that compliments and rewards where rewards and compliments are not warranted can be more damaging than helping. Offering individual attention at times when the entire class needs to be addressed would be inappropriate. At some point during the day or during the semester or school year, every single child needs to be touched by a caring, sensitive, astute classroom teacher. In a lecture in Independence, Missouri, Ron Edmonds (who did extensive research on effective instruction in New York City) pointed out that he observed an instructor who, after calling upon individual students, would place a tick mark on a piece of paper before calling upon the next student. Observing that the instructor was not putting these tick marks next to the individual names of students and indeed observing that they were tick marks, not grades for correct or incorrect answer, Ron Edmonds was moved to inquire of the teacher after the class what the tick marks represented. The teacher responded by indicating that he discovered he was guilty of calling on students in a particular section of the classroom more often than students in another section of the classroom. Ron Edmonds indicated that we will sometimes, being human as we are, call upon students who we perceive as being brighter or more cooperative, more forthcoming with their answers, more likely to offer the correct answer so we can go on to the next concept, than those students whom we perceive to be slower, less cooperative and less likely to give us the desired response. The instructor cited by Ron Edmonds said that putting down the tick marks regularly helped him to be more equitable, if you will, in his attention to students throughout the classroom. One of the reasons that we should "Lift Every Voice and Sing" was cited in an article in the May, 1986 *Learning* magazine entitled, "The Grey Child." The grey child, in that article, was defined as the student who, by virtue of their seeming self-sufficiency, received little attention because of our preoccupation with the best and brightest and the worst and most bothersome.

The grey child is a child who comes to school reasonably well dressed but not ostentatious, who responds in the classroom when called upon but may not be forthcoming with any enthusiastic initiatives, who causes no particular trouble, may not be the greatest athlete, but is one who seems to be faring fairly well, may receive grades of C and an occasional B, no failing grades, and would appear to be well enough adjusted to suggest that they come from a stable home environment. Consequently, we just let them fade into the background. Thus, the grey child.

I am suggesting in "Lift Every Voice and Sing" that the grey child is just as deserving of and perhaps in as much need of our attention as the student who demands our attention by acting out behaviorally or the student who commands our attention by being such a great academician. To ignore the student who acts out is to ask for more acting out and more demands of our attention, Also, students who do well on an ongoing basis and whom we might tend to treat similar to the way we treat the grey child because we feel they don't need any extra attention because they do so well all the time anyway may cause that child to demand our attention behaviorally because they haven't been able to command our attention academically. Sometimes it takes some years of experience to determine what equity and parity is based upon the acute needs of the behavior problem and the psychological needs of the grey child or the personal needs of the academician or the athlete whose great performances are indeed that because of their need for attention.

We are not all professional psychologists, but by definition of our profession we are lay psychologists to a significant degree based upon our observation skills in the classroom. We must look at students and try as best we can to determine what those students' needs are and then further determine whether or not we are the ones who can give them what they need or if we need to call upon support systems. In the case of the anti-social child who may act our behaviorally, we may be able to handle the situation in the classroom with a small degree of appropriate reprimand. It may be necessary to offer a psychological referral because the behavior is to the extent where it is not only disruptive but seemingly abnormal and recognizing our inability to make the determination as to what is clinically abnormal, we may need to call in the psychologist. For the grey child it may very well be that we recognize our own neglect but have not unlocked the mystery of what makes that child so nonresponsive we may have to call upon their parents and find out about their home environment and history, in order to determine the appropriate attention needed by the classroom teacher and/or those at home or in the community. The athlete and/or the academician may need extra attention in guiding their academic and ultimate professional careers. We may not be able to give them all that they need or all that they deserve in the way of career and academic guidance. As for the day to day activities in the classroom where we are not considering special attention we simply need to call upon students, and if we're concerned about embarrassing those who may not have the answer that we want we might call upon them for certain duties in and outside of the classroom, we might want to talk to a youngster informally outside of class if we realize that we have not called upon them in class. Our lifting of every voice and singing their praises might be informal and/or formal. The need is great, because we are working with a modern day student who has been taught to expect attention both by the media and, in many cases, by guardians in the home. Outside of the classroom, we have catered to the material needs of young people, the media has catered to their need for entertainment, and peers have catered to their need for approval and support. Therefore, the classroom needs, to some degree, to reflect and complement the larger society and smaller societies to which our students belong. Obviously, we must be careful that our recognition of the need to pay attention to our students does not deteriorate into catering to the whims and fancies of students who manipulate us into thinking that they have some dire psychological need when, in fact, they have simply become accustomed to controlling situations and people.

We need to be very sensitive to signals that young people give us as to the deeper psychological needs that are far more than manipulation or casual requests to be seen and heard. If students evidence extreme mood swings, sudden changes in behavior, shifts in friendships and types of friendships, unusual hostility, we need to pay close attention. If there are students who are academically "superior" and who have a need for perfection and who complain bitterly when they do not get perfect scores on exams or who punish themselves verbally for missing a question or plead with teachers to let them have the "A" because they only missed it by a half a point, and who are so meticulous that they spend an inordinate amount of time getting everything "just so," we need to pay particular attention. If there are young people who do not care at all, not only about what goes on in the classroom and the rest of the school, but who seemingly don't care about themselves, their community, their dress, their friends, who otherwise seem to have the normal capability of doing work if they just would, or participating in group activities if they just would, but just do not care, we need to pay attention. And if, in our classrooms, we have 100% "normality"— everybody is participating to the fullest, dressing right, and interacting with each other, we need to pay attention because there is just that possibility that there is some one student who needs to be called upon in class or complimented for winning a trophy over the weekend in some outside event, or who needs to be understood because their parents have received a divorce, or there has been a death in the family, or they've lost (in the case of the adolescent years) a boyfriend or a girlfriend who they "loved dearly" and now the world is going to come to an end. Because of that possibility, we need to pay attention. We should seize upon every opportunity to see the student least likely to respond, least likely to succeed, as clearly and even as favorably as we see those most likely to respond, most likely to succeed, because we might be able to turn around that student who we thought might not, would not succeed and make of that late bloomer, something special in our lives, in their own lives, and in the lives of others whom they touch subsequent to their experiences with us. This would be the place to mention the 5-Ex cycle of instructional and learning excellence. The five Ex's in this cycle are these: **Experiences, Expectations, Exposure, Excitement,** and **Excellence.**

EXPERIENCES. I believe that every student comes to my class with some body of positive experiences, cultural or subcultural, intellectual or recreational, shaping the child's basic personality or potential. Every child has a body of experiences that can be called upon to enhance his or her performance in the classroom and which can enhance the learning climate. If, indeed, every child does come to class with some body of positive experiences and it is very difficult for me to imagine any child by the age of five that does not have something within their background that is significantly positive; then my expectations for the child's potential are heightened by virtue of the fact that I know that the child has some positive experiences in his or her background. If those experiences are not apparent, it may require an interview with the child's parents to find out the kinds of things that the child does well and has an aptitude for or the kinds of things that the child particularly likes in terms of interacting with other people. The kinds of things in the child's ethnic heritage that can be pointed out even to the child, as well as to the rest of the classroom, that suggest that this child has a meaningful background. The child then should also be able to do well in the classroom based upon understanding from whence he or she has come. Once the belief is present and strong in that teacher, then the teacher needs to find ways to pull out from that child's experiences examples of the positiveness that is there. If

EXPERIENCES

EXCELLENCE   EXPECTATIONS

EXCITEMENT   EXPOSURE

Art of Positive Teaching ©1989

a child has a particular aptitude for conversation that seems to be a disruption in the class it might be well advised to call upon that child's aptitude and have the child recite in front of the class, read in front of the class, tell about personal experiences, etc. If the child seems to be quiet and introspective but indeed seems to have some degree of intellect in that introspection it might be well advised to give the child an assignment and perhaps that child who does not want to present in front of the rest of the classroom can then write what they know and the teacher might get the verbose child to read, and there you have some cooperation between the two and an opportunity to draw from each child's positive experiences.

If the child's background suggests, as in the Native American, that his ancestors are close to nature, it might be well advised to call upon that fact and where there are opportunities to study outside of the classroom perhaps, without embarrassing the child, indicate that this is the kind of appreciation for love of land that environmentalists are now, within the last decade or so, calling to the fore when indeed this child's ancestors have always had that love of land and perhaps he or she would like to participate at a meaningful level in this outdoor study. If a child's background because of the Asian Americans' emphasis on the family and its elders can be called upon as we study certain units, it might be a good idea for that Asian child to participate at a significant level. If a child's local environment is such that play is a big part of the child's development in terms of teamwork and character and motor and cognitive skills it might be well advised to call upon that child's aptitude for play and teamwork in those particular settings. These are not in-depth examples of the experience factor in the 5-Ex cycle, but they are examples which suggest that every child has some set of positive experiences that we can draw out as we attempt to help them feel comfortable in the classroom setting.

EXPECTATIONS. Based upon the fact that I truly believe that every child has a set of positive experiences, my expectations for children's abilities to perform well are high. In effective schools research, high expectations is one of the elements that is at the top of the list of characteristics of effective programs, effective climate, effective schools. High expectations do not come from a child's superior aptitude and intellectual performance in a classroom. High expectations are precisely what the definition of the word suggests—we expect that because of the kinds of experiences to which children will be exposed in our classroom that they will be able to learn as well as and learn as much as any other child, even though some will learn more rapidly than others and some will require alternative approaches toward mastery of certain materials. Our expectations are based upon the fact that they have positive experiences in their background that they have faced and worked with to some degree of proficiency, and that they can do the same in my classroom if I have the energy and if I have the commitment to find out what is positive about the child and what I need to do to tap those positive resources.

EXPOSURE. Our high expectations of every child's ability to do well should be exposed not only to that particular child, but also to the child's classmates. It is not enough to say to that child in private, "You are a great young person. You have a great heritage. You have tremendous abilities and I expect great things from you." It is far more significant when those expectations can be exposed to the rest of the class, suggesting to the class that not only do I have great expectations and not only do I have great appreciation for who this child is, holistically speaking, but that the rest of the class should also have great expectations of this classmate because of what they bring with them to this class. It is important for everybody to know that no one is better than anyone else, no one is worse than anyone else, and that all of us have great things to contribute. This helps, in terms of positive peer pressure, because oftentimes children's attitudes about each other are enhanced when a person in authority approves of particular young people. Their attitudes about the young people are shaped by how that young person is perceived among others in the classroom, friends as well as authority figures. So it is that the child whose clothes may not be quite so clean or the child whose ability to use standard English has not been developed to the capacity it will be upon sufficient practice, can be a very unpopular child and a child who might suffer form the ridicule of the rest. At a point when the primary authority figure in the class begins to talk about great expectations from this particular child whom others had found reason to ridicule it is very possible that the child's attitude will change about himself or herself and so will the collective attitude of the classroom toward that child. We need to appreciate experiences, have high expectations, and expose positive attitudes based upon the realization of those experiences and our own high expectations for every individual child as well as the collective classroom.

EXCITEMENT. When I am included in a positive way, I begin to look forward to coming to school. I will begin to say that I like subject matter when, in fact, what I am enjoying is the way I'm treated in that atmosphere that appreciates who I am, my parents' background, my local community, and this appreciation comes from someone who has high expectations for my ability to achieve and succeed in this world. I am suggesting that when I am included in every way in the learning atmosphere as well as learning activities, school becomes an exciting place to me because I can declare some ownership in the classroom. I am a part of the accomplishments and the shaping of an excellent reputation because I am a student in a classroom where everybody is special, and I know that I'm special because my teacher has been able to draw from me the special experiences that I bring to class when I get there. The teacher has let everyone know that she or he has great expectations for me because I come from such a special background. The exposure that I have gained has caused me to be a part of and, consequently, I am excited about this thing called school.

The fourth grade syndrome is what Jawanza Kunjufu talks about in his book, *Countering the Conspiracy to Destroy Black Boys*. Jawanza's book is not the only one that talks about what happens to youngsters after the primary grades. My theory is when you come into kindergarten where there is a lot of recreation, a lot of caring, a lot of nurturing and you get that from someone who obviously loves you because they dare to put their hands on you and hug you and smile at you and say nice things to you, between kindergarten and third grade it is a let down, to say the least, when you get into the higher grades and suddenly you are expected to be responsible and independent. You are too big to be held and you no longer need that nurturing and you're no longer participating to the same degree in games, show and tell, and blocks, etc. Suddenly at a very young age you are "on your own." Sometimes that lack of significant inclusion makes you an outcast, particularly for young boys who, until that time, were cute because they were all boy and they played aggressively and that was part of the teamwork that they learned as they were growing up and now they are asked to sit in rows quietly, and the little girls who are "dainty" become the apple of the teacher's eye and the little boys are disturbing the rest of the class when they continue in the fashion to which they have grown accustomed and were encouraged to be. Excitement is a result of inclusion based upon positive exposure and the teacher's appreciation for who I am holistically because I come with a great set of experiences.

EXCELLENCE. Excellence, is not an education product, it's an educational process. Part of the process of excellence in education is appreciating experiences, having high expectations, and exposing those high expectations in a positive light. Creating excitement is excellence in education because it is participatory, positive, progressive, inclusive not exclusive and if, indeed, that excellent climate is present, then based upon the exposure of one's classmates one's range of experiences are enhanced because now one has more in their own body of experience. And when the cycle begins to repeat itself the student is even brighter, sharper and more well rounded because of what is going on around him or her in that positive, excellent classroom climate. This process of excellence properly practiced and embraced at an early age, should become a habit for life. Human beings (should) never stop learning. The degree to which they learn how to learn affects how/if we continue learning until we die.

SELF—STUDENTS

Lesson 9
Allow this Generation to Be this Generation

A definition of adolescence is to be different from their elders. It was true when we were adolescents, it was true when our parents were adolescents, it was true when our parents' parents were adolescents, it is true for our children now at their adolescent age. This generation of young people looks to us to be some of the most peculiar creatures ever created on the face of the Earth. Their hairstyles are peculiar. The propensity for young men to want to wear earrings in their left ear seems to be peculiar. Their styles of dress are far more colorful than our style of dress when we were at an adolescent age and that is coming from a man who is 49 years old now.

Some teachers far younger might disagree with that. When we listen to the peculiar slang that young people use nowadays, particularly when that language includes profanity and profanity to a degree that is or ought to be intolerable, I would suggest that we have some great concerns about "this generation." We talk about the high incidence of drug trafficking, not only in impoverished inner cities, but in high socioeconomic level suburbs and in what would seem to be isolated rural areas. We talk about young people who seem to be growing up too fast. We talk about their need for immediate gratification. We discuss the fact that perhaps our wanting to ensure that they would not have to work as hard for things that they want as we had to, perhaps created the kinds of expectations among our young people that are unrealistic in terms of the world just giving them things or owing them things, including an education and careers. We discuss in the teachers' lounges, for instance, the lack of emphasis on school attendance and a seeming lack of respect for school rules and lack of discipline among young people. We just wonder aloud what indeed is the world coming to with this so-called lost generation. And as we wonder aloud, it occurs to me that perhaps we ought to also wonder aloud as to whether or not our judgment of today's generation speaks to a distorted perception of our own generation.

When we talk about today's generation, I am speaking in terms of adolescence because I would suspect that our characterization of today's generation, or the lost generation, is one that cites young people somewhere between the ages of 12 to 19 years old. The way that we discuss this generation almost suggests that we were very good when we were that age. We were disciplined, our study habits were keen, we paid attention to our parents, we used nothing but the most acceptable and understandable standard English. Somehow our perceptions of who we were seems to speak of some mystic generation that was just perfect in all ways, behaviorally and academically. We discuss the need for this generation to clean up its act, but when we begin to admit our own faults, we do that in muffled tones or in the secrecy of our own hypocritical minds. What we need to do is to discuss the way we were and why we were the way we were. One of the reasons that we were not perfect either is that, by definition, adolescents are rebellious. If you find perfect teenagers I will find a contradiction in terms. Part of the growing pains of adolescence is to begin to sever the psychological familial umbilical cord and in so severing it to make mistakes. We would like for adolescents to follow our advice rather than our lead. But we cannot learn for them—they must learn for themselves. And part of that learning is to experience some downs as well as some ups. The other part of the severing of the umbilical cord is the painful time span that it takes for both parents and children to recognize, as Khalil Gibran suggests in *The Prophet,* "Your children are not your children. They come through you but not from you." During the time when this realization is reaching its peak, some arguments are going to occur within the household between the adolescent and the parent. Some demands are going to be made on the teachers and those in the school in positions of authority from young people who are all wise at age 14 and recognize so well in their own minds that we don't know what we are doing and certainly don't know how to run a school. And these youngsters, if we would just give them a chance, would run it for us. There is also that realization that if, indeed, we said, "O.K., you've got it," these youngsters know all too well that they need us to run the schools, they need us to show them how to do things and to help them learn how not to do the wrong things. What they don't need, however, is for us to impress upon them endlessly the fact that they need us so much.

We bring up our young people playing team sports, cooperating and developing an attitude where they can listen to others. We want them to cooperate with friends. We compliment, we reward in our society popularity, we speak in glowing terms about youngsters who get along well with others. As a matter of fact, on the report card that was signed by my parents when I was in school there was indeed a line that said "gets along well with others" and if one did not the teacher would put a check mark. The assumption was that one should be able to get along with others, thus, the check mark was the exceptional mark rather than having teachers put a check mark in the cases where youngsters did get along well with others. There is the sociop-sychological need within each of us to get along well with our peers. Part of adolescent growth is fighting with the umbilical cord to sever that cord and in sometimes very peculiar and other times very profound ways. We did it and young people are doing it today.

We also had a need for originality. Didn't we have to discover our own music even while appreciating some of the music of our parents that spans the decades and the centuries? We also had to get some strange music of our own. Did we not have our own slang and did not that slang become obsolete as soon as our parents learned what it was? It is natural and necessary for generations to be able to mark their place in the sands of time in order that historians can look back and characterize the ME generation, and the Roaring '20s, the Cold War period, the Civil Rights Movement, even beyond adolescence. Even now, at age 49, many of my peers and I continue to look for something that approaches the turmoil and romance of the volatile and yet historically significant '60s. When I say, allow this generation to be this generation, I am suggesting that to do otherwise is to be on the wrong side of inevitability. We cannot do anything else. But when I talk about **allowing** this generation to be this generation, I am talking about it attitudinally. Approach young people in positive ways and accept them for whom they are.

I am not saying that we must accept all that this generation represents. If, indeed, we are in the throes of a massive struggle against a growing drug culture we cannot allow acceptance of persons with bad habits or criminal behavior. When I say allow this generation to be this generation I am not suggesting for a moment that we accept foul language throughout the halls of our schools and classrooms in our presence. We cannot accept that. We can allow young people to be assertive, and work toward channeling that assertiveness in positive directions so that they lead more toward reformation than revolution, attempting to help straighten out the society within the confines of what is legal and acceptable, rather than having no constraints and being chaotic in one's approach. I am suggesting that we encourage young people's creativity and that we have an obligation to be examples of that which is highest and best in a creative spirit, so that young people, while testing their own independent wings, can see us in flight doing positive, healthy, nonprofane things in their presence and suggesting that we would like to include them in drawing upon the exuberance of youth while giving them the benefit of the wisdom of age.

We must allow this generation to be this generation in terms of accepting differences, making suggestions at to what becomes obscene and/or ostentatious and its appropriateness or inappropriateness in the school room and/or the work place. We can encourage peer pressure, but on the positive side, suggesting to those who have a bent toward positiveness, optimism, and healthy living (and by the way, there are far more of those young people than there are negative young people) while encouraging them to use their influence on their peers, particularly those on the borderline between being good and being bad. Encourage positiveness, sobriety, health, and proper use of language. Encourage by rewarding accomplishment, achievement and congratulating cooperativeness and friendliness. Let me caution our educational social institutions here on the issue of rewarding positive behavior. When I talk about rewarding accomplishment, I am talking about rewards for positive and exceptional accomplishment. When I talk about congratulating positive attitudes and behavior, I am talking about encouraging young people to continue to be positive. The distinction I am making is this—I believe that there are too many suggestions for rewarding behavior that ought to be the norm as opposed to offering rewards only when one's accomplishments rise above what is expected. There are those who say that disciplined youngsters ought to be rewarded for being disciplined and controlled. That bothers me a bit in that I think that youngsters should be expected to be disciplined and controlled. They should be rewarded when that control and discipline sees them go above and beyond the call of duty where they initiate some action program involving their classmates or teammates in something that is exceptional, and that says we want greater school spirit or we want to develop particular programs that will help us develop habits of control that will follow us for the rest of our lives. If it is not exceptional, let us not be elaborate in our rewards.

We must allow this generation to be this generation not only because we demanded that we be allowed to be who we were at the time of adolescence but also because this generation is our hope for a future that will reform a society that is far less than perfect. And that reformation will only come through a group of young people who, when they are in positions of power, will be able to act upon creative expertise developed at a time when they most needed guidance in that development and who were not restricted from that development. They sit in front of TVs and computer games too much; but they are also computer literate. They are too independent at an early age; but they are also becoming responsible at an early age. They use too much profane language; but they also understand foreign languages. They have too much to do with sex; but they also know what not to do. They are belligerent; they are also confident. We have an obligation never to compromise our own values but at the same time we must realize we cannot impose our values on anyone else. Exposing our values and holding to them collectively may cause them to follow our lead as they hone their skills to become leaders of tomorrow.

SELF—STUDENTS

Lesson 10
Practice Parallel Perking

Parallel perking is offering more than one compliment at a time to young people who need to see themselves as whole persons. Oftentimes we inadvertently cause young people to see themselves as one dimensional or put them in embarrassing positions among their peers because they are so often singled out for a particular skill, talent, or accomplishment. I am suggesting parallel perking for at least two reasons. One reason is to reduce the embarrassment by offering "complementary compliments," if you will, continuing to encourage young people to do well what they already do well while at the same time helping them to enhance skills in other areas where perhaps they are not doing quite as well. The second reason is I think that it is equally important for young people to see themselves as whole or well-rounded persons, not dependent upon some particular skill or talent but persons who have learned at an early age that it is less one's talent and more one's habits that cause him or her to be successful.

What, for instance, is a parallel perk? Let's take a student in one's classroom who always seems to get 'A's. This is the young person who is surprised and disappointed when they receive a 97 on a test. This is the young person spoken about in a previous lesson who may have an unrealistic view of self based upon singular perks in early life about how smart they are, and so becomes very disappointed if this singular aspect of their character is not constantly reinforced and they cannot constantly prove how smart they are based upon test results. And so it is that you have a young person who always gets 'A's and a teacher who always holds that student up in front of the rest of the class, not only complimenting the young person for how bright they are but inadvertently and sometimes overtly suggesting to the rest of the class that they should be like this person. What happens sometimes is that the person becomes overly disappointed when they don't get an A; and, what happens, perhaps more often than that, is that person is derided by the rest of the class for thinking he or she is so smart or for what we used to call brown nosing the teacher or perhaps just left out of some activities because the classmates feel that they get enough recognition. Consequently the child, while wanting to continue to do well, does not want to continue to be embarrassed or disliked. A parallel perk would be to compliment the youngster for doing well on an exam and then offering a complementary compliment, about a social skill that they are developing or perhaps need to develop. Such a compliment could be: "George, once again I'm proud of you for getting an A on the test, but I'm even more proud of the fact that you are helping others by tutoring in the areas where they need some assistance." Or, "Susan, I really like the grades that you are getting and I don't think you have to worry too much about getting an A in this class. If you continue to do what you're doing no doubt you're going to get an A. I also appreciate the fact that you are participating in extracur-

ricular activities and encouraging your friends to run for office."
Or, "Mattie, your grades are great, but what's better is the
development of your personality. You seem to be more outgoing
and making an effort to get more friends and I think that's just
great." The idea here is to say that, while grades are great,
scholars do not live by grades alone and it is important that a
teacher look for something that a child needs to emphasize to a
greater degree in order that they are not led down a one-dimen-
sional path.

If you find a young man who is 6'8" tall and weighs 240
pounds and is not fat, nine out of ten people (if not ten out of
ten) will approach a conversation with that young man by assuming that he is an athlete, not asking whether or not he is, but
simply saying, "Do you play football or basketball or both?" We
would say to that young man if he isn't that he's missing a good
bet. He might go to college free and, as a matter of fact, may
become a millionaire by exploiting his size and latent talent if he
would just "go for it." I am suggesting that it is very possible
that the 6'8", 240 pound male muscle may want to be a concert
pianist or a neurosurgeon and should not me made to feel
ashamed for wanting that. It is all right to say to the star of the
basketball team or the football team, "I was at the game and you
were great. I also appreciate the fact that you're doing better in
science and that in your interview you were absolutely eloquent.
Keep working on your conversational skills because you may
want to become a lawyer some day." I am suggesting that we
owe it to young people to practice parallel perking in order that
they understand that we see them as more than jocks or brains.
See the young lady who dresses and looks nice as more than a
prospective model in this sexist society in which we live. We need
to help young people develop character and a desire to conquer
worlds that they hadn't previously considered because everybody
was working on them to enhance that one skill for which they
are well known. I am suggesting that any opportunities we get
to practice parallel perking will awaken within the young people
we encounter on a regular basis a real desire to develop all that
is within them rather than to make all that is within them one
aspect of their character.

SELF—STUDENTS

Lesson 11
Seize the Rare Moment

The rare moment about which I am speaking is that interruption in what we would consider to be the normal flow of the day which might ordinarily appear to be a disruption because, for example, some science equipment is broken in the laboratory or because two youngsters have a tremendous argument that might erupt into a fight or the curiosity of a particular student or several students is aroused and prompts them to ask questions outside of the outline of the lesson being presented at the time. A rare moment might be the nervousness of young people preparing for an assembly program and allowing that nervousness to manifest itself in behavior that would ordinarily be unacceptable. Capitalize upon that moment to teach a lesson that might be outside of the curriculum but might be a lesson for life. One of the great rare moments that I can remember in my own experience was the teaching of eighth grade science concepts marked for a gifted class to a seventh grade average-to-below-average class. It was a moment during which questions were asked based upon the previous classroom's experiments that had nothing to do with the lesson that appeared in my lesson plans for that seventh grade class. Because we did not have time to clean up after some experimenting had been done, the odor of the previous class's experiments lingered until the seventh grade class came in. Smelling the resultant odor from eighth grade introductory physical science experiments, one of the seventh graders said, "Mr. Boyd, what is that smell?" When I answered the question and showed that one seventh grade student the test tubes and flasks that were used in the eighth grade gifted class experiments, other questions followed as to why those test tubes were used, how the Bunsen burner was torched and set, what material state the wood was in when we began and how it changed and what were the indicators in terms of volume and color, seven minutes of answering questions of two or three curious students ensued. Upon observing my willingness to answer the questions and seeing that it was all right to leave their seats and come to the lab table to see what was going on, other students in the classroom continued in the questioning. By the end of the hour, the seventh grade average class had received a lesson in introductory physical science that was given to a gifted eighth grade class just prior to their coming in.

It was a rare moment because the quality of interaction among young people at the height of their curiosity and interest made the lesson an excellent one for all of us. It was a rare moment because those asking the questions were students who did not ordinarily participate in class discussions but the informality of this particular discussion helped them to feel at ease and they began to question as long as I would answer. It was a rare moment for me because it taught me a lesson about flexibility and helped me to understand that flexibility helps create a climate with the classroom that is as human as it is academic. It was a rare moment that taught me a lesson about what Madeline Hunter refers to as the "anticipatory set" wherein I saw that it was good to engage the youngsters in a lesson that was to follow. It was a rare moment that might have been perceived as a disruption had I been intent on following the lesson plan I had written for that seventh grade class but I felt then and I feel now that when students are at the height of curiosity and interest (and at the height of a willingness) to participate in something that we have to impart it is not always a bad idea to break for a moment, responding to their immediate needs in order to teach a lesson that involves more than subject matter but involves the human element to a degree as great as the academic element. It also led to more dynamic lessons from their regular unit, because they continued to ask questions, in subsequent days, on the lesson they were studying.

There can be a rare moment when students have a verbal misunderstanding, indeed an argument that seems destined to become a fist fight. Understanding, as most of us do, that many arguments, in fact, probably most arguments, are the results of misunderstanding, miscommunication, or the lack of communication altogether, it is important to assist our students in learning lessons for life. Among life lessons that can be taught at these moments of misunderstanding would be a lesson in conflict resolution. Over the last 7 to 10 years, many school districts are beginning to form secondary school conflict resolution committees who indeed intervene among their peers to ensure that misunderstandings do not get out of hand. When we look at the unpredictability of the human experience and recognize that every day we find ourselves in situations where we cannot predict from one moment to the next what is about to happen we ought to be flexible and receptive to the rare moment not only because of this practical value in terms of the opportunity to teach lessons, but also because of the psychological value to be able to cope with mundane "everydayness" looking for the possibility of sudden change.

Seizing the rare moment not only is part of the maturation process in becoming effective teachers, it is also a statement in front of the class that sets an example for them as they go through the unexpected eventualities in life so that they too, following our lead, will be able to make stepping stones out of stumbling blocks and lemonade out of lemons, so that they can look at obstacles as opportunities and indeed, upon many instances, they too can seize the rare moment.

SELF—STUDENTS

Lesson 12
Always Grade English

Always look for opportunities to correct students when they utter phrases that are grammatically incorrect. "Always Grade English" suggests that it does not matter whether one is in a science, math, or English class, teaching the rules of proper writing and speaking is important because we are teaching, in the U.S., both by example and by instruction, in order to guide young people toward mastery of this nation's language of power. Standard or mainstream English is the language of power. If there are those of us who realize that we are not proficient in the use of the language ourselves and therefore are reluctant to always grade English, let me suggest that doing so will also help us to master the language of power. It is important because school is where things are supposed to be done right. If young people are going to learn how to do those things which will make them successful in life subsequent to their elementary and secondary school years it is important that they matriculate in a climate where things are done right as a matter of course.

Grading English does not necessarily mean assigning essays in auto shop, but it certainly does mean that anyone who plans to be a mechanic and wants to communicate what is wrong with a vehicle ought to learn how to state the problem succinctly and accurately and that is best done by understanding Standard English first and then the mechanics, if you will, of shop talk. To only talk shop would make one suspect in the eye of the customer and would cause the cultivation of future customers to suffer because of the confusion of doubletalk. Whatever field one goes into—whether it be engineering, mathematics, botany, etc.—if one thinks that the only place it is important to master conversational Standard English is in broadcast journalism, then recall your frustration when you were driving out of town and asked for some simple directions. Standard English is important whatever your field at the time of one's job interview because, second to dress, the way one communicates is among the first impressions noted. And when one acquits himself or herself well conversationally, doors can be opened and an opportunity to show what else one knows will be presented.

Always grading English not only deals with that part of communication where one is transmitting but it also says that in order to communicate clearly from the standpoint of speaking to someone, one must also listen carefully to what others say as well as listen carefully to what one is saying himself. There have been colleagues who have asked because I taught science whether or not I graded for content or for grammar. My response to that was, and is, content suffers for lack of grammatical correctness. If one wants to communicate to a math teacher and cannot set up a problem in proper terms it will be impossible to solve that problem. The setting up of or the statement of the problem in clear, concise terms is certainly as important as solving the problem. There is a statement that was used often in the rhetoric of the '60s—if one does not know where he's going, any road will take him there. To paraphrase that statement as it pertains to being able to state a problem clearly in order to solve the problem, I would suggest that if one knows not what his problem is any solution will do.

We need to help our young people to write and recite clearly enough so that their casual conversation can speak to anyone at any level. As I suggested, in Lesson 9, I think that we should allow this generation to be this generation and let them have their colloquial terminology. But I think that colloquialism or slang, have their place and that place is not in the classroom. That place is not in the office of prospective employers during a job interview. That place is not when discussing one's future seriously with a college counselor who might be responsible for a scholarship. It is not only common, but it is necessary, for young people to be bidialectical, i.e., understanding both Standard English and slang. Being bidialectical also suggests being bisocial—that is, knowing what is appropriate in the streets and in the suites. If slang is all right among friends in the streets accompanied by peculiar handshakes as well as "appropriate" street dress, then it must also be realized that Standard English, the ability to listen, and appropriate dress is required in executive offices where one will find employment and perhaps a career. Throughout *Plain Teaching* I will emphasize the importance of the teacher as exemplar. It is certainly important that teachers practice proper grammar for all of the hours that we are in school. Again, if there are teachers who find that difficult, and there are some, it is important to seek help and to practice on an ongoing basis getting better at one's delivery. It will enhance your ability to communicate, it will enhance your professional image, and it will certainly help students who emulate you even when we don't know it, to learn the proper way to communicate.

SELF—STUDENTS

Lesson 13
Use Students' Special Talents and Interests

In the 5-Ex Cycle, I mentioned that education becomes exciting when we feel included. The quality of that inclusion depends upon a child's perception of his or her real acceptance in the classroom. As we call upon the significant experiences that children bring into the classroom and expose those experiences within a climate of high expectations, the believability of that calling upon is enhanced by our real knowledge of what interests those upon whom we are calling. In cases where there seems to be a reluctance to participate on the part of some young people it is certainly wise for us to explore not only their backgrounds and aptitudes but also to attempt to tap whatever is of special interest to them or tap whatever special talents they might have. Because of our academic orientation we do not want to emphasize athletics and entertainment to a degree that it would seem that all we are encouraging young people to do is become the court jester of a larger society. Also, we don't want to give them an unrealistic outlook as to their chances of becoming professional athletes and professional entertainers, nor do we want our classrooms to become theaters simply of entertainment rather than laboratories of learning. Sometimes when we think of youngsters' special talents and interests we think in terms of their academic talents and their intellectual interests. What I'm addressing here is using your students' special talents and interests in whatever interests them to a high degree and whatever their proficiencies are, whether indeed it is entertainment, athletics or dressing well and being able to mediate disputes or get along with others, whether it happens to be being able to sew, draw, recite, etc.

A good case that would serve as an example in using a student's special talents or interests was the case of a summer school student whose name is Emanuel. In the seventh grade, Emanuel had to come to my remedial reading summer school class at a time when school did not seem to particularly interest

Emanuel. During the course of our reading lessons, since I was
not enthusiastic as I might have been during those hot days
during the summer months, I looked for ways to make the reading lessons interesting and one of the approaches that I used was
group discussion. Oftentimes we would preview a lesson and
discuss what we were about to read rather than reading first and
then reviewing. The discussions were informal and allowed for
youngsters to participate in a spontaneous fashion, with
laughter and challenges from young people. Emanuel, even
during the discussions that seemed to have as much levity as
substance, never seemed to be particularly interested in the
reading lessons. One day Emanuel brought a small golf trophy.
Evidently, he had participated in a local tournament and was
good enough to have placed in the tournament thereby earning
a trophy. Because it was small I didn't see it well. Emanuel had
it in his hand and seemed to be preoccupied with the trophy and
I asked what it was and he said, "Oh, it's just a trophy." And I
asked what kind, and he said, "Golf." I said, "I didn't realize you
golfed," and he said, "Yes." I asked, "Well, how good are you?"
Another student, Marilyn, initiated, "Mr. Boyd, Emanuel is real
good at golf. He can beat Mr. Mosely." And I said to Emanuel, "Is
that right? Can you beat Mr. Mosely?" And Emanuel shrugged
his shoulders modestly as if to say "sometimes," or "I guess so."
As I began to discuss golf with Emanuel I suggested that he
bring his trophies to school the next day and let us see them.
Emanuel agreed, again not with particular enthusiasm, but certainly with a lot more interest than he had regarded the reading
lesson prior to our discussing golf. Sure enough, the following
day Emanuel backed up his U-Haul trailer to display the
trophies he had amassed over the course of his involvement in
golf from a very young age. Certainly while that is an exaggera-
tion, the point is that this was one of Emanuel's special talents
and interests. My suggestion was that we read *Golf Digest* and
similar magazines and begin to build reading lessons around
golf. Emanuel perked up, we developed a new relationship, and
he developed a new interest in reading, leading him to read with
comprehension and attention.

In another case, a young lady, Latanya, who was not one to
participate in everything but who certainly got along well with

all the students did not have an extreme interest in what was going on in school except that students liked her and she seemed to like students. But it was very difficult to tap what there was about Latanya that would cause her to become excited in a particular lesson or activity. One of the things that I noticed about Latanya was how neat she was—very neat all the time, not only in the way that she dressed, but what she wore (not only in terms of how neatly her dresses and skirts and pants were pressed, but also her obvious attempt in seventh grade to coordinate her fashions—not in any ostentatious way—but with an obvious appreciation for dressing properly and neatly). The interesting thing, I guess, about her dress was that she came from a very down-to-earth family who did not spend a lot of time trying to make impressions; but this particular daughter (not to make an impression but simply because she thought it was proper) was one who apparently went to some length to be an extremely neat young lady. Of the many questions that I asked along the lines of music and athletics, particular subject areas and extracurricular activities, the question that she responded to with enthusiasm was, "Have you ever considered modeling your clothes?" And when we began to discuss her modeling that opened a new relationship and a renewed interest in what was going on in the classroom because it now included something that she was particularly interested in and had a real aptitude for.

As human beings, most of us have some particular aptitude or talent, if somehow we, as educators, can tap those interests and talents in each of our students, and I know that I'm reaching here, but in each and every one of our students, we would find a level of participation consistent with that interest. It only makes sense. And I think that we have an obligation to our young people to look for those special talents and interests. And I think that much of the success in teaching is creating a climate that is conducive to learning. Part of creating that climate has to do with working at looking into the character and personality and interests of the young people whom we teach.

A Kansas City, Missouri teacher summed up what success in teaching was all about this way: "Preparation, preparation, preparation." The better prepared we are as educators before attempting to capture the minds of our young people, the more we are likely to succeed. Part of that preparation is getting to know as much as we can about each of our students. Impractical as it may seem, preliminary work in understanding attitudes and aptitudes of young people, interests and talents, and experiences that they bring with them to our classroom is valuable and, in fact, while it may be a great deal of work, it may save a great deal of strife during the course of a teaching year. Students may spend a lot of time doodling when we think they ought to be paying attention to our lectures. It may be that the student has a special interest in or talent for art. Young people may seem to be verbose when we want them to be quiet. It may very well be that the student has a special interest and talent in public speaking. Young people may spend an inordinate amount of time at a craft or hobby. It may seem to us to be a waste of time. But if we can develop lessons around some of those talents and interests, the involvement and participation of those students with those interests will heighten significantly and again create new relationships. The new relationship is created as young people see us as being interested in them as more than just students but as people. The relationship is enhanced because being a part of what is going on in the classroom can positively impact youngsters' attitudes toward their classmates who are also becoming involved in something that is of interest to them. It is as basic as show and tell. It is as significant as psychotherapy.

Teaching in settings where we have more than one class and where we might see upwards of 120 students per day does not seem realistic for investigating the lives of every one of those 120 plus students. One of the ways that we can use the special talents and interests of these students is to look at the groups, where a particular group of students had an experience over the weekend that involved their team or their choir and perhaps seven or eight were involved, it then makes it a little easier and yet is still personal. To the degree that it is practical we should try to explore every child's talents and interests. A good example of something that is popular and can be explored and positively exploited is that idiom of expression of the '80s and perhaps the '90s rap music. I have heard what I would consider to be some good rap music and I have heard what I would consider to be some awful rap music, but as an idiom of expression and entertainment, it is popular among young people. Rap music should not be used to give a signal to young people that this is the only form of acceptable social expression at the colloquial level. We also need to help young people understand that we are willing to become involved with "their" medium of expression but we also want to expose them to the jazz of John Coltrane, the preludes of Lizst, the blues of Billie Holiday, the poetry of Smokey Robinson, the music from "Oklahoma" and the talent of Pavarotti. One of the positive spin-offs of using students' special talents and interests is that we explore our own special talents and interests too.

SELF—STUDENTS

Lesson 14
Fight Fire with Water

The twist on this phrase speaks to the need for teachers to be different than their students inasmuch as school is the place where things are done properly. The examples that teachers set ought to be not only for the moment but for the future as well. When there is chaos, or confusion it is the teacher who must establish a conducive climate and must be the exemplar of being in control of one's self in order to control a situation. I have seen professional educators say to students in cases where it appears that a particular student or group of students have just absolutely gone crazy, "If you think you can go crazy, you haven't seen what crazy is until I go crazy on you." Now when the teacher goes crazy as well as the students, you have a situation where there is no one to diffuse the situation because a "crazy" teacher has exacerbated the situation by determining that he or she will fight fire with fire.

One of the things that is important as we exemplify what the world ought to be like in the future of those whom we teach is to be calm in the face of a storm and collected in the face of chaos. If school is where things are done right then those who make sure that things are done right in school are those who are charged with the responsibility of setting the proper educational climate. I suggest fighting fire with water, not only from the standpoint of diffusing a situation and projecting the example of how things ought to be, but I suggest fighting fire with water as a lesson in how to handle any situation in life. One of the ways that people who are bent on confrontation are totally disarmed is to confront someone who is smiling, who is congenial, who is receptive, and who is even agreeable. A person who wants very much to fight finding no opponent (or the supposed opponent being very congenial) will very quickly either refuse to fight himself or will be embarrassed by actions that appear to be illogical in view of the fact that nobody is fighting back or no one is shouting back or acting "crazy".

Actual wars are fought based on the need to fight fire with fire. If we trace the histories of several conflicts that surround us we might be hard pressed to find the true origin of the conflict.

We are extremely critical of youth gangs because these gangs fight over turf, and yet, world conflicts see formidable foes, indeed, fighting over turf. The kinds of arguments that are given for major confrontations are arguments that sound very similar to the arguments that our students give us for confrontation, i.e., "We were here first and they came and tried to overrun us" or, "We did not hit them until they hit us" or, "They disrespected us. They violated our space." When you look at students who are fighting each other on the playground, one student might describe the event as, "The sucker got up in my face." Well, face is equivalent to space. Each of us needs some sense of security within the confines of a geographical comfort zone.

We have become so proficient at fighting fire with fire that major studios producing block-buster movies seem to feel that a movie cannot be a hit without a great deal of fire power and a great many fires. Those fires might represent themselves in exploding vehicles, bombed-out buildings, or flame throwers that are aimed at human beings running to get away from the fray. We are a world that glorifies fire. If we, as human beings, are bent on killing each other in large numbers, the role of education ought to be to seek ways to co-exist peacefully and productively.

It is difficult for me to imagine creating a world of peace within laboratories of violence. If we suggest that one of the ways to keep students from fighting is to beat up on students, that seems to me to be illogical. If we suggest that one of the ways to keep a class quiet is to shout—telling our students to "shut up"—that too seems illogical. If we suggest that one of the ways to create nice young people sitting in front of us in our classrooms is to be hard, mean teachers, that also is illogical. If we suggest that one of the ways to get parents involved in school is to ignore or refuse to contact parents in positive ways, that too is illogical.

If you keep on doing what you've always done, you'll keep on getting what you've always got. If you keep on fighting fire with fire, you will keep on getting more fire. If you greet students who have determined that they are not going to respond in class with an attitude, "Then I will not include you in activities in the class," you'll keep on getting what you've always got—students who are not actively participating in class. Our responsibility is not to fight fire with fire—an attitude all too often experienced by the students most likely to show us the fire that is inside of them—but to use water or the opposite of fire in order to douse the flames of fear, insecurity, and animosity that cause young people to be confrontational rather than cooperative.

If we determine that it makes sense to fight fire with water in order to create a new climate and to reach toward what can be rather than regret what is then classroom leaders need to practice ways to fight fire with water. In order for it to become a natural reaction in chaotic situations, we will have to fight fire with water repeatedly so that it is the normal response rather than the rare response. If we believe that it is reasonable to fight fire with water, then that means that even outside of the class-room our demeanor should become such that we react to as many situations, if not all situations, with the attitude of calming the waters rather than precipitating the storm.

When students want to fight, teachers must teach them to reason. We must also teach them that reasoning is better than fighting. When students want to argue, we must teach them the art of debate so that they understand the basis for the argument and the way to have that argument heard within the context of reason rather than within the context of disagreement for disagreement's sake. When our students want to become loud, repeating vociferously the two favorite expressions of adolescence "Boring" and "Unfair", we need to approach them quietly and enthusiastically so that perhaps our enthusiasm becomes infectious, and they do not feel so bored. We must help them to also see that when they create a climate of confusion, even chaos, if you will, then that is unfair to their fellow students, teachers, and to themselves because they must gain an opportunity for understanding that fairness is more subjective than objective.

The traditional interpretation of the term, "Fight fire with fire," is, "Be as hard on others as they are with you. Be as confrontational with others as they are with you." I suggest that we fight fire with water. "Fighting fire with fire" suggests that it is necessary (for instance, in the business world) to be as assertive as one's competitors. Then I think that we could stretch a point and suggest, "O.K., fighting fire with fire is a reasonable approach toward keeping up with the competition." But I am afraid that the use of the term to meet the goals of encouraging young people to keep up, will lead toward an interpretation that we must be as tough as, rather than as enduring as, competitors or opponents.

Because it is a place to douse flames and to teach how to douse flames, teachers in the classroom have a responsibility to be the exemplars of fighting fire with water.

*　*　*　　*　*　*

The next section deals with how we relate to those who have the same professional responsibility as we. Whether they be teachers, administrators, auxiliary personnel, para-professionals, etc.—all who are charged with the responsibility of being team members, as it were, where we are interacting as adults with the young people in our schools. The adults in the building beginning with the chief administrator, if that be the school principal or school headmaster or dean, through the assistants and associates, faculty members, and others set the tone that will establish a learning climate that is either conducive to excellence or one that prohibits excellence. It is important, then, that we recognize the significance, not only of how we function by ourselves, but how we function with others as exemplars of a team determined to set a climate conducive, not only to productivity, but, indeed, to excellence.

SELF—COLLEAGUES

Lesson 15
Analyze and Update Team Assessments

When I had the pleasure in 1977 of working with Barbara Stewart at the Center for New Schools under the direction of Dr. Francis Holiday, I was introduced to something called "A Team Rating Analysis". I can attribute my exposure to the Team Rating Analysis to Dr. Holiday and Barbara Stewart, and am not certain when that particular instrument was introduced to the Center for New Schools. I have used the Team Rating Analysis with many faculties I've had the pleasure of working with over the last eleven years. A sample "Team Rating Analysis" appears below.

APT Team Rating Analysis

School (Institution, Organization) _____

Date _____

On a scale from 1 to 10, with 10 being highest (or most positive feelings), please rate the following (circle most appropriate number):

A. I feel that I have assistance and support from my fellow teachers.

   1   2   3   4   5   6   7   8   9   10

B. I am confident in the instructional and administrative leadership of the principal.

   1   2   3   4   5   6   7   8   9   10

C. This school emphasizes parent participation.

   1   2   3   4   5   6   7   8   9   10

D. Students respond positively to instruction from teachers at this school.

   1   2   3   4   5   6   7   8   9   10

E. Students are progressing, academically, at an acceptable pace.

   1   2   3   4   5   6   7   8   9   10

F. Students are progressing, socially, at an acceptable pace.

1   2   3   4   5   6   7   8   9   10

G. I feel good about my teaching.

1   2   3   4   5   6   7   8   9   10

H. I feel good about being at this school.

1   2   3   4   5   6   7   8   9   10

I. There is no problem at this school that cannot be solved within the present structure.

1   2   3   4   5   6   7   8   9   10

J. The faculty and administration, at this school, function together as a team.

1   2   3   4   5   6   7   8   9   10

The Team Rating Analysis is an instrument that can be varied to fit particular situations, but, in essence, it is a series of questions answered anonymously by members of a particular staff focusing on one's perception of how the team works, the principal leads, the students respond, and the parents cooperate. An example of a question would be "On a scale of one to ten with ten being the highest or most positive and one being the lowest or most negative, how do you feel about the instructional leadership capabilities of your principal?" The person responding, then, would circle a number somewhere between one (totally unsatisfactory) and ten (outstanding). In the team rating analyses that I have typed up for myself, I have asked those participating to respond to questions asked first person singular, wherein the item would appear like this:

1. I am confident in the instructional leadership capabilities of the building principal.

Then that person would circle one of the numbers deemed appropriate based upon his or her perceptions.

The value of a team rating analysis can be seen in situations where there is a particular need for team building. It can also be seen as an assessment tool if a new principal is coming on board and wants to get some sense of perceptions. As I indicated, team rating analyses would vary and obviously, if one is a new principal, the item on the instrument, "I feel confident in the instructional leadership capabilities of the principal," would not appear. The principal would then tailor-make a team rating analysis for purposes of assessment rather than necessarily team building. The assessment might reveal that team building is not an immediate priority because the team is so intact.

Another value of a team rating analysis is to have one who is part of a team either affirm his or her own perceptions about what's going on or to make them reflective of whether or not they may be out of step with what is happening around them. There is value in the fact that being asked to participate with such an instrument shows that their opinion counts. Their feelings are being taken into consideration, and there are possibilities for improvement where improvement is needed. The implication of doing a team rating analysis is: Once the analysis has been completed, suggestions would come forth as to how to improve upon what is bad and enhance what is good.

I am suggesting in this lesson that a team needs to continually assess and update team rating analyses. If things are not as they should be, and that fact is revealed in a team rating analysis after which suggestions are made and acted upon, it is important to then reassess in order to determine whether or not recommendations are working. Where there is an assessment based upon the team rating analysis that all things are going well, it is important to continue to assess and to update team rating analyses just in case a group has been lulled into apathy based upon the fact that a particular team rating analysis has said that everything is going well.

Faculties and leadership change, and because there are ongoing changes (some so subtle that a faculty might not realize that over a period of three or four years there's been a 40% change in the staff), it is important to continue to update the team rating analysis itself and, to monitor whatever action is being taken in order that the next team rating analysis will reveal more positive information.

One example of the value of a team rating analysis was seen at a secondary school where I was allowed three days interaction with the faculty. The approved first day's agenda included the

Team Rating Analysis. The second day's agenda included an analysis of the individual analyses. In the presence of the principal, I revealed what the faculty told me about what they thought of the school climate. Before the third day, the principal determined that we needed to change the agenda because the Team Rating Analysis revealed some areas that needed immediate and intense attention. Sometimes the value of the Team Rating Analysis can be seen as immediately as the time of instrument administration. Sometimes the value of the Team Rating Analysis cannot be seen until subsequent staff meetings or until recommendations have come forth based upon what the analysis reveals.

A team rating analysis—type instrument should be a constant and integral part of the ongoing activities of every school in order to ensure that there is continuity in the quality of the instructional climate in our buildings.

SELF—COLLEAGUES

Lesson 16
Share the Wealth, Please

As a neophyte teacher in 1964, I discovered that many teachers, not just a few, value some materials so greatly that they do not allow anyone else in the building to know that they have these materials in their possession. There are some items that are in such great demand that those who have them could probably develop a lucrative enterprise by offering, at a reasonable price, to share the materials with their colleagues.

In my first couple of years at the school where I taught the item most prized was masking tape. If you had masking tape and were willing to share it, your popularity stock would go up several points immediately with the person with whom you shared it, and eventually with the entire staff just by virtue of the fact that they knew that you were in possession of "the masking tape." I can recall meeting some teachers who, upon being asked to share construction paper of various sizes and colors, would open their closets, then the vault behind the closet, then the safe within the vault behind the closet, then the safety deposit box within the safe within the vault behind the closet, and reveal large packages of construction paper browning at the edges because it was so old. But these teachers were determined that if they were not going to use it neither was anyone else. It is interesting to note that this is a microcosm of our larger society where we are so invested in being the owners of, or having more than, or having something that someone else does not have, that even if it does not benefit us personally, we will not allow something that we have to benefit anyone else.

Not only is it a sad commentary on our attitudes toward each other, but it is certainly a terrible example to set before young people whom we punish for not sharing. Needless to say, there are many things that we purchase on our own. And if, indeed, one goes out of one's way to find something that is important to the classroom one is in, and whatever it is that has been found was not easy to find nor inexpensive and is extremely important to the lessons that we are teaching, you could make a case for not wanting to share because it might hurt the lessons we are attempting to teach.

From a practical standpoint, it only makes sense that when you share with others, it is likely that others will share with you. But even if one does not expect something in return, because all of us are working toward assisting young people in learning all that they need to know, we need to be willing to share whatever resources we have in order to enhance the learning climate for everybody, and the returns on our sharing investment are realized in students' increased capacity to receive and retain information. In many cases materials are reproducible and in most cases, we are not using all our material all of the time.

In speaking of sharing the wealth, I'm speaking of sharing resources whether they be material, human, or otherwise. I know that it is fun to have one's ego stroked as colleagues, parents, and students compliment you on being the only teacher who knows how to work the movie projector or, "This teacher is so popular, so well known, that she can bring in top-notch guest speakers on any given occasion." It is normal to want to be singled out. It is normal to want to be the best at something or the "only" at something, but in a school a big ego is not conducive to getting the most out of the learning environment. If one should stumble upon a magnificent teaching technique that you think others might be able to duplicate, say, "Eureka! I have found it!" And if your colleague's name is not Eureka, by whatever name they call themselves, go to them and share this wealth of information or methodology. There is still an opportunity for us to enjoy a rather singular recognition as we share with others as our school becomes outstanding.

Now as a member of an outstanding team that you have helped to form based upon sharing the wealth that you have, you can enjoy being singled out as a school, as perhaps being the only school that does certain kinds of things. I am suggesting that the school then consult with other schools interested in what you are doing that makes you such an effective educational machine in order that your sharing of the wealth can spread throughout the district in which you teach, throughout the county, throughout the state, and ultimately, throughout the entire U.S. Some decades ago to make such a suggestion might have sounded fantastic or fantasy-like, but in this modern age of advanced communications, it is possible through telenetworking to share the wealth immediately with satellite hook-ups around the country, and indeed, around the world.

Sharing of the wealth increases the wealth, and because school is the place where we show those who come to us to be taught how things are supposed to be done, it is an excellent example of what the world ought to be like when teachers share material, philosophies, and human wealth with fellow teachers in the presence of, and to the benefit of, our students.

SELF—COLLEAGUES

Lesson 17
Use Inside/Outside Consultants

Inside/Outside consultants is a term that I use to discuss our need to respect our neighbor across the hall as much as we respect our neighbors across the nation. Consultants generally get a great deal of respect when they are outside consultants just by virtue of the fact that they are outside, and the further outside a consultant is, the more credibility he or she is automatically given.

A Chicago consultant, for example, when consulting with colleagues in Chicago, is pretty much known by his or her first name and accepted as one who may, indeed, be quite knowledgeable and "in a pinch" might be one on whom we can call if we need some information. This very same Chicago consultant, who might be used in the hometown "in a pinch" is revered in San Bernardino, California, where endless calls are recorded on his answering machine beckoning him to come to the West Coast to impart pearls of wisdom that will be immediately used and everlastingly retained.

It is biblical that one cannot be a prophet in his hometown. If that rings true, then it is certainly also true that one cannot be considered a wise consultant in his or her own school. I think that this is unfortunate because the success enjoyed by many consultants is that success that has come from picking up information directly from those who are on the firing line in the classrooms everyday. The luxury that the consultant has is that of being able to work full-time on organizing the information received from the classroom teacher in a salable package that we as consultants can then use to write a book and come back as experts to the very place we received the information and sell that information at a premium. I am suggesting that we use inside/outside consultants. That is, we should begin to respect those among us to a much higher degree and even to the degree that we respect outside consultants.

Let's paraphrase another biblical concept. "How can I admire the wisdom of outside consultants whom I do not know if I have no respect for the inside consultant with whom I work everyday." It is not only important to respect our colleagues at the building level as consultants but it is also practical. As we fix our budgets in spring of the year for the following school year, much of the money from the budget is set aside to call in outside consultants to deal with specific problems. The money is sometimes well spent. Yet there are no guarantees that an outside consultant will speak to the peculiarities of a local problem. If, indeed, they are to do that, the chances are their ability to do that depends upon a local school's not only hiring the consultant and paying the consultant's fee but also spending countless hours and developing many materials to get to the consultant prior to the visit in order to ensure that the person coming in with their "expertise" will speak to the pertinent issues at the local level.

There are times when we leave a conference or a staff development in-service perhaps feeling good based upon the style of a particular consultant or consultant group, but then, upon reflection, have to admit that while we felt good at the end of the session, the person really did not address what we came here to solve.

Now the person next door oftentimes is not respected for professionalism or expertise, if you will, because we are so close to them that we like them or dislike them based upon their personality, not their professionalism. The person who is across the hall is a person with whom we are familiar, and "familiarity breeds contempt." It is not necessarily so that we are contemptuous of our colleagues, but we are at least casual in our attitudes toward respecting their expertise. Another reason that we are casual is because if we give credence to their expertise, we are concerned about the fact that we have to live with them everyday gloating about the fact that they have some expertise that we do not have. Those of us who have worked closely with professionals know that those who would be called upon to help us work through particular issues are, indeed, professional enough not to gloat about the fact that they have been called upon. An inside consultant because of their closeness to the situation, can attack a problem with a degree of expertise that no outside consultant could possibly have.

I think also that not only should we respect and admire the expertise of those close to us, but I think that they ought to be paid similar fees as an outside consultant for bringing their expertise to us. Even if a person in the local school building is paid the exact same amount per day that an outside consultant demands, a savings is still realized as it is not necessary to give them a per diem to pay their airfare and their hotel and local travel fees. In the previous lesson, I suggested that we ought to share the wealth. I believe that such a sharing of the wealth ought to be done with no regard to the possibility of being paid extra for sharing that wealth.

In this lesson I am talking about sharing expertise that other faculty members do not have. If, for instance, there is a computer expert on staff and one's school is now going to get a windfall from a major computer company that will seat every student in front of a computer at any time they need it during the day, and computer efficiency will enhance the ability to keep records including grades, attendance, follow-up services, etc., then this is the person we can call on to give us instruction based upon their expertise. I think that it is only fair for those persons to be seen as experts and paid accordingly. What we so often do is decide that since we have a windfall which represents a savings, we can now go into the budget to hire someone from outside who is highly paid to come in and tell us what the technical use of these computers might be. I say technical use because his or her examples are theoretically based upon the fact that he or she has no personal knowledge of the local needs. This person is paid and revered before the person on staff is ever approached, and so time is wasted waiting for that person or, perhaps, even that group of people to come on board to help us out. And not only is time wasted, but it is not long before we realize that the information given was based upon a theoretical foundation. Even after hiring the outside expert, schools sometimes find it necessary to then assign the local expert to the computers on his or her own time, or whenever they can get around to it, to help us out. So, in fact, they become the on-hand, second-string, non-paid professional in this whole equation.

I think it's also reasonable to assume that teachers are in as great a need for esteem building as students, and in respecting what one has to offer above and beyond the normal duties, one's self-esteem will be enhanced and, consequently, a person will be encouraged to offer more of him- or herself. It's also practical from the standpoint of team building as those on the local level see that bringing their expertise in has many benefits, and they are more likely to enhance their skills and make them known.

I recognize the philosophy that suggests that if everyone embraces what being a teacher is all about they ought to be willing to give of themselves above and beyond the call of duty anyway. I understand that. But, I think that there are many who do not understand that teachers are doing that already.

I think that two approaches toward using local expertise would be: 1) to develop a local skills bank and 2) to survey our own in cases where issues need to be paid special attention before going outside.

The skills bank would be something where, at the beginning of the school year, teachers are asked what they have in their backgrounds that suggest that they might be called upon to do some special things relative to that background. I think that in the skills bank information would be filed based upon teachers' special interests and things that they particularly enjoy doing. So, the first thing that would happen when setting aside staff development time would be for us to look around and say, "Who among us will be able to address these issues?" If, indeed, there is no one, then we might begin a search for outside talent.

One of the things that is important in this issue of using inside/outside consultants is to make sure that we put ego and personality differences behind us in cases where even the most obnoxious person with whom we deal with everyday has the expertise needed. There are two reasons for this: 1) it is a matter of professionalism and 2) it may be that a person might lose some of their obnoxiousness if they perceive themselves as being respected by those who have heretofore considered them to be obnoxious.

Needless to say, the use of inside/outside consultants does not need to be exclusive. I believe that there is merit to outside consultants coming in from time to time to assist in staff development. One reason is an outsider's objectivity. For instance, if there is an analysis of a team rating analysis, the outside consultant is one who can look at the information and say, "Based upon what you have told me, your principal is perceived to be one who is not an effective instructional leader." The outside consultant saying that is not confronting a building administrator personally. The outside consultant is simply reading the information given, at which point, the outside consultant can say, very soberly and comfortably, "If I read the signs properly, it would appear to me that there are certain things that can be done to relieve this situation. Among those things being, one, the principal taking a good look at himself or herself to determine whether or not this team rating analysis is accurate based upon what I am seeing as one who doesn't know what's happening everyday, or if it is a reflection of some differences that we might have that represent personality differences rather than actual performance. Since the evidence of the analysis is overwhelmingly skewed toward this perception, the administrator has some work to do."

The inside/outside consultant would not be one to interpret the team rating analysis because they put themselves in a precarious position if they say, "The principal seems not to be doing their job," because now they may have to suffer the ire of that principal. Or in the case when the evidence may suggest that the principal is wonderful, the inside consultant then appears to be overemphasizing how wonderful the principal is, therefore, perceived by colleagues to be attempting to gain points with the principal. So, an outside consultant's objectivity is one reason that from time to time we might call upon someone from the outside.

The second reason is, while I believe it doesn't happen often, there are times when an outside consultant may bring something new. When that is the case, and the "something new" actually enhances the local situation rather than a particular school being impressed by the newness of an approach whether it has anything to do with that school or not, it makes sense to call in an outside consultant. When all of those on faculty are just absolutely overloaded and do not have the time to commit to get across what's needed in a particular instance, it is imperative to call upon an outside consultant.

We owe it to our local school community, we owe it to each other, and we owe it to ourselves to end the ancient ritual of disregarding experts within close proximity, and because, as I have stated over and over, school is the place where examples of doing it right are given, it is time to make this whole idea of using the inside/outside consultant a natural part of what goes on in the local school building.

As each section begins with the word "Self", I am suggesting here that to hold in high regard our inside/outside consultants who teach next door, and across the hall, and down the hall, and downstairs, is the responsibility of every teacher. It is not ours to wait until the principal discovers these people, but when we see a problem, we ought to encourage that principal or those in control of the budget or in control of particular staff development or in-service to scan our colleagues. We ought to give them information where we know that we have colleagues who are just great. Our responsibility is to be respectable and to be vigilant, to be on the look-out for those among us who can do as good a job as anyone we hire from whatever distance they travel.

SELF—COLLEAGUES

Lesson 18
Display a Team Atmosphere
Throughout the School

One might wonder how a single person can display a team atmosphere. The obvious answer is: by being a complete team player. Does being a team player suggest that one is a "yes man" or a "yes woman"? Does being a team player mean that the team is right at any cost because a majority agrees? Should one de-emphasize one's own creativity or assertiveness in favor of those things that the team deems valuable? The answer is a resounding, NO.

To say in the U.S., "My country, right or wrong," is to suggest that there is no such thing as one person, one vote. My vote is extremely important. Therefore, if this is my country, if my country is wrong, it is my responsibility to do all that I can to set it right. If I'm a member of a team in a school building, if my real feeling is that the team is wrong, then I must do all that I can to set the team right. This does not mean that I am not a team player. This means that I intend to be a team player to the highest degree. One would not be a team player who ignored the fact that the team was headed in the wrong direction and decided simply not to become involved, but has, later on when things do not go as they should, an "I knew that was going to happen" or "I could see from the beginning that we were doing the wrong thing" attitude. Well, if you could have told, why didn't you? And since you didn't and could have, please don't even discuss it at this point because this speaks to the paralysis of analysis that Dr. King discussed during the civil rights years when he talked about the propensity for some in the struggle to become so enamored with their ability to analyze problems that they did not take the step further toward solutions.

When I talk about creating a team atmosphere within the school, I am suggesting that the school needs a clear and succinct mission that is understood and embraced by all. Here again, even in arriving at a mission statement, it is important that an entire staff be included in the process in order that the statement that emerges reflects the ideas and opinions of the whole team. And where one is out voted, it would be after reasonable deliberation in order that all involved feel that they received fair treatment in the development of a meaningful mission statement. Once the mission for the local school has been adopted (a mission that would be in keeping with the mission of the school district) all who are employed on that campus as team members are bound by that mission statement based upon the democratic process through which the statement emerged and the clarity and succinctness of the statement which means that everybody understands precisely what it is that they are embracing.

An extension of a clear mission statement for the school and those in charge of setting the climate is the development and implementation of uniform rules and standards. In order for young people in a building to regard seriously the few rules that govern their behavior and the standards of excellence that are expected by the teachers, it is imperative that the professionals be the exemplars. All members of the team must have had an opportunity to discuss the rationale for all school rules and upon consensus or at least majority vote, embrace those rules. And every professional in the building must be a part of enforcing those rules.

If we are concerned about dress as reflecting high standards in our building, then the professionals must be the exemplars of that standard. It is important to me when I visit secondary schools to be able to distinguish between the teachers and the students, not only in their demeanor but also in the way that they dress, and if, indeed, we are all a part of the school team, then each of us, even if we are not particular about "dressing up", should see it as part of our job and part of being a professional team that adheres to high standards, to dress in a manner that suggests to all in the building, the students in particular, that they are a part of the best that the society has to offer.

In terms of standards, it is not necessary that a school rule indicate that all students must at all times use Standard English, a subject discussed in Lesson No. 12. But what is important is that our standards demand that everyone on the team be conscious of their use of Standard English in front of their students. Most of us have an answer for students who say to us that they should not be held to certain standards when they observe Mr. Lackadaisical neglecting to live up to their standards. We say to them that Mr. Lackadaisical is not responsible for your behavior nor your future and consequently, if you should find one of my colleagues guilty of observing and seeming to embrace low standards in your presence, because your future is only in your hands, it is not for you to imitate one who does not hold to high standards.

But I think it's unrealistic for us as the exemplars to expect young people to adhere to high standards that we obviously do not embrace as a team. It is sometimes embarrassing to see professionals among us who make no attempt to use proper grammar. I would suspect that there are few people in the U.S., aside from the likes of Edwin Newman, who are so proficient at the use of the English language that they never make a grammatical error. I am certain that we all do. I am most certain that I do, but in my work and in my travels, I take advantage of every opportunity to learn from colleagues who speak and write well. And I am especially careful to attempt to project a professional demeanor in the way that I dress, in the way that I speak, and the way that I carry myself in the presence of those who are to learn from me.

So being a part of a team and helping to create a team atmosphere in the school can be done by understanding the school's mission, and understanding is helped by being a part of the development of the mission statement, by embracing and enforcing agreed-upon school rules in order to ensure that one of our colleagues is not left out on a limb with students scoffing at them because they are the only ones who are attempting to enforce a particular rule, and observing in practice high standards in all that we do, the way that we dress and the way that we speak.

As it pertains to the importance of projecting a team atmosphere, let me relate to you a true incident that occurred in one of the schools where I was privileged to teach. At one of the schools where I coordinated science fairs, I had a number of young boys borrow chairs and tables from classrooms to set up in the gymnasium and in the halls for students' science exhibits. When the boys borrowed the chairs and tables, they used masking tape (that I was able to uncover from the vaults of hard-to-find school supplies) to write room numbers and affix them to the bottom of the chairs and tables they borrowed. Later, the same young men collected the chairs and tables and looked on the bottom to determine the rooms for those chairs and tables.

On the particular day the chairs and tables were returned, there was a certain room where a substitute was teaching and on behalf of the absent teacher, he allowed the young men to return the chairs and tables to his room. The teacher across the hall indicated to the substitute that one of the chairs that was returned to his room should have been returned to her room because, indeed, that was her chair. The substitute, in an effort to be cooperative and not having a vested interest in the extra chairs and tables, traded the chair that was returned to the classroom where he substituted for a chair that was returned to the classroom across the hall.

On the following day when the regular teacher returned, I was confronted by a student who insisted that this particular teacher needed an immediate audience with me. I indicated to the student that as soon as I finished the lesson that I was currently engaged in, I would go over to the teacher's room and find out what it was that she wanted. A few minutes later, the same student came back and this time with an "attitude," and said that the teacher wanted to see me NOW. It wasn't particularly amusing because, in the interest of being a part of a team, I do not think it's a good idea for teachers to share with students their attitudes toward each other.

But, at any rate, I smiled and said, "Well, if it's that important, I guess I'd better go." I engaged my students in some book work and lab table work and proceeded to see the teacher who had been absent the previous day. The teacher confronted me in a very "concerned" way with the statement, "Where's my chair?" Now the interesting thing about the question was the attitude suggested that the chair had a lot more import than I ever imagined a chair ought to have. But the question also need not have been asked because the teacher asking knew full well that the chair in question was in the teacher's room across the hall. In fact, the other teacher was present when she confronted me with the question, "Where is my chair?" Before I could respond, not knowing fully what was going on, the other teacher said, "That is not your chair. That is my chair and it had no business in your classroom." At which time the teacher who was inquiring about the chair in the first place, said, "They got that chair out of my classroom for the science fair and I want the chair back." The other teacher said, "You borrowed that chair from me seven years ago and never gave it back, and now that I have it back, I'm going to keep it." The first teacher then said, "I did not borrow the chair from you seven years ago. That chair belonged to me. I let you use it eight or nine years ago. Seven years ago I got my chair back."

The interesting thing about this conversation was, in addition to the fact that it sounded very silly to me, was the fact that it was being held in the presence of a growing crowd of students who found the whole scene quite comical. Students began to say that the two teachers were just crazy.

At this point during the discussion, it was necessary for the assistant principal to intervene. Now obviously, this is an extreme example of how not to function as a team, but the purpose of the example is not to cite how silly an argument was that happened between two teachers who should have been a lot more professional.

The point of this example is to show where we fail to function as a team. Young people, just as older people, pick up on the negative far quicker than they pick up on the positive, but they have an acute need to be in a positive climate, and then they see us operating against each other rather than with and for each other, it gives them an unreasonable rationale for behaving in an undesirable manner because they can cite examples when they observed us operating in a undesirable manner.

Creating a team atmosphere goes beyond understanding the mission and adhering to uniform rules and high standards. It starts where we initiate cooperation, where it wouldn't seem necessary but is altogether desirable. Let us imagine that in a particular building all things are going smoothly and a cohesive faculty is functioning as a team and students are matriculating in an acceptable way. Part of being a team member and helping to create a team atmosphere is to initiate even when all is going well, something that might enhance the school situation so that we will go out of our way to, as stated earlier, share the wealth. We would go out of our way to include other classrooms in something that we are doing that may be relevant to something that the classroom is studying. It may not be necessary but it is certainly desirable.

Let us say that, for instance, our classroom in a discussion on the history of the civil rights movement has determined the desirability of looking at some of the video tapes from the series entitled "Eyes on the Prize." Because we are engaged in a unit dealing with civil rights, getting copies of the video tapes is directly pertinent to our discussion in what we are doing, it would not be necessary but would certainly be desirable to invite another class or other classes who are discussing the Civil Rights Movement or multicultural relationships or non-violent, direct action to cause a society to look at the plight of the disenfranchised, to come and observe the video tapes with us. If we get an opportunity in a particular classroom to be exposed to Asian cultures by virtue of the fact that we are getting ready for an exchange visit with students from Cambodia, Laos, Vietnam, and China, it might be a good idea to survey others in the school who are interested in foreign cultures, foreign languages, or whatever else might be pertinent to things that they're doing in their class and invite them to come with us.

The point is that the creation of a team atmosphere does not begin with the team, it begins with the individual, and since we have no control over any individual other than self, then we need to initiate things that enhance a team atmosphere. We must be the ones to help others interpret the school mission, and every opportunity we get to point out that what we are doing is in keeping with the school mission, ought to be seized upon because we are a part of a team that believes in that mission. One person can impress upon colleagues at every opportunity that is it important to observe the school rules and high standards, not as an individual but as a part of a team.

We hope to create a team atmosphere when we refuse to allow students' criticism of our colleagues to divide us. Once again, on the issue of ego, students being manipulators, sometimes know how to stroke our egos, and so it is that they might come into the classroom and say, "Mr. Notsogreat doesn't know how to teach, but you really know what you're doing, and I wish we could just get rid of him because he is really out of it." In one sense, we like to hear that we are accepted by the students in a better light than someone else, and students can stroke our egos with statements like that. And we might say something like, "Well, maybe he won't be here next year," or "Oh, give him a break. He's trying the best he can." And, in fact, what we're doing is assisting the students in putting him down. We have a professional responsibility to indicate to the students that it is inappropriate to discuss a colleague's failures in the class, and,

158

in fact, to point out those positives that we see in that colleague. As part of our team-building responsibility, it is important that if we have a problem with that teacher, that we should go to the teacher personally with our concerns or leave it alone. But to allow students to manipulate us into thinking that we can be elevated by putting someone else down is then to become the student and allow the students to become our leaders in the wrong direction.

Key terminology in creating a team atmosphere includes the terms "professionalism" and "common courtesy." If we are professional, we do not allow personality to interfere with our charge. If we observe common rules of courtesy, then we will do what we can to support the positives in others and to improve upon the negatives we see in ourselves and others. It is important not only to be supportive of colleagues and instructive where there needs to be some instruction from us, but in the creation of that kind of climate, it is altogether important that all of those things that we do individually to promote our collective sense of positiveness must be done within the presence of those who will learn from our example: the students.

SELF—COLLEAGUES

Lesson 19
Consider Substitute Teachers As Guest Teachers

It is important when you are a regular classroom teacher to sympathize with the plight of those who are engaged as substitutes in your school. The substitute teacher is in need not only of clear emergency lesson plans he or she will teach from but also in need of feeling some sense of belonging which is difficult to impossible given that so many substitutes travel from school to school.

In situations where there are building subs or teachers who have substitute status but remain at the same site on an ongoing basis, a sense of belonging can develop and even acceptance based upon becoming familiar with the surroundings and the faculty and students therein. But in many cases, the substitute is regarded by students as a kind of junior teacher, an outsider, one who, by virtue of the fact that one is a substitute, does not know what's going on in the school or in the classroom, and therefore should be taken advantage of. One of the ways that the regular teacher can assist the substitute is by making the substitute a guest teacher, finding out from the substitute whether or not there are things that they need, routines with which they need to become familiar. finding out if one's physical presence at any point during the day might assist in getting order, introducing the guest teacher to the rest of the faculty, indicating when faculty gets an opportunity to come together in the teachers' lounge in an informal way, making sure that the substitute is familiar with the mission of the school and making sure that the flow of instruction has little disruption when it is necessary for the regular teacher to be absent.

The reason I use the term "guest teacher" is based upon what the term "guest" connotes. When we invite guests to come see us, we welcome them, we try to arrange for a comfortable, enjoyable setting, we are courteous and attentive, and we try to see that a guest goes away with a good impression of us based upon our treatment of them while they are in our presence. I use the term "guest teacher" because even when I go into a classroom as a substitute, when I am introduced as a guest rather than a substitute teacher, not only do faculty members treat me as a guest but so do the students. It is important for students to be taught how to treat guests in the school much like they are taught how to treat guests in the home. When we regard substitutes as guest teachers, not only do we take advantage of whatever opportunities we have to treat them well, but we also allow them to seize upon opportunities to treat us well and then they become a part of a reciprocal arrangement to do each other favors. In fact, when it is a matter of course in every school building, it will not be regarded as a favor either from the regular teachers or from the guest teacher.

The whole idea of substitute has a connotation of "less than." If one is on an athletic team and the first string takes the field, it is the substitute who must sit out and watch and be called upon only in cases of total low productivity by the first string or in case of injury for real help. And while, indeed, the substitute teacher is one who is called upon due to ill health or injury or extenuating circumstance, the connotation of "less than" might be removed if a teacher, knowing that they have an appointment or some other situation coming up, should say to the classroom, "Students, you will have a guest tomorrow (rather than a substitute tomorrow), and I'm not sure what will be presented by the guest, but I do know that they have some valuable information to impart, and I would hope that you would be as kind to our guest as you are to me."

In fact, I think it is important for us to instill within our students that they should be even kinder to the guest than they are with us on a day-to-day basis because, based upon the closeness of our relationship, there are times when the students might become familiar with us. That is inappropriate with a guest teacher. If we could refer to those who take our places as guests, then our own attitudes might change toward them as we are reminded each time that we refer to them as guests, that, indeed, they are people who are coming to our schools at a total disadvantage and yet, they are our guests and we need to make their visit as comfortable as possible.

As I was discussing in the lesson dealing with creating a team atmosphere, the fact of the matter is, sometimes our egos will dictate that we should allow the guest teacher to fend for himself or herself so that, in contrast when we return, we look good. We return to the classroom and we have students saying, "I sure am glad that you are back because that substitute didn't know what he or she was doing." And somehow this gives us a little tinge of pride because we are the ones who can now set things in order when our students come to us and then say, "That substitute let these kids run over and we could get away with anything while that substitute was here." Rather than our attempting to instill within our students the need to understand that they looked bad taking advantage of our guest rather than the guest who looked bad acting as a substitute, we seize upon that opportunity to say something like, "Well, I'm back now and I will make sure that nobody runs over me."

The poem, "Desiderata," has a passage that suggests, "Do not compare yourself to others or you may become vain and bitter for always there will be greater or lesser persons than yourself." It is interesting how we spend a great deal of time measuring our competence based upon someone else's lack thereof. If that becomes the measurement by which we declare ourselves efficient or inefficient, then unfortunately we can get a terribly distorted view of who we are because there may be someone who is so superior that we would never measure up and consequently remain in a state of depression because we've made the mistake of comparing ourselves to someone who is just a natural in the business and doesn't even know themselves how they came to do such a good job. Or, we will compare ourselves to someone who is so terrible at teaching, that whatever we do looks good and consequently we won't bother to measure ourselves by how good we were last year or by what potential we have and are failing to live up to. We will be satisfied and thus complacent based upon our measurement and comparison to someone who is at a disadvantage.

The guest teacher, acting as a substitute, is clearly at a disadvantage when they come into a school where not only are they ignorant of procedures and the members of the staff, but also they come into a situation where the expectation is that students will act up because they have a substitute teacher. The problem often manifests itself in our waiting to be heroes. That is, rather than anticipating that a substitute or guest teacher is likely to have some problems based upon the fact that the regular teacher is gone, we wait, allow problems to arise, then come in on our white horse and save the day to the undying gratitude of the students and the "poor substitute."

We must regard those people who have chosen to help us out in this thankless way as our special guests and ought to set up a climate where there is a likelihood for success rather than the all too common likelihood for failure. There are some real problems that can result based upon a substitute's lack of knowledge. Students who are being bused can miss their buses because a substitute doesn't know the schedule and the procedures. There are students who might have special free lunch privileges who have forgotten their lunch tickets or for some other reason may not be required on a particular day to conform to absolute rules governing paid lunches, and because the substitute wanted to abide by the rules of the school, a child has perhaps missed lunch, and it has not been the guest teacher's fault. It has been the fault of the administrator and faculty members for not ensuring that the guest teacher's day goes in a smooth, orderly, and productive fashion. We have not only the opportunity but the responsibility of making those who visit with us in whatever capacity feel like guests and consequently want to return as guest teachers at a later date and become public relations persons and ambassadors in our behalf as they spread the good news about their reception and treatment at our local school.

As I believe that principals should spend at least one day a month teaching in the classroom, I also believe that regular classroom teachers should spend at least two days per year as substitutes at other schools where, should the word get around, they too will be received as guest teachers. That two-days-per-year experience will, more than likely, help us to appreciate our regular classroom duties. Proper treatment of guest teachers and others, for that matter, boils down to age-old wisdom that suggests that we should "Do unto others what we would have others do unto us."

SELF—COLLEAGUES

Lesson 20
Shame the Bad Teacher

At a 1985 in-service (dealing with team-building) for the staff of Faxon Elementary School in Kansas City, Missouri, I was asked the question by a staff member, "If there is someone in the building who absolutely refuses to be a team player, what should you do?" At that time I suggested to the person who asked the question, "You cannot keep me from loving you." That response is based upon a statement that I heard often in the 1960s when there were a number of spiritual people attempting to tap into the hearts of those who seemed not to like them, and the statement, oft repeated was, "It doesn't matter what you think of me. It does matter what I think of you." My interpretation of that statement manifested itself in the answer I gave the staff member, and that is to suggest that while a person may be totally uncooperative and even perhaps hostile to anything the team does, that does not matter as much as my making sure that I do not allow that person to create a hostile attitude within me.

It is important that I recognize that there is one person over whom I have any degree of control and that is self. Therefore, I cannot make another person become a team player. Since we are colleagues at the same level of authority, it is not within my purview to fire that person. Since I do not have the authority to reprimand or fire the person, and since I have no control over that person's actions, then what I have some control over is my level of professionalism in that person's presence. When I suggest that one should shame the bad teacher, or better, all other team members should shame the bad teacher, what I am suggesting is that the rest of the team's level of professionalism ought to be so high that any person who is hostile, uncooperative, indifferent, or mediocre, should feel uncomfortable in the presence of such professionalism. When I suggest shaming the bad teacher, I am suggesting that any person in your presence ought to know by the very way you carry yourself that you are a person who believes in taking care of business and you surround yourself with others who take care of business, and those who do not embrace the same high standards have no business around you.

Think of people whom you know who never receive gossip because gossipers are ashamed to bring gossip to these people. The way those people carry themselves is such that a person that has nothing on their minds but gossip "mess" would not dare take that to a person who has so much class. There are people whom you know who are so serious about school and the students therein, that anyone who would dare to come to them with a derogatory anecdote about particular students or classes of students would be immediately embarrassed by the response, or lack thereof, of that person who is serious about the duties of being a professional classroom teacher.

For example, if one became a member of the Korean National Martial Arts team, just joining the team seemingly would increase one's proficiency a significant amount because one feels that he or she is with the best.

In your school a person from outside, upon approaching the doors and placing a hand on the handle, ought to feel such a surge of excellence that upon entering the building, their demeanor improves. We shame the bad teacher when the bad teacher is in the obvious presence of a high degree of excellence on an on-going basis, not just for a particular day, or week, or unit, but on an on-going basis. The fact that you have not confronted the bad teacher, a situation that might exacerbate the problem, would put the teacher in a posture where they cannot respond negatively based upon the rationale that they have been treated negatively. The fact that you have not only gone on about your professional work but even heightened the level of your professionalism in that other person's presence gives them no reason to think that if it were their purpose, they can't disrupt the flow of efficiency based upon some peculiar private agenda that they have because they're disgruntled about the way things are handled.

It is certainly possible, if not likely, when the uncooperative staff member observes that excellence will go on anyway (in fact, will increase) then they too will find a way to become a part of the team. One of the reasons I suggest heightening the level of one's professionalism rather than confronting an uncooperative teacher is that there may be a circumstance that would explain that teacher's attitude. Suppose a teacher whom we evaluate as being ineffective just has a terrible year and suppose each time they are confronted, they respond in a negative way. Based upon the negative attitude and response of every confrontation, we determine that this person is not a team player and ought to be ostracized and ignored, and, indeed, criticized at every opportunity. And let us just suppose that person who has that terrible year because they are a "bad" teacher reveals to someone who decided to be professional and even congenial in spite of the person's attitude, that during that year their spouse had a terrific battle with terminal cancer and, indeed, died during that year, and perhaps, in explaining the situation, apologized for a negative attitude. While that may not be the case very often, just the possibility that such extenuating circumstances might exist ought to dictate to us, inasmuch as we don't know the circumstance, that we should not try to control that person's life, but we should love them anyway. If it turns out that there are extenuating circumstances, it's hard for love to be wrong but easy for spite to be an error.

One of the ways that we can shame the bad teacher is to make sure that our habits are professional at all times. One of the habits that I had when I was teaching at Douglas Elementary School in Chicago was to stand in the hall talking to a fellow teacher after the tardy bell had rung. When the bell rings, we expect students to be in their seats prepared for work. When we have our students properly trained, those students will, indeed, conform to the standards we set before them and be prepared to go to work when the tardy bell rings. There are times when the tardy bell would ring and even though the students were prepared, because I was sharing some juicy tid-bit having absolutely nothing to do with what I was about to teach, I would stay in the hall a few extra minutes. One of the ways that some of the more professional teachers embarrassed me was simply to walk away, not hesitate, not apologize, but walk away immediately upon hearing the bell. On those occasions when everybody walked away, I was afraid that I might be suspect if I remained in the hall and continued to hold a discussion when there was no one there but me and find my way into the classroom because I was embarrassed or ashamed of myself for even wanting to keep up the conversation when I knew that I was supposed to be in the classroom where my students were. If you want to see the height of non-professionalism as it pertains to projecting a peculiar habit in front of the students, imagine two teachers in the hall discussing irrelevancies beyond the time that the bell rings. After a while because the teacher is not in the room, the students become lax and begin to make noise, and then the teacher who is outside of the classroom, upon hearing the noise, shouts back angrily, "Don't make me have to come in there." It should occur that someone ought to make him or her come in there because that's where they belong. I was made to "come in there" simply by virtue of the fact that my colleagues walked away to do what they were supposed to do. It didn't take a terribly long time for me to get the message. Not one time did anyone say to me, "Carl, I really think you're being unprofessional and you need to go into the classroom where your students are because staying out here in the hall makes you a bad teacher." Nobody said that. Their walking away was a simple indicator of what was supposed to be done and it also helped me to understand the kinds of standards the teachers had pertaining to that particular habit.

When we do what we are supposed to do in the presence of, and in spite of, non-cooperative team members, the likelihood is that they will come around for they will stand out to the degree that the administrator will feel compelled to do something about it, or they will stand out to the degree that they will feel ashamed, embarrassed, and decide to go elsewhere where their mediocrity can find aid and comfort. The other outcome of heightening an individual's professionalism and indeed, of the entire team, in spite of non-cooperation would be that excellence does not suffer based upon our being rendered inactive waiting for somebody to come around. We can control self but not others, and that very control might be a factor in causing someone else to be moved to behave differently.

One of the observations I should have made earlier as it pertains to shaming the bad teacher in cases of non-cooperation is that in some cases it may very well be that the person has not been allowed to feel as though they are part of the team, or the person may recognize their deficiencies but have not been made to feel comfortable enough to confide in others and consequently, as a defense mechanism, responds negatively. But as I said to the staff member, "You cannot keep me from loving you." When one's willingness to accept a person for who they are (even if they are not willing to accept their lack of professionalism) might cause the person to confide in the receptive individual the need for help and upon making up the deficiency, they could become a more productive member of the team, and, from a psychological standpoint, even a more productive individual.

SELF—COLLEAGUES

Lesson 21
Develop and Participate in Some
Teacher Extracurricular Activities

One of the things that helps us to do well at work is doing well at play. A peculiar interpretation of teacher dedication is that interpretation which suggests that we are dedicated when we work all the time. There are people who have become so work-conscious that their ability to enjoy their families, their ability to know what it is to take a vacation, is significantly stifled because they feel that the work ethic in America is one where the workaholic is the prototype for a successful individual. The fact of the matter is, success ought to be measured, not by how much one earns, but by how many one helps, beginning with helping one's self. And if we think that the only way we can help ourselves is by seizing upon every opportunity to earn more money to earn more recognition based upon working all hours, then our sense of reality is terribly distorted and we are looking for short life-spans and certainly short career-spans ended by burn-out.

And I think that not only is it good to enjoy Sara's Hour and to enjoy whatever hobbies one has, but in the interest of enhancing school climate, I think it's a good idea for faculties to take advantage of opportunities to enjoy life with each other. It is not a requirement of professionalism that we play with each other, but it can enhance the work environment if we become a team in some areas and those areas can be defined by whatever extracurricular activities we might be participants in. For instance, a school may have a faculty chess club that not only plays chess among themselves and challenges students in the local school, but the faculty chess club may challenge other schools and perhaps even develop an invitational tournament that involves faculty members from throughout the city.

There may be extracurricular activities such as volleyball where, again, the faculty finds time to play with each other but also compete against other schools in the interest of building a team spirit, in the interest of exercise, and in the interest of getting to know each other as people outside of the confines of the "professional" school building. It might be fun to have an extracurricular committee to come up with activities that might last through the years or to come up with different activities for different years. There are people who enjoy sports with which we might have been previously unfamiliar, or board games we have no knowledge of, or they come from a geographical region of the country where certain kinds of activities enjoy a greater degree of popularity than the location where they are, and an extracurricular activity might include that person or those people proficient in that particular activity teaching others how to participate.

The idea behind creating and participating in extracurricular activities is not only for us to see each other in a more human light, but also to give students an opportunity to see us in a more well-rounded way giving opportunity for students to see how we compete, respond to defeat, respond to victory, interact with fellow teammates, and how it looks for us to come out of our professional clothing and come "down to earth" as it were. The extracurricular activities cause us to develop and enhance different parts of our personality just like our "parallel perking" assists students in developing different aspects of their personalities.

Our participation in extracurricular activities can also put the "extra" in extracurricular in proper perspective. We can compete and compete vigorously in the presence of our on-looking students and show them that we can become totally involved in the competitive aspects of extracurricular activities, and then leave that competition, vigor, and enthusiasm for the activity on the gameboard, the court, or on the field when it comes time to be professional in the classroom. To set that example for students is to show that it is only one aspect of group development and maturation that can enhance academia, but it should not replace academia. Who better to set the proper example than the very teachers with whom they interact on a day-to-day basis?

Developing extracurricular activities and participation also gives an opportunity to invite parents to be a part of the extracurricular activities. They then become a part of the school outside of the fact that they are the parents of students. It gives an opportunity for developing a relationship between faculty and parents, and it gives an opportunity for parents to see themselves as being proficient in certain skills so that they are not intimated when conference time comes and they have to listen to the labeling and technical jargon that we are sometimes guilty of using when we are attempting to help parents to understand the problems or successes their children are having. It is important that we see each other on an equal level and that equality can certainly be enhanced when we make efforts to develop opportunities for us all to, at one point, be the person who is the expert. The president of the school advisory committee may not be the same person who is captain of the after-school volleyball team but both may project a leadership respected by all.

In the development of extracurricular activities it means that we may have to seek out in the community people and places who could be first-line resources for the activities agreed upon, and it means that it would give an opportunity to offer the school as a community resource during after school hours, not only within the jurisdiction of the engineer who can open the doors, but also as an extension of the day where the teachers are regarded as members of the community because they are, indeed, participants after school. We then become social resources, as it were, to be the role models the community needs to see beyond the perceived staid professionalism of the classroom.

If it should appear that it just is not possible to develop extracurricular activities on an on-going basis, I would certainly suggest that every school plan some one or two activities outside of the regular instructional program that would include not only colleagues in an informal setting interacting with colleagues, but would also include students and their parents. It would be a good idea also where there are school-business partnerships to plan activities that would include the business partners and/or businesses in the local community that have a potential for partnership so that the interaction, once again, informal as it is, offers an opportunity to expand upon the relationship and also gives students an opportunity to see the business people as friends, upon whom they can call because of the peculiar relationship that they have in cases where students are in need of tutoring or perhaps career counseling and the like.

* * *   * * *

The next section deals with "Self—Classroom Atmosphere." The classroom climate is the responsibility of everyone who functions in that classroom on a day-to-day basis. That means that it is the responsibility of the classroom teacher and/or aides and the classroom student. Anyone who is in the classroom on a day-to-day basis has an individual responsibility to do what he or she can to enhance the climate within that classroom. To suggest that the responsibility is solely on the teacher because the teacher is the leader in that classroom is to deny students the opportunity for full participation in their learning. We have a responsibility to instill within the students an appreciation for their role in setting the climate in the classroom. In helping them to understand their role in setting the classroom climate, we can extend that to helping them to appreciate their role in setting the climate throughout the school.

Without the students, obviously there is no such thing as a school. A great student body means a great school. When people evaluate excellence in education, what they are evaluating is those things that students do to reflect the learning that they gain at the institution being evaluated. It is important that all the players, all classroom team members, understand that each has an equal responsibility for setting the classroom climate. But inasmuch as it is the paid professional, or the teacher, who is perceived as the leader in the classroom and, indeed, ought to be, it is important that we see our role as a key to setting the atmosphere, because we are the only ones in the classroom who, indeed, get paid for insuring that optimal conditions exist for learning to take place. Part of our responsibility as classroom leaders is to make sure that everyone understands that they have a role in setting the climate, but we must take it upon ourselves to show students, based upon our experience, education, professionalism, how to set a climate that is conducive to excelling.

This is a country of one person, one vote, and every individual has as great a responsibility to make sure that this society is what it ought to be as do other individuals. However, those elected have the responsibility to assume more leadership based upon the fact that they have been put in particular positions to see to it that the wishes of their constituents are carried out. In the classroom no individual is more equal than others but we, as classroom teachers, have been put in a position of greater leadership than others, and so we must assume the responsibility of setting the tone even as we encourage others in the classroom to take on a similar responsibility. And while the responsibilities may be similar, the roles are different.

SELF—CLASSROOM ATMOSPHERE

Lesson 22
Consider Constraints, Concerns,
and Complaints vs. Care, Confidence,
and Consistency
(or, the Paralysis of Educational Analysis)

In many communities across the nation, school districts seem to be in some degree of turmoil. In some cases the reason for the turmoil is because of the attempt to implement a desegregation plan. In other cases there is turmoil because school systems are going from a traditional central office management organization to a school-based management situation or some variation thereof. For various reasons there are districts struggling to become as efficient as we think all districts should be. Perhaps it is because of the politics and personalities of the school board, or the lack of interest of the business community in what is going on in the schools, or if it is because of significant demographic changes that seem to occur faster than some school districts can prepare and make adjustments for, if it is because after the 1983 "Nation at Risk" report by the National Commission on Excellence in Education many districts have initiated several different kinds of reform that puts the classroom teacher on the firing line to attempt to implement whatever the organizational structure might become, even if it has not been adequately tested. Our school districts across our nation are suffering from transitional turmoil.

In the heat of the various debates concerning educational reform, there are a number of opinions as to why schools are not run as efficiently as they ought to be. If one should listen to the various debates, one might draw the conclusion that the definitive answer to what is wrong with our schools goes something like this: the problem in our schools today is the lack of concern and participation on the part of the parents. Inasmuch as the parents are children's first teachers and because the children are the responsibilities of the parents until they are of legal age to be responsible for themselves, it is without a doubt the parents' responsibility to monitor their child's progress in school and, indeed, to insure that youngsters get the best possible education. If parents are not involved with their child's education, then it is obvious that the children are not going to get the kind of education that they ought to because educators are not going to be held accountable unless they are held accountable by a concerned community of parents. Where there are effective schools, there is usually an involved community of parents. Therefore, where there are ineffective schools, there are most likely uninvolved parents.

But then one might conclude that what's wrong with our schools today is the fact that we have too many unprepared teachers who are not dedicated to what they've been hired to do. If we had more teachers who were more dedicated and better prepared, we would, indeed, have much better schools.

It is without a doubt that where there are effective schools, there are, indeed, dedicated teachers who come to that school well-prepared, or who are so dedicated that they will dedicate themselves to getting the tools in order that they can become the kind of teachers that insure the highest quality education for every child. Indeed, the two critical problems with ineffective schools are uninvolved parents and unprepared teachers.

Actually, the problem in our schools is a total lack of leadership at the local school level. What's happening is: there are too few principals who have the proper leadership skills and too many principals who are so inundated with paperwork and cosmetic activities that they really don't have time to show their leadership skills if, indeed, they have them. In effective schools research, it is revealed that one of the chief components of an effective school is an efficient instructional leader in the form of school principal, headmaster, or dean. The absence of that leadership creates a climate where there is neither direction nor continuity. If there are a great many schools across our nation lacking the proper leadership, then we are in dire straits, indeed, as we can easily conclude that the real problem in our schools is that the parents are not involved, the teachers are unprepared, and the principals are not providing leadership.

But then what we really need to say is that the problem with our schools is a great deal of overloaded bureaucracy that serves to stifle creative movement at the local school level and serves to make what ought to be an academic climate a political climate. Consequently, it is difficult for schools to move forward if the people "downtown" are so involved with saving their image, thus saving their job, that they cannot lend the kind of administrative support that is imperative if schools are to function properly. There are many people at the downtown administrative level who seem to be overpaid and underused, who have a flair for the cosmetic and crisis orientation, but who fail miserably when it comes to the mundane issues of running a school district day-to-day-to-day-to-day. Then it seems quite evident that we can sum up the problem of our education institutions across the nation. The problem obviously is: uninvolved parents, unprepared teachers, unskilled principals, and uncommitted district administrators.

Or, the problem with our schools is the fact that the large community does not support education as one of the major priorities in the local or larger society. If we function within a society that does not see education as a major priority, then the examples set by those who are in power positions will be imitated by those who seek power or the support of power and we will begin to make our priorities in the areas of politics and economics, or looking good and finding jobs. If the larger society has a great emphasis on politics and economics, then those of us who teach will teach toward getting a job rather than a career and making a living rather than making a life. If the larger community makes a determination that education is the number one priority and that being the case, we are going to commit resources toward enhancing the educational climate across that nation, then that would make the critical difference. So, actually, what's wrong with education is: uninvolved parents, unprepared teachers, unskilled principals, uncommitted district administrators, and unconcerned communities.

But then, to the truth now, what's really wrong with our school is the fact that electronic and print media seem to be on a smear campaign to insure that the only thing they have to report about education is bad and that which they report at length is that which is bad in a sensational way. What do they report of a sensational nature that is bad? Youth gangs storm school buildings and shoot teachers. The drug trafficking now in junior high schools and elementary schools is one of the major activities aside from the regular instructional curriculum in which our students are participating. The media seem intent on making our schools look bad so they are the problem, and I guess what we must do then is sum up by suggesting that the problem in our schools is uninvolved parents, unprepared teachers, unskilled principals, uncommitted district administrators, unconcerned communities, and unkind media. Now that's what is wrong with our schools.

Actually, it boils right down to the level of the student because what's wrong with our schools today is students who have poor study habits, low school spirit, a total lack of discipline, and an air of "Somebody owes me an education," rather than, "I must participate in getting the best possible education that I can." I mean, let's just be real about it. Since there can be no such thing as a school without students, then there cannot be good schools without good students, and frankly, our students are just too bad so we have students who have no desire to do what they are supposed to do to enhance the educational and social climate in our schools, and that, of course, is what causes the image of the schools to really suffer and, consequently, we can surmise unequivocally that the problem with our schools is the terrible students that we have and, perhaps, we might say that the problem with our schools is: uninvolved parents and unprepared teachers and unskilled principals and uncommitted district administrators and unconcerned communities and unkind media and undesirable students.

And, don't you see that if parents are not involved, then the teachers feel no reason to become prepared, and principals feel they have nothing to lead, and district administrators have nothing with which to work, and local communities have no need to be concerned about the current situation, but to work toward something new. The media had nothing good to report because students are so terrible and the students are terrible because their parents are uninvolved and their parents are uninvolved because the teachers are poorly prepared and don't even know how to help parents become involved. The teachers are poorly prepared because the principal doesn't hold the teacher accountable because they're busy with paperwork, and the district administrators are not hiring great principals because the local community is not passing levies or giving school district budgets that will allow them to hire the best and the brightest. And the local community is not going to enhance local school budgets as long as the media finds nothing good to report about the schools and the students are not going to be good students when the media seems not to reward good things but seems only to report on the bad things. And if students are not going to be what they really ought to be then that does not make a citizen who is going to become an involved parent and if we produce students who have such terrible school experiences, who, as a consequence, grow up to become parents who are not involved, then we are likely to have teachers who are not dedicated because the parents don't care anyway. Administrators are not skilled because so many administrators come from the ranks of those unprepared teachers and district administrators who are shuffled around based upon politics and cosmetics and local communities which will not grow because they would rather leave and try to find a good school district somewhere rather than stick around. And the press will reflect upon the fact that our local community cannot attract a society of committed people because our schools are so poor and our children, hearing from the media how poor they are, make that a self-fulfilling prophecy and become parents who are the extensions of these undesirable children, and so on.

I think perhaps you see what I'm getting at. And that is, that if we wanted to, we could expend endless energy in the rhetoric of blame when, in fact, if there are problems, we are all to blame, and where there are possibilities for solutions, we must all play a part. We can fill up volumes with complaints about what's wrong—who is really to blame—why we cannot do what we are supposed to do in the absence of support we are supposed to get. I am suggesting that there are, indeed, some constraints. We do, indeed, have some complaints, and while we may have a great deal of concern about what's wrong with somebody else, our responsibility is to take care of self. If teachers want to blame administrators for a terrible climate within a particular school building, their blame may be accurately placed, but placing the blame does not necessarily change one's behavior.

If we understand that someone else is not doing what they are supposed to be doing, it should not keep us from doing what we are supposed to do. In fact, it ought to make us more committed to doing what we are supposed to do. If students are angry with media for negative reports, then students may not be able to make media change but they can certainly bombard media with good reports based upon their commitment to changing themselves. If parents are concerned that teachers are not doing what teachers ought to do, then what parents must do is what parents ought to do, and that is, take more care in seeing that youngsters get what they need of an education background after school and lobby in whatever appropriate form available to them for the removal of incompetent teachers.

As long as we are mired in the milieu of negativism, the changes of forward movement are slim to none. But in the worst situation, there are good teachers. In the worst of communities, there are good parents. In the worst of newsworthy situations, we can find some good news, and we must not put the onus on someone else to change their ways. We must change our own. Therefore, rather than being a teacher who deals with constraints, concerns, and complaints, let us deal with care, confidence, and consistency in ourselves. Whatever chaos reigns at the top, during the school day there are youngsters in your classroom who deserve an education. I might be very upset with what's going on in the district where I teach. I might be very upset with the personality of the principal for whom I work. I might be very concerned about the apathy among students' parents, but whatever else is going on, at the moment that I close my classroom door, I must commit myself toward giving those who face me the best possible education they can get under the circumstances, and circumstances must be extremely extenuating to keep a teacher from teaching their subject to the best of their ability if they are committed toward doing that. History has shown teachers in one room schoolhouses with little more than a chalkboard and a couple of pieces of chalk who have turned out astro-physicists and world leaders. If we have the commitment, we can make a classroom an oasis in a wasteland of mediocrity.

When I talk about care, confidence, and consistency, I am suggesting that young people will respond favorably to their perceptions of consistent care. If a student regards a teacher as a caring person, the student is likely to respond to the requests of the teacher because the student likes the teacher, not necessarily because the student thinks that the request is so reasonable. And if the teacher's care manifests itself consistently, there is likely to be consistent positive returns on that caring personality. Our caring will help us dare to do things that are innovative even if we do not have the equipment and materials needed. The more we try out creative approaches toward enhancing the classroom climate, the more confident we will be.

Our confidence in the presence of students is as important as our caring. The reason confidence is so important is because, unlike some popular opinion might assert, our students long for a person to be in control. A teacher who is confident and projects an air of confidence is half-way toward controlling the classroom atmosphere just by being in control of one's self. When a teacher appears to be confident in what they say and do students will act upon what the teacher says based upon that confidence. When a teacher is confident that they can control the classroom climate, young people tend to be more relaxed in their responses in the classroom because one who is in control will insure that classmates will not laugh at wrong answers, ridicule the way one dresses, or take unfair physical advantage of one's weakness if one is not as strong as someone else. A confident air helps students to realize immediately that there will be one person responsible for running the class, and while we continue to encourage students to participate in their learning at a very high level, they must know that one person is in charge, and without confidence, a teacher is not in charge, is not perceived by students to be in charge, and there is a possibility of a lack of order or in some extreme cases, chaos to reign in a classroom where the person at the head of that classroom is lacking in confidence.

Students need that air of confidence from the teacher so that they know that the time will not be wasted when they are attempting to get the most that they can out of every class period. The confidence is not necessarily, and, in too many cases, absolutely not, borne out of how wonderfully the local school or district is run, but is borne out of one's personal knowledge of their ability to overcome adversity which we must do in this age just by definition as classroom teachers. And having that personal knowledge and confidence allows one to function efficiently even in the midst of problems that surround the classroom or local school situation. Confidence also manifests itself in projecting high expectations. Students appreciate teachers feeling confident that whatever else is going on in one's life, around this school, in this district, you can emerge with excellence. You can learn whatever you need to learn to be successful in the society in which you live and in other societies you might visit as you travel through life.

There are often complaints about things that hamper our ability to do the best job that we can. If these complaints deal with things over which we have no control, then complaining frustrates us. If the complaints deal with things over which we have some control, then our responsibility is to get busy. In either case, simply complaining solves nothing. If there are constraints, generally we consider them to be constraints out of a sincere desire to do more than we are presently doing. If the constraints are legitimate by board rules or school standards, then we must do what we can within the limitations of those constraints. If the constraints are simply due to our lack of creativity or initiative then we need to go to our down-the-hall colleagues, and get them to assist us in how we might get off of point "A" in order to reach point "C" because we seem to be stuck by our own doing. In either case, to simply allow constraints to stifle our overall productivity is to be controlled by something that is not only counter-productive, but might find us in a pattern of allowing constraints to be our rationalization for not doing all that we are supposed to do.

Where we have concerns, not only is that natural, but I think it is healthy. We would need to be more concerned about our attitudes if we had no concern about wanting to do a better job. But having those concerns should spark us to do more, not to do less. We can wallow in the swamp of complaints, concerns, and constraints, indeed, sink in the quicksand of complaints, concerns, and constraints, or we can care enough about our students to use care, confidence, and consistency to make something exciting happen even in an atmosphere that doesn't seem conducive to educational excitement. And I guess as we consider care, confidence, and consistency over complaints, concerns, and constraints, one way to sum up what the real problem in today's education is: **The fact is that I am not doing all that I could do.** But since these lessons deal with becoming a positive teacher, let me put the analysis of what's going on in education in a positive context and suggest that the reason I know that whatever the assessment of what's going on in education today happens to be, that things are going to get a great deal better because I know that I am getting better and that I am going to make things better.

SELF—CLASSROOM ATMOSPHERE

Lesson 23
Don't Spruce Up—Stay Up

I can recall in one of the schools where I taught a Tuesday afternoon when one of the students said to me, "Mr. Boyd, are we going to clean up for Thursday?" Not knowing what the student was talking about, I asked, "What do you mean, clean up for Thursday?" The student said, "Those people are going to be here," and I said, "What people?" And the student was talking about the accreditation association for the district in which I taught. And I said to the student, "Well, no I hadn't planned on cleaning up. I was aware that they would be coming but I hadn't planned on doing anything special." The student said, "Well, some of the teachers are doing their bulletin boards," and he went on to describe the various ways that people in the school were "cleaning up" for those people who were coming on Thursday. And while I didn't go to any lengths to explain to the class why I was not going to clean up for those people, I will explain here that my philosophy is that we ought to be doing what we are supposed to be doing every day. And if someone wants to determine whether or not we do what we are supposed to do, then they need to catch us doing what we always do. If it is necessary to clean up especially for visitors, then it may very well be that we were not doing what we ought to have been doing before they decided to visit us.

Now I don't want to carry that logic to unreasonable extremes or, if you will, illogical extremes. It is a matter of courtesy, for instance, if the auditorium for an assembly program is cleaned up for guests. If someone is coming to the school for whom you'd like to put out a banner saying "Welcome" to the school with the person's or the group's name on the banner, fine. When parents visit the school, it's nice for them to feel welcome and to feel that they are not taken for granted, and that we would do our part to make sure that they're going to be comfortable with their visit even if that entails getting extra chairs out or providing for their comfort by borrowing some furniture from a neighboring school or from a community center. All of those things are reasonable.

But when I talk about staying up rather than sprucing up, what I'm talking about is inside of the classroom where we teach where someone might come to observe. I think that the observation has no validity if we spruce up. I think that the continuity of the lessons being taught is disrupted, and, consequently, unfair to the students. And I think that we begin to lose confidence in who we are when we attempt to project an image that is different. I believe in a very simple open-door policy. Anyone may come and observe me teach at any time as long as those who observe do not disrupt. I think that it is important that every day I teach as though those people are here. I think that it is important that every day the climate in my classroom be conducive to the optimal learning experience available to my students. And if I am confident that during the course of a particular lesson, it is educationally sound to introduce an anthology of Smokey Robinson's greatest hits, and if visitors should happen to walk in, as Smokey is singing "If that don't do, I'll try something new" then that's O.K. with me because if they should ask after the class is over, why that particular song was playing, I ought to either be able to justify why that song was playing at that time, or it should not have been playing whether I have visitors or not.

If a student is absent but whose turn it is to fix bulletin boards, and it turns out that the student is absent at a time when the bulletin board is not complete but the students and I feel that allowing that student to complete the bulletin board is more important than the information being put on the board, then it would be unfair to that student if he had an excused absence to have somebody else do "his" bulletin board in his absence just to appease somebody who's going to be there for one day when that student is going to be there for the rest of the school year. If those who visit have any difficulty understanding what's going on, then, at the appropriate time, they can ask. But to adjust, and especially those who would radically adjust, the continuity of what goes on in the classroom in favor of impressing some outside guests, is to risk losing one or two or perhaps more students in the adjustment without any risk toward losing those who come to visit. And if the continuity were kept intact, not only would there be a very low risk of losing the students valuable to us, but, believe it or not, there would be little risk of losing face or reputation.

Parents should be welcome in any classroom where their student matriculates as long as parents do not disrupt. Every parent ought to be welcome as a visitor in a classroom where their children are sent to learn. Parents, of course, must be astute and courteous enough to know when their presence might, in and of itself, represent a disruption; for instance, after an altercation between two students, one of whom happens to be the child of that parent. If the parent decides on an occasion like that to just "happen to" stop by, his or her presence then could be a disruption so that visit would not be appropriate.

In some cases, after visiting, those who visit may volunteer to come up and spend time in the classroom and do more than just observe at the direction of the teacher. An open classroom policy also establishes a powerbase, if you will. As mentioned earlier, shared power is increased power, and when the community feels that one is receptive to their visits, and/or volunteering, they will begin to spread the word that this is an effective and cooperative teacher. Not only will they spread the word which enhances one's powerbase based upon good PR, but in cases where students become critics or media print negative things, those who have had the personal experience of the classroom visit may very well become advocates on behalf of the accused. There is little ill will that can come from an open classroom policy and a great deal of good that can come from it. It's good because it keeps us on our toes. It's good because it establishes a support base. It's good because the students are less likely to misbehave in the presence of community adults than they are in the absence of community adults. It is good because it gives us a greater knowledge of those who are part of our community. Again, don't spruce up, stay up!

SELF—CLASSROOM ATMOSPHERE

Lesson 24
Anticipate Behavioral Changes

The anticipation of behavioral changes is something most of us do intuitively. In addition to allowing our intuition to continue to express itself, it is also a good idea to consciously anticipate behavioral changes. But when should we anticipate these changes?

One time to expect changes in students would be when students graduate from pre-adolescence to adolescence. This would be a behavioral change that we as teachers have all gone through, and if we would but take some time to reflect, we should recall that it was a very awkward stage in our lives, and therefore we have every reason to expect that it is an even more awkward time in the lives of today's adolescents than it was for us who lived in a simpler, more community-supportive time.

In the anticipation of the change from pre-adolescence to adolescence, and the many changes that occur during adolescence, we should not to be surprised at some of the peculiar antics that are part of the lives of middle schoolers and young secondary schoolers. We ought to be able to get ready for the slowness of the maturation in the boys and the advanced adult-stage of the girls, and "adult" ought to be in quotes because I am not suggesting for a moment that the girls are truly adults.

Among adolescents, you might witness students who come in at a particular time and everything that they do looks quite mature and quite adult. They'll do things that will make you proud. They are young people who will be courteous, responsive, respectful, bright, optimistic, patriotic, mature—everything that you would want in any 27-year-old. And the very next day—sometimes the next class period—you will find an adolescent who is silly, wild, poorly dressed, discourteous, disgruntled, upset, depressed, and, indeed, in both cases it is the very same adolescent. Because we know that is part of the adolescent experience, we ought to anticipate where we can deflect it and, where we cannot deflect it, be sensitive to the way that we respond to adolescent behavior.

But beyond physiology and psychology, there are behavioral changes that can be dictated by the time of day. Young students act differently when they return from recess than before they went out to recess. They act differently immediately after lunch than they were acting before lunch. If there is a celebrated holiday coming up, then young people will act differently than they acted during the course of the regular school year. Behavioral changes can be observed when a popular student transfers to another school, when the school teams in secondary climates do particularly well, or particularly poorly for that matter. Behavioral changes can be observed in cases where personal lifestyles have been impacted—the death of a family member, moving, etc. These instances should be taken into consideration in terms of how the youngster fits in or fails to fit in. There are so many possible effects on children's behavior that as many effects as we can anticipate, we should. Somehow it seems that we learn to teach as though events and personalities are going to be static in our schools.

There are some examples of obvious times for group behavioral change. Unfortunately, in many schools today there are students who commit suicide. This is a time when not only the immediate family is affected but all of the students who attend the school of the person who committed suicide. We can anticipate behavioral changes in this obviously traumatic situation without any great knowledge of psychology, and yet, even though in every situation of suicide during the school year among young people that I have observed, there has been a person or a team of persons called in to work with young people to get them through this trauma. There are still those who suggest that the best way to deal with this is to simply go back to the everyday format to which we are accustomed, almost as if nothing happened, in order that we do not have students dwell on the incident. The fact of the matter is: the chances are great that students are not going to be the same, and, consequently, will not be able to simply go back to the normal day-to-day routine after something of that magnitude occurs, and experts, indeed, need to be brought in.

Another obvious group response in terms of behavioral change would occur if there is a gang fight or a major altercation in the school, and when these kinds of things occur, oftentimes we will take students back into the classroom and say, "Now, we're through with that. Now, let's go on to what we were doing, and I don't want to hear any more about it." This may be a great opportunity to discuss interpersonal relationships, conflict resolution, and how one deals with one's self in order to cope with any of the eventualities that might come up in today's world of students.

We should not suspect that students will react to major events in a comfortable manner that is conducive to going back to business as usual. We can anticipate behavior changes. Obvious behavioral changes will occur in the physiology of an adolescent female who must experience the menstrual cycle for the first time and, in some cases, if they have not been prepared for it at home, are very embarrassed by it, don't know what to do about it, become awkward, sometimes shy, sometimes withdrawn, sometimes wanting to stay home. Depending upon the pain involved at that particular time of the cycle, there might be some evidence of actual hurting.

But in terms of anticipating behavioral changes, there are also more subtle signs that we need to be conscious of. Sometimes a particular student, for personal reasons, may change their behavior or become sullen and withdrawn if there's abuse in the family. Here again, while this is an obvious causal effect for a behavioral change, the subtle change that we might not notice is what happens to the close friend of that student who may become withdrawn or overactive. Students get new sets of friends. We may be engaged in observing their behavior with their new set of more mature, more active friends. We may even be happy for them if it represents a positive behavioral change, but let us also take stock of the old set of friends who may be affected by this person choosing someone "over them." The behavioral change may not manifest itself as pronounced as the person being observed, but we need to anticipate change because this is a change in the life of that child.

A behavioral change might result from classwork becoming harder for a student who is accustomed to doing well on tests, exams, and classwork, and then suddenly confronting subject matter that is not as easy to deal with as previous subject matter had been. It may be that we should concentrate on the change in grades, but we might also concentrate on the recent change in behavior. We might, at least, ask the question, "Which came first, the lower grades or the change in behavior? Did the student become less enthusiastic about school, less involved, less participatory as a result of poor grades, or did poor grades result from these behaviors?" And we need to take a good look at that. If a student had been in classrooms for seven years, taught by females, and then the eighth year confronts a male teacher, many students will adjust very well to that, but a particular student may change their behavior based upon the fact that this is the first encounter with a male teacher. And that student who responds differently to the teacher may be either a male or a female student depending upon their personal orientation, depending upon whether they have father and mother in the home or all brothers or all sisters. We don't know, but we need to look at the causes and effects of behavioral changes as extensively as we can in order to make sure that we are providing for the individual differences in the different students whom we teach.

It should not surprise us that in the spring a young boy's fancy turns to girls and vice versa. It should not surprise us that just prior to summer vacation, students' enthusiasm for academic pursuits decreases. It should not surprise us when parents go through a divorce that children will also go through changes. We are not surprised when a classroom loses a regular classroom teacher at the middle of the year that the classroom behavior changes, and, most often, changes for the worse rather than toward the good. There are many ways in which behavioral changes manifest themselves where there is an obvious cause and effect, but in terms of anticipating behavioral changes, the suggestion here is to look for causes where the effect is an extreme behavioral change because it may very well be that we are looking directly at the student's behavior with no regard to what might have prompted that behavior. But even better than looking for the present cause of behavior, would be to anticipate the possibility that behavior will change based upon some things that we see that are potential causes.

Some students' behaviors change when they get a hair cut, especially if the hair cut that they get presents a radically new hair style from the way they have been wearing it. Their behavior changes, and other students' behavior changes toward those students. Some students' behavior changes when they get a new outfit. Some students' behavior changes in the secondary grades when one or the other gets a new girlfriend or a new boyfriend. Some students' behavior changes because they made the basketball team or the soccer team or the team won or the team lost. What I am suggesting is that it is very difficult for us to change students' behavior, but it is altogether possible for us to create the kind of climate where students feel comfortable enough to share the reasons that their behavior might have changed, or the reasons that their behavior is as it is. And that climate depends upon our sensitivity to the different causes that might result in an adverse effect if we are sensitive. That means we'll be "on-the-lookout-for." Being "on-the-look-out" means that we can properly anticipate. If it turns out that our anticipation is wrong, then it is better to err in the direction of being overly sensitive, and perhaps apologizing for it later, than it is to err in the direction of being totally insensitive or ignorant, and not having an opportunity to apologize later because the student flunks out of school, gets expelled, leaves the community, etc.

Finally, what I would say about anticipating behavioral changes is also anticipate behavioral changes in yourself. We are as human as our students. We are just as vulnerable to changes in life as our students. That being the case, if we understand ourselves well and know that certain things spark a change in our attitudes prompting a change in behavior toward people, our sensitivity to that coupled with our professionalism as teachers will keep us from having students suffer the brunt of whatever problems we are encountering that are not caused by those students. We need to be able to anticipate how we might react should a creative approach toward a lesson not work. We ought to anticipate how we might respond if, after thinking that we have really taught the concepts in a particular lesson, 80% or 85% of the students flunk the exam. Will we then indict the students for being poor learners, or will we investigate our teaching methods so that the next time the concepts are taught, they might be better presented? It is far better to prevent than to attempt to cure, and our ability to prevent may, indeed, be based upon our ability to anticipate behavioral changes in our students and in ourselves.

SELF—CLASSROOM ATMOSPHERE

Lesson 25
Create a Team Atmosphere in Your Classroom

Students seem to enjoy participating in, or watching the performances of, precision drill teams and dance teams. In my classroom, I like to suggest to students that the classroom is similar to a precision drill team in this way: I ask students if they were on stage lined up in rows of four and everyone was precisely where they ought to be except one person, who looks bad on that team when that one person is out of place? The response to the question is almost always overwhelming when the students say in unison, "Everybody looks bad." I go on to ask those students: If you are on that drill team and in practice this one person continues to be out of step but they had to perform and there was not a replacement, what would you do?" Students then say, "Teach the steps," and I say, "How?" They will say, "However we can." I say, "How much time would you invest?" "We would teach until the person learned the steps because we are not going out on that stage with that person until he or she is ready. However much time it takes, we're going to make sure that before we walk on that stage, everybody is in sync."

Now, that exercise is reasonable to me because I believe the students when they say that by the time they walk out on the stage, they're going to be ready. Then I say to them, "This class, being like a precision drill team, will look bad if anyone walks out on the stage of life out of step. What, then, must I do to insure that each student is in step?" The answer to that question is: I must teach everyone the steps. How will I teach everyone the steps? By whatever means necessary, but I must insure that we must not walk out on the stage of life until everyone is in sync. And, I must also take the time necessary to make sure that everyone on the team knows the steps because the stage of life is as much a reflection of that classroom as the performing stage is a reflection of the preparation for the performance of that drill team.

This analogy is easily understood by the students and if not that particular analogy, then some example needs to be used in order to convince homeroom members that they are part of a significant team. The rationale for creating a team atmosphere has to do with students seeing themselves in the position of supporting, encouraging, and helping each other rather than ridiculing and making fun of each other. If we are all a part of the same team, then I have a vested interest in your performance. Therefore, I will assist you in becoming as proficient as you can be. And because your achievement represents me, then I harbor no jealousy when you excel but I have a sense of pride. When we are working together, in order for the team to look good, the process of working together as a team is excellence in learning in and of itself. As recent examples of cooperative learning indicate, when students function as part of a team, not only do they encourage and support and help each other, but they also hold each other accountable because they recognize that the group is evaluated based upon the individual performances within the group and the overall collective performance of the group as a whole.

Students should be helped to realize that a current classmate may be a future employer or employee. Knowing that should prompt one to be a part of that other person's success and to invite that other person to be a part of one's own success. We are attempting to instill within our young people a cooperative attitude toward other young people. That has merit in and of itself by virtue of the fact that human beings ought to be civil to other human beings. The practical aspects of it deal with the fact that there are people with whom they are going to school today whom they will meet later on in life, perhaps on a continuous basis. Many of us are old enough to know that. Many of us have had experiences in education where someone with whom we grew up called to hire us for a particular position or to ask our recommendation for them to be promoted, and because we feel that having grown up together, having gone to the same school, that they, indeed, are a part of our personal team, and we have been more than happy to offer the recommendation or to accept the position offered.

If that climate can be created, then the rest of what goes on in the room can revolve around the whole idea that we are all in this together, and we will all succeed together. Creating a team atmosphere in the classroom can come about from the teacher's example of being a member of the school team and also can come about with the teacher encouraging students to work cooperatively rather than competitively. The student who is the perpetual "A" student must be encouraged through parallel perking and other means to help other students who may not be as academically astute. Students in the classroom who have very sharp social skills must be encouraged to assist other students whose social skills are lacking, that later in life those youngsters practicing those sharpened social skills may get feet in doors otherwise closed to them based upon qualifications, but now open to them based upon personality. There may be students who are withdrawn and introverted, or less talented than others. These students must be teamed with their academic, athletic, social opposites in order that they can become reasonably well versed in that which is deficient. They may not become extroverts but at least will feel comfortable in holding a decent conversation on various subjects and in various settings.

A team atmosphere in the classroom is obviously designed to give students an appreciation for being a part of the overall school team. The logical extension of being a part of the team in this year's classroom is looking forward to being a part of a team in next year's class. Later, students can look forward to being a part of a team with their fellow employees or with their fellow faculty members when they determine that they will teach in years to come. A team atmosphere can be created when on a given day the classroom teacher comes in with a large certificate for the bulletin board citing the entire class for their excellent behavior over the past month. A teacher may come in and put up a large certificate citing the students for increased attendance over a given period of time. The teacher may enlist the assistance of students who write well in a particular class in generating a press release for local print and/or electronic media extolling the virtues of things that are happening within the classroom for a period of time this year or for a particular campaign or a particular unit so that the classroom itself has reason to feel proud as a unit as well as those individuals in the classroom who get good grades or who become the captains of teams or the officers in the school elections.

We can create a team atmosphere in the classroom by seizing upon every opportunity to point out that students who do well individually have done well for the team, saying things like, "I told you, this is the best classroom that there is in the best school that there is." By saying to visiting parents, "Your child adds so much to making this a really good class, and I hope that you are acquainted with your child's friends in this class because this is a great classroom with some great young people, and I hope that they stick together and know each other throughout their school career."

Whenever it is possible, even under negative circumstances, to point out that we are a team, teachers should seize upon those so-called negative situations and consider them opportunities. When two students fight: "Students on the same team do not fight. And it is important that the rest of the class make sure that this kind of thing does not happen because it hurts everyone on the team. A chain is only as strong as its weakest link and we cannot have any weak links refusing to do what they are supposed to do because that tears the whole team apart." Or: "When you are absent, it does not just affect you, if affects the entire class because we need everyone here if we're going to learn everything we need to know to make it this semester. You need to be here because, as the teacher, I am not a genius. I'm not brilliant enough to be able to impart all of the information all of the time in a way that all of your classmates can understand. It may very well be that on the particular day that you are absent, that you would have been the one to be able to explain a lesson better than I, but because you were not here, someone didn't get it, and we need you in this mix. It may very well be that the pertinent question that needed to be asked was not asked because other members of the class were embarrassed to ask the question, did not have the nerve to come forward and admit that it was something that they did not know, and we missed you. You needed to be here to ask that question because it was such a significant part of the lesson."

Wherever opportunities present themselves, a teacher should seize upon the opportunity to create a team atmosphere within a class. Youngsters, perceiving that their working together is advantageous, will not only work together and continue to do so, but the quality of their individual efforts will be improved because they want to be perceived as a significant contributor to the team. Creating a team atmosphere reduces discipline problems, increases attendance, assists in youngsters learning team-type lessons for life, and assists those of us who are in positions as teachers in being exemplars of what being a part of a team ought to be like.

One of the things that upper classes in elementary schools and secondary classes can do to help create a team atmosphere would be for the lower grade teachers to call upon upper grade students to assist in peer tutoring or inspirational and motivational lectures to young people or to help out in other ways with younger students. The same can be said for upper grade students making presentations to businesses who might be interested in what's going on in the school, at the local library for citizens, community groups, for youth groups at the Boys' and Girls' clubs, YMCA, etc. And younger students in the school should be introduced as members of the classroom team.

There are schools that have dress-up days and dress-down days and other kinds of particular days. Certain days might be theme days where the classroom participates as a team with people helping each other to dress in the appropriate attire and to learn the appropriate terminology if that has to do with the theme. It's all designed to help create a team atmosphere within the classroom.

A classroom may, indeed, have a drill team, class choir, dance team, chess team or a debate team. There may be competitions within the school that have classrooms participating in academic affairs such as a science fair. The idea, of course, is that all of the competition is friendly competition, and once the local competition is held and students from particular classrooms win, then, or course, they understand that at the next level they will be representing the entire school thus expanding upon the team concept.

Creating a friendly team atmosphere in the classroom will enhance the team atmosphere throughout the school and hopefully enhance a child's attitude toward citizenship for life.

SELF—CLASSROOM ATMOSPHERE

Lesson 26
Employ Flexible Structure

Teachers know the importance of preparation in order to teach meaningful lessons in the classroom. It is important for teachers to use lesson plans, to have long-range goals, to have in mind certain outcomes based upon the lesson plans that teachers make, and when, indeed, teachers have the plans that they have, the chances of lessons being meaningful and outcomes being met are enhanced. It is because we recognize the importance of having structure that we do have lesson plans.

Because no youngster likes to function in chaos, the appreciation for structure on the part of the teacher is a very important aspect of what teaching is all about. And emphasizing that important aspect of teaching is not only helpful to the classroom teacher himself or herself, but is extremely helpful as an example for the way students should go about learning as they create habits for life in their school years. Much of what has been said in *Plain Teaching* has emphasized the fact that we are dealing with human beings. One of the peculiarities of the teaching profession is that we encounter different situations from day to day, from class period to class period—in some cases from moment to moment—and part of our psychological preparation for the differences that we will certainly encounter ought to be that of employing what I call flexible structure. To maintain rigid adherence to lesson plans when opportunities present themselves for larger lessons is to be unreasonable for whatever personal, selfish reasons we might have to the learning detriment of students who might benefit from our being flexible enough to seize upon an opportunity that might otherwise be considered a disruption.

Flexible structure says that, "In my lesson plans I will go over metric conversions because that is important to the overall unit dealing with measurement." A student comes into class with a pet iguana and I say, "That's nice, but this is not the time for us to study iguanas and I would appreciate it if you would take your pet and put it in your locker until the end of the school day," or, "Please excuse yourself until you can get rid of your pet," or I might say, "Did you realize the family from which the iguana comes?" and engage the students in a conversation about exotic animals. In so doing, students see me as human, and they recognize my flexibility, and enjoy the lesson not only because it may be less boring than metric conversions but also because it is a departure from whatever the routine is. It also gives an opportunity to introduce metric conversions in a more relaxed setting because the students feel that the previous day they had gotten away with something so they're ready to go back to the "routine" the next day.

It is also important to note that the student who brought the pet may very well have expected a reprimand—did not get it—

and thus he or she feels a lot better about you and about the class. The student may have brought the pet for the shock value of putting something in the teacher's face that might look frightening or perhaps to show off the nerve that the student has to the other students, and so the shock element is disarmed by the receptivity of the classroom teacher, order is maintained, and students learn something about iguanas that they did not know. It is an opportunity to show that the teacher, being a part of the team, does not ridicule or reprimand unreasonably.

Now, needless to say, flexible structure maintains the structure aspect in the terminology rather than suggesting that one simply be flexible because if students are allowed on an on-going basis to bring in pet iguanas, then prepare for a menagerie. If students are allowed to deviate on an on-going basis from the lesson plan, then prepare for discontinuity on an on-going basis. What I am suggesting is that there are times when it is good to deviate from structure to enhance the classroom atmosphere, and even to relax one's self as long as that momentary deviation does not detract from the overall lesson or the expectations in the classroom for doing what is supposed to be done.

Let us suppose that in an English literature class a teacher is attempting to assist young people in appreciating great writers, and because the popular idiom for youthful expression today is rap music, a student suggests that they would rather listen to and recite a popular rap than study great writers. Employing flexible structure might be, "If you can bring in some rap music that you feel has artistic merit and is positive, has a message, and you can explain the message in the music and the structure of the rap, then I will permit that provided that you also pay attention to Langston Hughes' *Life for Me Ain't Been No Crystal Stair* or a Shakespearean sonnet or Gwendolyn Brooks' *Raisin in the Sun*. And after you recite your rap, then I will request that you also recite *Raisin in the Sun*." The flexibility comes in allowing the rap and, the structure comes in the trade-off—the rap music plus the great writers. And again it is important for the teacher to observe that in making the concession and employing flexibility, one must not allow the class to become a six week unit on rap music.

One of the reasons that flexible structure is important is because it does lend to the creativity of one's teaching style, and creativity should be an important part of delivering the lesson. The creative approach is important as it pertains to the quality of the lesson. It is also important as an example for students in how to get the most out of what life has to offer. When we are rigid, we might, indeed, get results, but when we are intelligently flexible, we can get optimum results and that's what we want. To employ flexible structure does not require an apology to the school principal for not being on the very page of one's lesson plan that is outlined. It does not require an apology to the students' parents for not following the lesson precisely as the syllabus outlines, and it does not require an apology to one's self for lack of discipline as long as we realize that it is a temporary departure and not the rule.

SELF—CLASSROOM ATMOSPHERE

Lesson 27
Solve Classroom Problems in the Classroom

If we can instill within our students a desire to function as a part of the classroom team, then we should be able to create a climate in which the statement "What goes on in this classroom stays in this classroom" can be an appropriate statement and an achievable objective. What that statement and objective embodies is the team's ability to have the kind of camaraderie and confidence in each other that says, "Once that problem is solved, we will not then leave the classroom telling others about the problems that we had in our classroom."

The idea behind solving classroom problems within the classroom is to teach students problem-solving skills rather than simply reprimanding them for creating or being involved with problems. To solve classroom problems within the classroom enhances the teacher's image among the team members in the classroom because all know that whatever trouble they might get into, it will be handled and dispensed with without the intervention of other teachers, the principal, or outside intervention specialists, and, in some cases, without the need of involving the parents (depending upon the severity of particular offenses). Solving classroom problems within the classroom is more expedient than involving others and more personal.

Teachers who frequently call upon others to solve their classroom problems are regarded as incompetent and sometimes weak. If the incidence of asking others to come into one's classroom grows frequent, colleagues will begin to avoid a particular teacher or simply begin to say "No." A principal's evaluation of a teacher who seems unable to deal with things that come up in the classroom will obviously be low and the confidence that students have in a teacher who frequently calls upon others will also be lowered and possibly eliminated.

Gaining skills toward solving classroom problems within the classroom involves researched practice. When given assistance, the idea is to make one more proficient at solving one's own problems, not to make one more dependent on others to solve one's problem.

One of the reasons that I think it is important to solve one's problems within one's own classroom is that administrators are hired to do a lot more than mete out punishment for classroom discipline problems. Personally, I am not impressed with schools that employ the instructional principal/disciplinarian assistant principal-type organization. It suggests that the assistant principal has few intellectual skills that can be used to enhance the learning climate, but heavy disciplinary skills which may or may not enhance the academic climate.

I think that discipline must be viewed as one aspect of an over-all climate and instructional plan for any particular building. If it is but one aspect of the over-all plan and can be seen as a small but integral part of the whole, it then becomes quite necessary for those most closely involved to determine the degree to which it impacts upon the over-all atmosphere as opposed to simply viewing it as an isolated incident that must be treated with some particular disciplinary formula at the level of the principal's or assistant principal's office. If our problems are seen as part of what we do throughout the day within our classroom, then they would be viewed more as opportunities to teach lessons than disruptions against what we are attempting to do. If we can do that on an on-going basis, not only will our problem-solving skills be enhanced, but the incidence of problems is likely to be substantially reduced because things that come up if, indeed, students regard themselves as part of the classroom team, will often be solved even before the teacher is aware that a problem existed.

Among the ways that we might approach solving classroom problems within the classroom would be to have a mock court, and in some cases call upon that court to conduct mock trials. Have students become involved with being "attorneys for the defense" and "attorneys for the prosecution" and serve as a jury that might be appealed to vote, not only on whether one is guilty or innocent, but also in terms of what punishment might be appropriate. This also affords an opportunity to illuminate the problem and perhaps give us the chance to discover that it was not as big a problem as originally perceive by those involved. It would also stop the rumor-mongers from making it appear to be more than it was or different than it was, and it varies the approach to conducting class which might be not only a learning opportunity for young people but fun in the process.

Another way to approach the idea of solving classroom problems within the classroom would be to have those young people who are involved in the problems explain their motives before the class. They may have a case and if it is found that the offense is not as great as we originally imagined it to be, then there may be some small consequence depending upon their ability to explain what is was that occurred that made us think that there was a problem. It gives young people a hearing that they feel that they have been treated fairly. Once again, as in the mock trial situation, it illuminates the issue and we can get at the truth of the matter rather than a distorted version. And, it gets rid of the situation quickly without the necessity of investigating a lot of different stories and helps youngsters feel as though they are a part of a unit comprised of people in whom they can confide and in an atmosphere where they can comfortably air their concerns or their defense.

Another way that might be employed to solve classroom problems in the classroom is to have the teacher isolate the offender and converse with him or her after class in a private place where they do not feel that they are being ridiculed or reprimanded in front of their friends, and in a situation where they might feel more comfortable and, consequently, be more forthcoming in their responses to the teacher's questions about the nature of the problem that they are confronting.

It is important to young people to not be embarrassed in front of their friends. If there is a mock trial, it should be done in cases that are not severe, or do not involve situations of a sensitive nature that might require young people to reveal their personal lives. In this case the youngsters going before the class should be interviewed to find out the nature of the problems so that something is not revealed during the mock trial that will exacerbate the problems rather than eliminate them.

To lose control in front of the class and make some of your students suffer the brunt of that loss of control can, indeed, embarrass the individuals confronted as well as the rest of the class, and some young people find it very difficult to forgive a teacher who has embarrassed them in front of their peers. So there will be cases where it is good idea to isolate the offenders so that the intricacies of the matter can be discussed soberly and honestly. This also helps young people to feel like they are a part of a unit because they are being respected and because the leader of the class—the teacher—is sensitive to the personalities of the individuals involved.

Another way to solve classroom problems within the classroom would be to have mediators within the classroom itself. Many schools have mediation teams. It might be that a mini version of this could be a part of classrooms where either a particular group of young people form a mediation team, or where the entire class gets an opportunity to be involved by having rotating mediation teams. Conflict resolution skills are taught as young people act upon their assignment as mediators, and classroom problems can be solved at that level through the use of participation on the part of students as mediators in particular conflicts.

In severe cases, many parents do not want to have to come up to school to confer with the school administrator, principal and/or the assistant principal, teacher, or other parents and their students. Where it is possible, they would much prefer having a problem solved at the local level—the classroom level—and alleviated so that it takes less time, less embarrassment, and, again, increases the cohesiveness of that small unit or team because those involved do not only interact with each other when things are going well, but have enough confidence in the local situation that when things are not going well, they can confine the solution of the problems to those directly involved rather than going outside.

Another approach toward solving classroom problems within the classroom is to ask those directly involved with whatever the problem might be to offer their ideas for solutions. "This is what you have done, and having done that, what would you suggest we do about the matter?" Sometimes we find that when students are engaged in offering suggestions for their own punishment, they are far more harsh than the teacher's would have been. It does not mean that we should accept a student's harsh punishment for himself or herself, but what it does offer is the opportunity for us to see how honest young people really are, and how willing they are to accept the consequences of their actions. If they are never polled on what ought to be done based upon their offense, we might never find out that there is remorse and acknowledgement of the offense and that there is some sensitivity to the fact that a consequence must be paid. Again, this allows students to participate in their own learning and expedite the process for resolution.

I would ask classroom teachers when they summarily send students to the principal's office because the students are not doing what they are supposed to do, "What do you expect the principal to do with the youngsters once the principal gets them?" I know that in some cases teachers become very upset when they send a student to the office because the student has misbehaved and the student arrives 7 minutes later with a note from the office, not excusing the student's behavior but acting as a messenger for office personnel. Therefore, the desired result of sending the students to the office was not only missing, but the student has been rewarded for being sent to the office because now the student has permission to walk through the halls carrying messages from office personnel. This may reflect a disregard by office personnel for the needs of the teacher to see to it that this child is "taken care of" or it may reflect miscommunication; that is, office personnel not knowing why the child was sent to the office and assuming that they were sent to work as office messengers. It may also reflect the fact that one teacher was not the only teacher who decided to send a student to the office for behavior problems at the same time, and the principal simply did not have time to look after that matter at that moment.

In any case, can we expect the principal to do more for the social development of that child than we can do in our own classroom? If the answer to that question is "Yes", then I suggest that we need to do more to find out how something that can be done in the classroom would at least equal but, ideally surpass, what a principal could do with the child's short visit to the office considering that we have the child everyday over an extended period of time.

It speaks to the team orientation of a classroom, the competence and confidence of the teacher, and the trust in the seriousness of the parents when we determine that problems arising in the classroom will be taken care of in the classroom. If the classroom is a microcosm of the larger society, let me suggest that the classroom then is analogous to the local family. It is not often that a family, when children misbehave, send those children to the neighbors to be reprimanded or straightened out. If my classroom is my family, then I don't think it's a good idea to send students away from where the problem occurred to be reprimanded or straightened out. I think that we should view problems as opportunities to teach even if the lesson that must be taught is to help youngsters appreciate that they must suffer the consequences of their actions and assume responsibility for things that they do. I think that it needs to be presented to those closest to the offences and among those directly impacted by the offense which is, indeed, that classroom. I think to do otherwise can weaken the strength of the classroom unit.

I would be remiss if I did not point out that nothing is absolute. Obviously, there are cases severe enough that nothing done in the classroom would resolve the problem or alter a child's personality. Obviously there are times when professionals need to be called in—psychologists and others. I think that the psychological referral should be a rarity. I think that America does too much labeling of young people as it is, and in some cases, the label need not have been prescribed had an issue been looked at to the degree that it might have been at the local classroom level.

Unfortunately, when I talk about the classroom being a microcosm of larger society, it is that we seem as a people to be comfortable putting children out of the house. I am suggesting that we don't have control over the house, and only to a limited degree do we have control over the entire school. But we do have control over our own classrooms, and having that control, we ought to employ whatever skills we have to insure that we keep our young people all year long, and part of keeping them is to make sure they benefit from what we think is valuable in the way of what we teach when we solve classroom problems in the classroom.

SELF—CLASSROOM ATMOSPHERE

Lesson 28
Teach A Full Day

The issue of teaching a full day is mostly, if not strictly, psychological. We need to end the school day with the same degree of enthusiasm and energy as we began the day. We sometimes begin our days already programming ourselves to wind down sometime before the end of the day. There are people who work in offices and the quitting time is 5:00 p.m. who begin to wind down at 4:00 p.m. There are people who work in plants and the quitting time is 4:30 p.m., and they begin to wind down at 3:00 p.m. There are people who are engaged in strenuous activity and their mind is already made up that "It's going to be a lot less strenuous by the time I finish than when I began," so psychologically the wind down process has begun even before they start because they have already determined that it's going to be a lot easier at the finish than at the beginning.

In U.S. schools we suggest that reading and math courses should be taught at the beginning of the day. The suggestion here being that there is greater alertness on the part of students and teacher at the beginning of the day, and if we have as part of our curricula things like music and art, then they ought to be taught after lunch or more toward the "wind down" time of the day.

When I suggest that we teach a full day, the suggestion is based on personal experience when I was guilty of the wind down mentality as a science teacher whose schedule was set so that teachers who sent students to other classes for other subjects would have their own class for the subject they taught at the end of the day. When I knew that I would have my homeroom for science at the end of the day, I found myself being guilty of teaching less science to my homeroom than the other classrooms because, this being my team, I could relax with them a little bit. When my homeroom came to me at the end of the day, this was the time for me to question certain students about their behavior in somebody else's classroom. And if we were preparing for a presentation at an assembly program, this would be my time to rehearse rather than conduct a class in science. I realize that this is an admission of a total lack of professionalism but I am admitting it in the interest of suggesting that it is unfair to students for us to wind down on them, both from the standpoint of what we fail to give them and from the standpoint of the example that we, indeed, do give.

We have an obligation to teach a full day. The psychology of the afternoon being the wind down time sees some automobiles in the parking lot five minutes before the bell rings starting up with nobody in them in anticipation of the fact that teachers will get out of the building before the students because they have anticipated all day, the end of the day. Teaching a full day on an up beat so that whatever occurs after school is out finds us with an attitude of the day just beginning or at least finding us with an attitude that the day is still going strong. This is something that is absolutely "do-able."

To suggest that people are physiologically lazy after eating a meal is to defy that there are many nutritionists and physical fitness experts who see to it that after being strengthened with a proper meal that they walk, jog, or exercise. Much of our behavior is determined by our psyche. Obviously, internally there are involuntary reflexes to certain things over which we have hardly any control, but as it pertains to our ability to be alert all day, that is a decision that we can make, and in making that decision, we can carry it out just as those who take classes after school have found ways to matriculate.

We have an obligation to teach a full day, to show that we are serious about education, and there are no moments to lose. There are no wind down times of the day. Now, does that suggest that there are no times to relax during the day? Absolutely not. Obviously, in understanding that human beings need variety, times to relax and stretch and not tax their brains, certainly we ought to offer some opportunity for informal interaction between teacher and student. That's just fine, but to suggest that the informal moments are only appropriately experienced at the end of the day, and the more formal, more academic moments must be experienced at the beginning of the day is simply inaccurate., It is not true and a distortion of fact. It is just as important to teach a course in calculus at the last period of the day as it is at the beginning of the day. And a student who is not challenged throughout the day is a student who is being deprived of the opportunity to advance at the highest degree of potential.

If school is to be let out in June, there are some teachers who begin to wind down in March. It is to the detriment of students because they are not getting all the material that could be given them. And, by example, this will become a part of their lifestyle as they go into the workplace and begin to wind down at 3:00 p.m. on a 9:00-5:00 job.

How does it manifest itself over the years in secondary schools? Do you find students saying, "I'm going into my senior year. This is going to be my easy year. I really won't have to do anything this year, only have a couple of classes and, other than that, we'll just pretty much hang out." The senior year is a great opportunity for those young people who have attained enough credits to have but a few classes to be peer tutors, or to participate in work-study programs. There are some academic challenges that they can be part of in terms of advanced courses. Senior year might be the time for them to take college courses so that when they get into college, they have already done some of the work that can be used as college credits. It is not a time for seniors to roam the halls in a relaxed, casual, even playful way so that sophomores see them as the examples of what they're going to become.

Grades 9 through 12 represent either a four-year experience or they don't. If, indeed, nine through twelve represents a four-year experience, it is important that we begin to plan for that fourth year when youngsters are in their ninth year so that their experiences will be equally rich at both ends of that four year spectrum. If there is a class, for instance, that seems to be weak academically at the freshman level, then what we ought to do is shore up our resources in order to bring them up to par by the time they are in the senior year, and plan for that senior year being ripe in education experiences so they will not enter college with the same degree of weakness that they entered in high school. If a freshman class is particularly astute, and these are gifted students, then we have a similar obligation to them to plan on enrichment experiences by the time they are seniors so that the entire secondary school experience includes rich academic pursuits.

We cannot, in the interest of fairness, project to young people an attitude that there are times that are natural wind down times and therefore we will not be held, nor will the students be held, accountable for any appreciable degree of productivity because everyone knows that you begin to wind down at 2:30 p.m. during the day and March of the school year or in your senior year of your high school experience.

We teach a full day in order that we get the most out of what we are doing. Often, the discoveries that we make are at times when we least expect to make discoveries. There have been many times when teachers have determined that this is a lesson that they do not want to teach, and not only would they not want to teach it but especially at this time of day. So often they have found some major discovery, either in terms of student receptivity or in terms of trying an approach they had not discovered.

There are teachers reading this passage who know all too well that they have said to colleagues as periods were changing and a particular group was coming down the hall, "Oh, no. Not this class! This is the hardest part of my day." And then discover during that particular class period that someone on whom they had given up comes through as a bright shining star and was always a pearl but we just hadn't taken the time to polish it. Or during that class period the very thing that we were concerned about in terms of having to teach this class, that is, the collective personality of an overt class causes us to have one great class period because of that overt personality and the interaction, the life, that was in that class. An aside here would be to suggest that sometimes we need to see antics that students perform as possibly the manifestation of an exciting personality. Read the biographies and autobiographies of many of the people whom we idolize and you will find so many say that when they were in school, they were the kind of youngsters who "gave their teachers fits." Sometimes we might be able to find in those young people a spark of personality that is conducive to enhancing the environment rather than disrupting the environment. We don't know when genius is going to come through. We cannot prescribe the time, and since we don't know, every moment that we interact with young people ought to be a moment of optimum interaction between teacher and student. We have a professional obligation to, indeed, teach a full day.

* * *   * * *

I think that in a book of this type, it's a good idea to mention instruction, but I also feel that the book is more about principles of teaching than instructional methods. Therefore, the next seven lessons deal with considerations as it pertains to instruction and viewpoints that would fit into whatever instructional technique, methodology, or theory is employed. The importance of realizing this is to suggest that this is not a section on "Art of Positive Teaching Instruction Methodologies," but it is a section that suggest that to employ some of these ideas would be to use ideas that can fit into whatever program, methodology, or approach you happen to be using. This is not a book of innovations. I think that there is no particular merit in originality unless that originality comes up with something that assists in enhancing the learning climate to a degree not previously experienced. Personally, I believe that we have many approaches, techniques, and methodologies toward teaching that can be employed effectively already, and I don't need to attempt to be innovative to justify my speaking on these topics because the essence of *Plain Teaching* is to call upon the wisdom of colleagues with whom I have taught over the years and with whom I have conversed and educators whom I have met in my consulting throughout the country. Therefore, while the title of the section is "Self and Instruction," it does not represent a magic package of seven innovative teaching lessons that will cause a school to call itself an Art of Positive Teaching School based upon these instructional ideas. However, these are some things that anyone can consider immediately and by one's self to enhance the climate of instruction.

SELF AND INSTRUCTION

Lesson 29
Know Your ABCs

I am using the letters A, B, and C to refer to Adler, Bloom, and Comer. These are arbitrary names because they happen to fit A, B, C. They are also good names as it pertains to things that are going on in education and educational reform.

A: Mortimer Adler and the Paideia Program, **B:** Benjamin Bloom and *Mastery Learning*, and **C:** Jim Comer and his laboratory helping schools to become communities within themselves and employing human skills to enhance the rapport between teachers and students and students with each other. Obviously there are others involved in educational reform, many of whom, just as those I have named, were involved in what is termed "educational reform" before the educational reform movement. But I think that it is easy for us to remember the concept I am attempting to get across if I just say, "know your ABCs" or "Make yourself aware of what's going on in educational reform, especially where the practitioners have projected useful approaches toward advancing the opportunities for youngsters to fulfill their highest potential." And so it is that we should also hear from Madeline Hunter, Trevor Gardiner, Asa Hillyard, Janice E. Hale Benson, John Goodlad, the research of Ron Edmonds, Ernest Boyer, Nancy Arnez, Bob Brazil, Donald Smith, Haki Mahubuti, and others.

To hear from them and to attend conferences to learn the theories that are being projected and the practices being employed is not necessarily to agree with what is being said and projected and practiced, but it is to show one's seriousness about our profession. It is important that we be exemplars for our students as we thirst for knowledge in our chosen profession, just as we want our young people to thirst for knowledge as they attempt to prepare for their futures.

It is important that we know the ABCs of education in order that we grow individually and among the ways that we can become knowledgeable about these ABCs in education and educational reform would be to go to our local libraries, to attend conferences, and, indeed, to discuss the great ideas in education among our colleagues at the local school building level.

Let me also suggest that the essence of the book, *Plain Teaching*, suggests that having encountered great educational orators, and having been exposed to current theory in educational reform, and having adopted what might be perceived, indeed, as a magic package, there comes a point at which it gets down to plain teaching. I am hopeful that the lessons within this book can be internalized to the point where it doesn't matter who on your list in the ABCs in education you have determined you will follow. These lessons can be valuable from the human standpoint of plain teaching. If I had the opportunity to choose between a faculty well-versed in the ABCs of education versus a faculty whose main attribute was their total dedication to seeing to it that every student matriculate to their highest potential, then I would certainly choose the more dedicated group emphasizing human values because I believe that there are enough ABCs in education for a dedicated group to find that which is compatible with their teaching styles if, indeed, they are intent on seeing that every child develop to their highest potential.

I would also suggest that if one does not have the intention of insuring that every child develop, their knowledge of the ABCs will not help because no teaching theory, methodology, approach—no practice—will work within a climate of educators who are not determined to do their best for their clients which are our students. We can espouse theory to the hilt just as there are religious persons who can espouse particular doctrine to the hilt but if they have not internalized a true desire to live that which they espouse, then the rhetoric is empty and the practice will certainly suffer. It is important to be dedicated toward the young people whom we serve, but just as knowledge without dedication will not work, dedication without knowledge will not work either.

I think that it would be smug and unreasonable, indeed ignorant, to assert that all educational theory is simply sound and fury signifying nothing simply because I don't believe in educational theorists. I think that it would be equally ignorant to suggest that innovation is invalid because I believe that we already have enough basic principles from which to draw to have great schools. Obviously, by definition, education is a field that experiences on-going evolution because, as we awaken to the newness of life, that means that we have something new to study and to teach. So it is important to observe the innovative approaches that can be employed as new situations arise. But just as it does not make sense to reject a theory or innovation based on the fact that they are theory or innovation, it makes just as little sense to accept theory because it is from a respected institution or accept innovation simply because it is innovation.

What we need to do is study the different educational theories and practices from the standpoint of their longevity, the empirical evidence that what they project has resulted in higher learning capabilities and social skills for the students acted upon. We should pay close attention to the practitioners who forward certain kinds of educational reform ideas to determine whether or not there can be some kind of universal application or, if they have use as a laboratory that has some very peculiar characteristics that can only be used to a limited degree. And if that limited degree fits one's own local situation, then use that. But if it is so limited that it has no application for the local situation discard it, without discarding the fact that it can work in some instances. I think that one of the things we need to do in this potpourri of excellent educational reform is select one or two ideas upon which we wish to work and give that idea an opportunity to enjoy a meaningful test period.

Sometimes we are so anxious to allocate funds that have been given to us that we send faculty members and administrators and others to a number of different conferences and in so doing, they come back and try to implement every idea that they have heard or they try a particular idea for a year, and if it doesn't yield the desired results, then they go to others. Most of the time, it takes years for an idea to work.

Now, the reason for knowing one's ABCs and the reason a school should know its ABCs is because it is a risky proposition to have to wait several years to determine whether or not particular ideas are going to work in your local school situation.

Unfortunately, some ideas, given a proper test period, prove to be poor ideas—that is a risk that we take when we determine that we are going to adopt a certain program for our school. But the risk is significantly reduced when we are well-versed in the ABCs of education. When we can see programs measured against other programs, and when we can collect demographic data so that we can determine whether or not ideas were employed in settings reasonably similar to our own, when we can question those who have been involved with certain programs, and investigate data of the program prior to the implementation of certain ideas and then the post-data to determine what the outcomes were the better we will be able to serve our own local situation.

And as it pertains to one's self and instruction, obviously, the more we know about instruction, the more we will be able to vary the lesson when it needs to be varied, the more we will be able to give a reasonable time period for the development of a desired outcome based upon our research and knowledge of how long it took in several other situations. The more we know about our ABCs the more we will have to call upon if, indeed, a particular approach does not seem to be working. The more we know about our ABCs, the more selective we can become as it pertains to going to certain conferences. The more we know about instruction, the more pertinent notes we can take when there are in-services and staff development meetings. The more we know about instruction, the more fun we will have doing what we do because we have a significant base of knowledge upon which to call so that the most difficult problem that arises in our class will be met with an intelligent response based upon our enthusiasm with which we have sought all of this wonderful knowledge.

It is important as we approach instruction that we are experts in the field. When we graduate from college as students of education, what we need to be first is experts in instruction. In many instances there are instructors who are well-versed in their subject but cannot get it across because they know nothing about instruction. In many cases there are teachers with a great deal of enthusiasm, but the enthusiasm means little until that enthusiasm translates into a quest for getting the tools for proper instruction. Becoming acquainted with the ABCs should not be an afterthought when one has graduated from an institution, but ought to be an integral part of the classes taken at colleges of education and teachers' colleges throughout the nation. When I talk about knowing the ABCs of instruction at the college level, I don't mean simply a shallow introduction to different teaching methodologies, but, indeed, some extensive research on the various approaches toward insuring that our students will be able to call upon a similar base of knowledge as they approach different levels of education.

I think that instructional techniques should be our first concern and our last worry because there are so many approaches that are being projected by experts in the field. If teachers are called upon to appear on the various talk shows on television, a given should be that teachers know how to teach. It would be expected that teachers would know about their particular subject area of emphasis, but all teachers ought to be experts on how to teach; or, if not already experts, ought to be on the way to becoming experts because there is such a significant body of information that is available to all of us.

SELF AND INSTRUCTION

Lesson 30
Build Upon Cultural Strengths

In 1977, I worked at the Center for New Schools in Chicago, Illinois. My supervisor was Dr. Frances Holliday. At the time that I was working with Dr. Holliday at the Center for New Schools, she was writing her doctoral thesis and it dealt with building on the cultural strengths of students. I was so impressed with her theme that it occurred to me that every teacher ought to have an appreciation of, if not knowledge of, the various cultures of the students whom they teach.

I suggest that the imperative here is not so much to be able to offer in-depth treatments on every single cultural point or sub-cultural point impacting upon the lives of every single student, but that our appreciation for the cultural differences ought to be acute. The knowledge and sensitivity to the different cultures will significantly advance the cause of team building, student achievement, and creating a conducive classroom climate.

To be sensitive to the cultural strengths is the first step in building upon the students' cultural strengths. The sensitivity being the realization that inasmuch as we all are impacted upon by culture, there is something that every student brings that can enhance the classroom climate. That's the sensitivity aspect. That is the employment of the first step in the 5-Ex Cycle. That is something that we need as an integral part of elevating our expectations as well as dictating our treatment of those whom we teach. Having the sensitivity, then, ought to prompt us to find out as much as we can about the cultures from which our young people emerge, and in which our young people continue to function. And when I talk about the cultures, the various cultures, I'm not only talking about ethnic culture, I'm also talking about a body of experiences impacted by the surroundings from which young people come, meaning local or family surroundings as well as larger societal surroundings. I am suggesting that, because of all of those elements in a child's life that represent culture, there's a great deal that can be called upon and built upon because each of us is a product of our surroundings as well as our history. The more we know about our students, obviously the more we have to build upon, the more we have to call upon as they contribute to the classroom team as we search for various ways to make sure that all students benefit at the highest level from our interaction.

Gan we build upon the "groupness" of the African-American child? Most certainly as we practice cooperative learning. Can we build upon the family orientation of the Asian-American child? Most certainly as we attempt to create a team atmosphere in our classroom. Can we build upon the nature orientation of the Native American child? Yes, we can as we seek to explore the innermost physical and psychological relationship with Mother Earth. Can we build upon the patriotism of the Anglo-Saxon child? Yes, we can as we seek to understand and then explain our need to discover within each of us a sense of belonging to the ideals of our country as we continue in a continuing quest to reach some degree of reason, somewhere between the blind patriotism of zealots and the unreasonable militancy of actual or would-be revolutionaries. Can we build upon the bilingualism of the Mexican-American student? Yes, we can as we realize the growing Mexican-American population along with other Spanish speaking groups and therefore realize the need to understand not only their language but languages in general with those students helping us to learn what is lost in the translation—not only in terms of languages but in terms of cultures.

And can we learn from, or build upon the cultural strengths of students from the lowest socioeconomic rung of our capitalistic ladder? Yes, we can as we observe their survival skills, whether they be crude street survival skills or smooth street survival skills. We can learn from them and employ their survival instinct as we attempt to show examples of the different ways to make a life as well as the different ways to earn a living. Now those questions and the answers to those questions just asked and answered represent generalizations that we need not accept at face value. That is to say, that African-American groupness is not the exclusive characteristic of African-Americans because obviously there are Italian-Americans who exist for and participate in the group. To discuss the family orientation of Asian-Americans is not to suggest that Irish-Americans do not have a family orientation. And to discuss the survival instincts of those on the lowest socioeconomic rung of our capitalistic system is not to suggest that others do not have survival instincts. To discuss the patriotism of Anglo-Saxons is not to deny the patriotism of others.

We can call upon cultural characteristics and couch them within the context of strengths rather than peculiarities and expose the positive nature of how they assist young people from the different sub-cultures in succeeding within that sub-culture and expand upon those life experiences to show how they can be used to experience success in the larger society. As we attempt to build upon cultural strengths, we are required to learn something about the cultures and sub-cultures that mark the young people who are our charges.

To build upon cultural strengths is to show respect for that environment from which our students come. It is not only to show respect personally but to show respect within our classrooms, and consequently find a team-building tool in the projection of the respect for the cultural strengths of individuals and groups whom we encounter. Building upon the cultural strengths is not a mystique. It is not something that requires extensive study. It is an opportunity to let the children lead us. When there are overt examples of building upon cultural strengths such as having a cultural heritage week, that opportunity ought to be seized upon to make the suggestion that while this is a special week we should not forget the great lessons learned as children discuss who they are and why they are who they are, and from whence they have come in daily classes.

Building upon cultural strengths allows personalities to emerge that might at first appear to be offensive, but upon further study are simply manifestations of a background where under the child's "normal conditions" (appearing, perhaps, initially abnormal to us), these "peculiar" characteristics can be used to form a new norm. So often we attempt to make students conform to our perception of a school's standards. Too often the perception is not the reality, but, because it is real to the perceiver, we create an estrangement between the teacher and the students because the students refuse to adhere to our "standards." Because the standards are more perceived than real, there are circumstances under which, the students will never rise to those standards, and when they do not, we sometimes compliment ourselves with the rationalization, "That's exactly what we want. We never want to be satisfied. We want to keep them reaching, and even if they are frustrated, that's O.K. because later in life the lesson that they have learned is 'You never do well enough'." Well, that rationalization can be harmful rather than helpful in life because it may very well be that the message that we're sending to the students is that their lifestyle is wrong or they can never achieve the degree of success that they desire.

If we could, because of the variety of personalities and subcultures represented by the mix of students coming into our classrooms today (particularly in public schools), determine that rather than make the students adhere to a set of standards that we prescribe or a set of perceived standards to which we aspire, we will, instead, develop a new set of equally high standards based upon the mix that we have rather than based upon making the youngsters assimilate into what our perceptions project. If young people in school can learn to appreciate each other for who and what we are, there are great possibilities for a future world of peaceful resolution to conflict based upon our realization that we are all human beings made up of a mix of experiences peculiar to our own set of circumstances that ought to be appreciated by others because they, too, have their circumstances that are not dissimilar to our own in their basic impact on our lives, but, perhaps, are dissimilar in the way they manifest themselves in overt behavior.

A lesson can be learned from building upon cultural strengths because young people need to leave us knowing more than and, indeed, feeling better than they did when they came to us. If we can offer opportunities for each child to describe something about their local environment that makes them the good, productive, and successful youngsters that they are, it can cause them to hold conversations with their parents and their grandparents and their great-grandparents. It can cause children to begin to develop an appreciation for their own strengths because they have found out that somebody wants to know. It can cause young people to feel less ashamed of the language that they use, or of the difficulty in getting a handle on Standard English. And even while it is important on an on-going basis to help young people appreciate the power of Standard English, they will also be able to appreciate the significance of whatever language is spoken in their own home.

When we build upon cultural strengths, we do not build upon one's strength by emphasizing another's weakness, but we put strength to strength throughout the whole team. Many of the characteristics that we will find will not enjoy exclusivity in one particular group. It may be a significant part of that group process to find that after thinking that they were so very different, they are quite similar and can begin to explore those similarities rather than regret the differences. And, as a student I will feel more comfortable in other settings because, even if I don't know what the cultural strengths are, I do know that there are, indeed, cultural strengths and I'll just be sensitive to that and keep my mind, my eyes, and my heart open to what there is to learn about the environment wherever I go.

It is important to build upon cultural strengths within our classroom and within our schools because inasmuch as the nature of American society is marked by the acceptance of so many different people from so many different places, the definition of who America is continues to evolve. If you were to get 50 people to describe or define what America is or America means to them, out of 50 responses you might get 37 different answers because there are those who think of America as a melting-pot or a salad bowl, and there are those who think of America as a land of opportunity. There are those who think of America as being more closed than they thought it would be when they came from their native land. There are those who think of America as simply being a place to earn as much money as possible and spend it all on material goods. There are those who think of America as a place where democracy definitely works, and there are those who think of America as a place that needs a great deal of improvement. There are those who think of America as a very white, Anglo-Saxon, Protestant-oriented, conservative society, and there are those who think of America as an emerging nation appreciative of all the differences that define who she is.

It is important to build upon the cultural strengths of students by revealing the cultural strengths of the teacher. As many examples as teachers can give about their own personal background to explain their behavior, the better the students will understand the teacher and the more comfortable students will feel in revealing their own backgrounds that have a causal effect on the behavior they project in the class and in society. And with the realization that there are certain things that cause us to respond to events and individuals in the way that we do, there can be efforts to grow as individuals as we share with each other who we are.

If culture is represented by the body of experiences and the environment encountered by young people and that culture can manifest itself in the music, art, literature, poetry, and the mores of a particular group, I believe then there is no student who comes to us without culture. And that being the case, we have an opportunity to build upon every student's strengths beginning with the student's culture rather than beginning with the student's behavior.

As we build upon the cultural strengths of our students, it is important that this does not manifest itself superficially or cosmetically, that it does not manifest itself in shallow phrases such as "I like your haircut," and "Your people are so colorful." But if, indeed, it is to be put within the context of something that is positive, it is better to delay the comment than it is to make the attempt to discuss the child's culture and have it result in saying or doing something that is offensive rather than complimentary.

With what I have discussed on the building of cultural strengths, then it should be apparent that I am talking about not only building upon the cultural strengths of a particular child to enhance that child's learning and feelings of comfort within the classroom, but I am suggesting that to build upon the cultural strengths of the different children in the class also impacts positively on the other children in the class and creates a learning environment where all feel comfortable with who they are because they understand that the teacher appreciates all of them wherever they come from because each of them has strengths upon which to build.

SELF AND INSTRUCTION

Lesson 31
Use Music During Certain Study
and/or Activity Periods

Use music to enhance the climate of students' learning certain concepts. There are obviously employers who believe that employees can concentrate better through the use of music so they employ "elevator music" in their plants in order to relax their employees. In the book, *Super Learning*, the authors Nancy and Shiela Ostrander talk about the University of Suggestology in Bulgaria and some of the American universities both in the state of Iowa and on the West Coast that employ an instruction technique that involves the use of music over or under academic instruction, and because the music appeals to the right brain and the instruction is internalized by the left brain, instruction is actually enhanced through the use of the music. In their assessment of using music as an instructional tool, they further suggest that it is a certain kind of music, for instance, that which has been composed by Wagner at a particular beat, so many beats per measure in a particular rhythmic pattern, that causes optimal retention of information offered using the suggestology technique. I am not here proposing something that is quite so profound. I have studied extensively enough to know the merits of the *Super Learning* study. I certainly find it intriguing and do not have a reason to doubt such a possibility not only exists but that such a technique is being used effectively. Don't doubt it. But all I am suggesting here is that the use of music can create a climate that is comfortable for students and therefore conducive to learning as well as positive and friendly interaction. The use of soothing music without lyrics can calm students after a rigorous and exciting activity, can engage students during transitions from lesson to lesson or class period to class period, can teach music appreciation without stating it as such, and could even be used to create a different climate when used for its dramatic effect.

Why should I suggest music in particular as a vehicle for enhancing a particular climate or offering a variation in teaching approaches? Couldn't I have just as easily suggested that we might use slides in the classroom because the visual effect of slides also assists in varying the teaching method as well as creativity in the classroom? The chances are there are any number of variations on a particular theme, but the use of music is an unobtrusive variation from the standpoint of students. With the use of music it is possible to focus on more than one thing at a time because the music is used as an undercurrent rather than the principal activity or the principal focus at a given time during a particular class period. Also, I believe that there is some merit to the adage that "music [can] soothe the savage br east." This is certainly not to suggest that we are teaching savages, but music certainly can make a difference in one's day.

Also students are accustomed to being in a climate where music is played. Much of their after-school activity—movies, MTV, television—involves different kinds of background music.

The reason I say "during certain study periods and certain activity periods" is because there are obviously times when the intervention or the use of music would be inappropriate. It is also, I think, inappropriate to use it all the time because it would possibly lose its soothing and/or dramatic effect if it is always used. But during an activity hour—activity meaning an hour where students are enjoying table games, decorating the classroom, watering plants, engaged in leisurely, personal reading or conversing with each other—an activity period like that could employ music that not only would not disrupt anything but complement the informality of the moment.

Just as was mentioned in "Allow this generation to be this generation," we can benefit from a cultural exchange, as it were; that is, to ask students to listen to the kinds of things that we listened to when we were their age, and allowing them to have us listen to the kind of things that they are listening to now. We might even find much of their music quite enjoyable, and, to the degree that we would not continue to call it "their music" but simply to refer to it as "music".

I have even used music during exams. I do believe that based upon exam results and the way students responded while taking the exam, that it had no detrimental effect on the exam. I cannot say that I used it long enough and evaluated it deeply enough to suggest that using music during exam time, indeed, helped, but I certainly can say that it is evident that it did not hurt. But I think that there is the possibility that it might, indeed, help if it is the right kind of music.

Among the practical uses of music in classrooms is using music to get the attention of the students in the class. There are times when students may be hyperactive. There may be in the transition from subject area to subject area or class to class on a particular day more excitement than on another day, and in the need to command students' attention sometimes playing music without saying anything at all can get students' attention as they begin to listen to what's being played. And when students express their curiosity as to why something is going on in the classroom, a teacher now has a point of interest from the students that can help to begin whatever lesson is coming up.

Music can be used after an altercation in the classroom to help settle students down. Music can be used in the background when students are asked to recite, especially if they are reciting poetry or the like. Music can be used when students' cultural strengths are being discussed as a way of setting the tone or the atmosphere in order to bring authenticity to a particular discussion by playing the music that is reflective of that student's culture.

An informal study of music can be used to distinguish between time periods or eras in a discussion with students about the differences between today's world and yesterday's world—not in the same vein as discussing "our" music versus "their" music, but to discuss historical events and the music that marked the times. Students might find it interesting to learn how the music of different time periods was reflective of what was going on during that time period—the peace songs of the '60s and the patriotic songs of World War II, the frenzied music of the Roaring '20s, the explicit lyrics and loud background of music of the '80s and early '90s. And whatever other kinds of music become popular and seem to wane as new generations of young people emerge, there are classics and standards that will always be with us.

It is also interesting to play music not only from different periods but from different geographical areas. I'm not talking about cultural music that might come from China or Cambodia or Egypt, but about music that might come from urban versus rural communities, southern versus western communities. There is so much music that not only will it be easy for teachers to find appropriate music to introduce during certain class periods, but it's also fun to look for music that will accompany things that are going on in the class. It is fun to discover that students appreciate a teacher's taste in music and it is sometimes fun to laugh at one's self as students seize upon the opportunity to show us just how out of date we are.

One can experiment with different kinds of music to see the effect that it has on the activities of students. I believe that when students are hyperactive, playing soft music might slow them down. When students appear to be bored or inactive, certain kinds of music might be introduced to pep up the classroom. Experimenting with different kinds of music, again, certainly cannot hurt the climate because, if an inappropriate kind of music were introduced at any particular time, it is very easy to simply stop the music. Most likely, however, the prudent use of music will significantly enhance the classroom climate and it is something that is simple to employ and can be called upon at a moment's notice. Because it is informal and non-threatening, students—particularly students who do not come forward to participate in other activities that might seem to be opportunities for failure—can be used as the designated DJ for a particular week or a particular period of time. And when I use the term "DJ", that is descriptive only for lack of a better term. I don't think it would be a good idea to say that a student is going to be a designated DJ because if you call a student that, it may very well be that when his or her week comes up, the person designated will come in to the classroom with a new haircut that bears hieroglyphics, sunglasses, sagging trousers, and a vocabulary that is hardly intelligible where adults are concerned, but the delight of the students in the class, in which case the idea of a designated DJ would set a precedent wherein students would feel that the introduction is fun-time and that is not at all what I am discussing here. But having the students become involved as designated DJs will show the level of trust that teachers have in the students' ability to bring the appropriate kinds of music into the classroom when the teacher says what it is to be used for, whether that would be a study period—in which case, quiet music, no lyrics; a cultural period—in which case the student would seek out the kind of music appropriate to studying a particular culture; or an activity period where a student would look for music that is popular enough for young people to enjoy, yet unobtrusive enough so that students don't begin dancing in the aisle.

SELF AND INSTRUCTION

Lesson 32
Use the "No-Cheat" Test

My original intent was to create a climate in the classroom where students would relax during quiz periods. It is a well known fact that there are people who are poor test-takers. There are some people who experience severe anxiety upon contemplating taking a test. Teachers who have taught for a while have encountered students who are obviously intelligent, but somehow do not fare well when it comes to test-taking time. Also, there are some teachers who have a great deal of concern about students cheating on tests.

The idea behind the "no-cheat" test was to have students help each other, and, in so doing, reduce test anxiety and remove any incentive or, even, opportunity to cheat. The way I introduced the "no-cheat" test, was to say to students, "You have 35 minutes to take this test. During the first 15 minutes, do the absolute best that you can, but if you find in those first 15 minutes that you're not doing as well as you should OR as well as you would like, then ask someone else to help you. And whether you get help or not, I will grade your test based upon the answers that appear." Again, the idea here was to offer students an opportunity to use the first 15 minutes in a relaxed state, to find out how much they retained from a particular lesson, and then to feel comfortable asking someone else rather than feeling guilty if their eyes happen to glance in the direction of someone else's paper.

The desired outcome was better grades based upon less test anxiety and better understanding of concepts that students might impart more effectively than I, the teacher, had. The unexpected outcome dealt with the second or third no-cheat test which saw students who started out being the "helpees" become helpers. During the first 15 minutes of the no-cheat test, several students seemed to be determined that they would not be the students who always needed help. In fact, on one or two occasions one of the students whom I had in my science class who previously had not done very well, during a no-cheat test, stood and boldly asked across the classroom, "All right, then, who needs some help?" (The suggestion being that "I have gotten myself so together that I'm ready to help somebody else.") Using the no-cheat test is an instructional technique that serves to reduce anxiety, serves to enhance the learning capabilities by using a variation on the peer tutoring theme, and serves to give an incentive for students previously in need of help to become helpers to other students.

But the use of the no-cheat test can have drawbacks if not property implemented. It is dangerous to use the no-cheat test with such frequency that students begin to anticipate that there will be a no-cheat test and consequently do not study as hard as they otherwise would. Also, I think that it is not a good idea to use the no-cheat as a mid-term examination or final examination, but on occasion, in order to reduce test anxiety, the use of the no-cheat tests sets up the kind of climate wherein not only are students comfortable because they can get help, but when the teacher announces that today's test will not be a no-cheat test, but everybody is on his own, anxiety might be reduced because the previous "helpees", now helpers, are so prepared that it's O.K. that they cannot get help from someone else because they came in not needing any help from anyone else.

I suggest that it would be a good idea to "play around with" the no-cheat test until one sees the relevance in application to one's own particular situation. Some teachers may use it more than other teachers, and some might find that the no-cheat test can be used with reasonable frequency. And because the teacher has extensive knowledge of the individuals in the class and the class as a collective, the teacher can make a determination as to whether or not something such as a different test will work, and the teacher's knowledge of the students will determine how often such a technique will work in a particular class.

I am always concerned when I meet a colleague who seems to want to catch students doing wrong, who seems to want to catch students cheating on tests in order that they might reprimand the student or show how tough they are as teachers. My suggestion is that we give every opportunity for students to feel good about the classroom, to feel relaxed, and to help each other because that's what education is about. Removing the possibility of cheating obviously removes the incentive to cheat. The more variations on this kind of positive theme, the more relaxed students will be as they matriculate and the more successful they will be as they, indeed, assist each other and determine that it is not productive to cheat but it is productive to prepare one's self with purpose because one is likely to be more successful when one does have purpose. If, as a student, I am asked to become a peer tutor, then my purpose for learning subject matter thoroughly is to assist someone else, and experienced teachers know that in the peer tutoring relationship it is more often than not the tutor who benefits more than the one tutored.

SELF AND INSTRUCTION

Lesson 33
Engage Students in the "You-Teach-Me, I'll-Teach-You Approach"

This is an approach similar to the no-cheat test approach; that is, to have students prepare by learning a great deal of subject matter to teach the teacher. When students are involved in teaching a teacher, they gain an appreciation for the difficulty in imparting knowledge to someone who does not have the proper basis of information. When teachers are involved in learning from the students, the teacher gains an appreciation for the difficulty of learning when they do not have a sufficient basis of understanding to begin with. With the "You-Teach-Me, I'll-Teach-You" approach the student teaches the teacher something that is almost totally foreign to the teacher's body of current experiences. It is also important that whatever it is that the student is teaching, that it be something with which the student is thoroughly familiar so that as the students run into problems in teaching, they have a great number of facts to call upon and examples to use.

If young people were to teach teachers things like the latest dance or jumping double-dutch or mastering video games or using slang, things that are peculiar to youth but not to the experiences of the teacher, it will probably result in some amusement, in some cases, perhaps, some frustration, but certainly would result in a renewed appreciation for the plight of the teacher. In some cases it would be a good idea to have students teach subject matter, but again, it should be something with which the class is unfamiliar but with which the student teacher is totally familiar.

We talked about appreciation for different cultures. It might be interesting to have someone from China demonstrate the interpretation of a Chinese folk dance or for someone who is from Puerto Rico to explain the subtle differences between the Spanish that is used by Puerto Ricans versus the Spanish that is used by Mexicans. It would be interesting to have students from rural communities conduct lessons on rural geography versus urban geography. We may have students who have expertise in such things as glass blowing, sign language, calligraphy, photography, self-defense, hair styling, or any of several other crafts, hobbies, techniques, with which other members of the class are unfamiliar. When that is the case, it is not a bad idea to give those students the opportunity to demonstrate their knowledge that might be fascinating to others, and also to gain the experience again of the plight of being a teacher and understanding what it takes to prepare, present, and evaluate a lesson.

The teacher, of course, will benefit from recalling what it was like to go into a classroom with some degree of enthusiasm and to find out that not one student could even generate the necessary question to get on track. It is good inasmuch as the teacher is the leader of the class to feel the pain of being looked up to by others in the class and having to be the one to ask the "stupid" question. The obvious advantage that the teacher has here is in knowing that there are no such things as "stupid" questions, only stupid attitudes when the proper question is not asked. But still, just recalling those feelings and having those feelings in the midst of others who look up to you can help in the way teachers present lessons because having that experience and recalling having had the experience of being the student some years ago helps us to refuse to make assumptions about what students already know, and to begin each lesson from the beginning in order that one student or those few students who do not have the proper base of knowledge will be up to speed with the rest of the students as the lesson progresses.

The "You-Teach-Me, I'll-Teach-You" approach is once again an opportunity to do some team building by having students as full participants in what goes on in the class. It is an approach toward team building and enhancing the classroom climate that gives students worth. It empowers students. It recognizes their value in front of the rest of the class and, in so doing, results in greater participation when the classroom teacher returns to that role. Students enjoy doing things with which they are very comfortable and people—students, those who are not students, young people, adults, senior citizens—get a great deal of pleasure out of being called upon to share their expertise with others. Videotape these sessions and allow the students to critique themselves and to have a copy of their own videotape that can be kept through the years and that they can look back on and see what a great job they did, or look back on and see where they, indeed, could have improved or, if it is appropriate, even laugh at themselves and the participants in their initial teaching experience.

I would like to see that one of the outcomes would be that a student decides that teaching is something that they enjoy doing and, perhaps, will decide to teach after they have finished college.

The second part of the "You-Teach-Me, I'll-Teach-You" exercise involves the teacher's role. The "I'll-Teach-You" aspect of this particular exercise is not for the teacher to teach just anything. It is not to say, "You teach me whatever you would like, and then you will pay greater attention as I teach you the regularly scheduled lesson." But the idea here is for the teacher to teach something that he or she particularly enjoys outside of the regular curriculum, to teach something that deals with a particular hobby, a particular field of interest, something that is informal and enjoyable, intriguing, interesting over and above the regular classroom lesson. We would not want young people to feel that the regular curriculum is either to be entertainment or a part of some kind of trade-off. Students must understand that whether or not a particular exercise such as the "You-Teach-Me, I'll-Teach-You" approach is engaged, they must come to school prepared to learn what is necessary for them to be successful in life and to pass the course. So teachers, when they announce that an exercise will be undertaken, need to emphasize that "We will all—that includes the teacher—bring something that is different enough, unique enough, so that others will want to learn it." If it turns out that a few students have the same hobby, interest, or particular talent and would like to team up, I would think that would be O.K. inasmuch as this is an informal exercise and an opportunity to get the highest degree of participation.

Students can find educating exciting when they are full participants in their own learning. In this case, the student teacher is learning communication skills and enhancing their study and preparation habits.

Students should not be allowed to develop lessons that are so extensive or so complicated that it requires more than one presentation. Students should present 20-minute lessons and, in some cases, perhaps students could be allowed to use a full 50-minute period, but students should not be allowed to develop a two-week course in introducing to fellow students and the teacher some particular hobby. This exercise is simply to give an opportunity for students to participate at the level of instructor, but it is not designed to give the teacher two weeks off as students function in the role of the teacher.

The "You-Teach-Me, I'll-Teach-You" approach should also be done in the presence of the regular classroom teacher rather than having an exercise such as this continue in the teacher's absence in the presence of a guest teacher whose benefits from the exercise would be limited in terms of their brief visit with a particular class. The "You-Teach-Me, I'll-Teach-You" approach could also lend itself to an opportunity for parents to come in while their children function as the teacher in an informal setting. However, if students suggest to the teacher that they might be self-conscious in the presence of parents, the teacher should not insist as this is designed to be a classroom rather than a community experience.

It can be fun to have the student who does the teaching evaluate the performance of the class including the classroom teacher as a student, and to have the fellow class members functioning as students evaluate the student who is, at that point, the teacher. But the evaluations should be informal and verbal rather than formal, written recorded. The idea here is to have a sharing activity that may have magnificent results or mediocre results, but even where there are mediocre results, the magnificence is in the participation, not in the ability of all class members to grasp whatever has been taught, and not in the "teacher's" ability to emerge as a superstar.

In large classes, or even not so large classes, the "You-Teach-Me, I'll-Teach-You" approach may be spread out over a full year in order that a lot of time is not taken up when there is a continuum of students participating in this particular exercise. The idea here is not to overuse the exercise to the point where the teacher loses continuity for those subjects that are called for in the regular curriculum.

In this particular exercise, every student should be encouraged to participate as teacher, but no student should be required to participate as teacher. There are some students who simply may not have matured to the extent, or gained enough confidence, to present an actual lesson to the class. Their participation as presenters may be fulfilled by the writing of a brief two-page paper on their particular skill or talent or hobby. It may be prudent to simply allow certain students to opt for non-participation at the level of teacher. (If it appears that students have a severe problem with appearing before the class, that might be cause for a conference with that student and/or with the student's parents, and even with a school psychologist, but that would be the rare exception.) I would suggest that in most cases if students are reluctant to teach anything, it is based upon a young person's natural fear of speaking in front of a group—a fear, by the way, which is also natural to older persons and old persons—or based upon a young person's self-perception that they don't have anything unique to share or enough expertise in a particular area of interest. This will give a teacher the opportunity to convince young people that they certainly do have something that they could offer that would be of interest to others, and, here again, this would represent another opportunity for teachers to get to know their students quite well. But when it is mutually determined that the student's reluctance to participate is not based on any severe psychological disorder, I would suggest that students be allowed to wait to participate, or to refrain from participating at that level.

Each time that I say "participate at that level" what I am suggesting is that all students ought to be required to participate as students when their classmates are teaching. They should certainly participate in these exercises but to require them to be a part of the "You-Teach-Me, I'll-Teach-You" exercise as teachers may prove to be counter-productive as it creates rather than reduces anxiety.

This approach, or exercise, is appropriate at grade levels from the primary grades through seniors in high school, and the earlier students participate and the more often they get opportunities of this kind, the more proficient they will be in the upper grades based upon their lower grade experiences. The more comfortable they are in appearing before a class the more comfortable they will be in appearing before large audiences or interviewers for jobs or wherever they might be asked to communicate on a greater scale.

There may be some natural follow-up-type activities where there is great interest in something presented by particular students and great value in more extensive study or participation in particular concepts, but particular students must not be allowed to preempt (because there's a great interest in what they have to present) other students whose subject area might appear to be less interesting. There may be occasions upon which teachers having a difficult time introducing or carrying on specific lessons might remind students of how they felt when they were attempting to teach, and those of us who were the students just didn't seem to be able to catch on or ask the proper questions or respond in the way that the teacher desired by saying, "That's how I'm feeling right now so someone who participated in 'You-Teach-Me, I'll Teach You' help me to get across what I want to get across. Tell me how you felt and what you did." Enlisting the cooperation of the students in this way reminds them that the job of being a teacher is not an easy thing and there are times when teachers need the help of the students to unlock what seems to be the mysteries of certain subject areas. But this call for cooperation cannot be done unless students have participated in such an exercise as the "You-Teach-Me, I'll-Teach-You" approach, and so it is that for purposes of varying the lesson, team building, building upon students' cultural strengths, enhancing the instructional climate in the classroom by having students empathize with the plight of the teacher, and gaining wider knowledge of subject areas not ordinarily covered, the "You-Teach-Me, I'll-Teach-You" approach is a valuable exercise at any grade level.

SELF AND INSTRUCTION

Lesson 34
Use Grouping for Academic and Social Growth

When I divided students into groups during the teaching of science classes, I did not call the exercise "Cooperative Learning", but students were, indeed, cooperating with each to enhance learning. Many of the approaches toward effective teaching today have labels on practices that many teachers have employed for many years without affixing a particular label to those practices. The two reasons for grouping students that prompted me to do so were: 1) To have students assist each other academically; and 2) To help students grow socially. The academic growth came as a result of two things: 1) Students assisting each other; and 2) Students holding each other accountable. The social growth came as a result of individual students' understanding that one person's accomplishments and actions affect people around them. The academic growth is important from the standpoint of students learning things that they need to learn, and it is important in terms of students getting grades that they desire. The social growth has not only classroom implications but societal implications as well. We encourage and require students to function in teams at the school level in order that they might enhance their capability to function with others in society after their school years are done.

In using grouping, my suggestion is that students are evaluated by the teacher, both for their individual academics and behavior performances and for their group behavior and academic performance. The way I employed grouping in science classes was to have students function within their group and at the end of each class period I would read aloud their group grades so that every group knew their class performance grade. Students are astute enough to know that the group grade, especially when it is a low grade that is read at the end of the class period, is often the result of some one particular student's antics. Being so aware, students will hold each other in check because they will let each other know, "Boy, I'm not getting a low grade tomorrow because of you. You better get your act together!"

Peer pressure often serves to tighten up a young person's future performance not because they are afraid of the other members of their group but because they do not like to be ostracized by their peers.

After work has been done, papers have been turned in, or students have recited, they would get their individual academic grades, but because that involves paper work that has to be taken home and graded in some cases, the only grade given at the end of a particular class period would be the behavior grade of the group. It is not proper to have an individual's academic grade suffer because of the behavior of the group, and therefore students must attach some significance, some importance to the group behavior grade in order that they see that as an incentive to behave properly during the grouping sessions.

The obvious way that the academic grade suffers from poor group performance is when students waste time or cause others' time to be wasted or when students on a particular team or in a particular group are disruptive or totally uncooperative. Therefore, it behooves all group members to behave not only in order that the group at the end of the period gets a good behavior grade but also to create optimum opportunities for all students to do well academically. The average academic grade for a particular group of students will be reflective of the group's behavior as it will be difficult for the average grade of a group to be "A" if any member of that group is wasting time for the others in the group or even for one's self. When the behavior grade is recorded as a group grade, that has some impact on the function of the group. Then when the academic average of the group is also read aloud, that ought to have some impact on the group even though the individual grades of those doing what they are supposed to be doing, and in spite of the uncooperative team member's behavior, will not suffer.

The importance of full cooperation among team members when students are divided into groups can be felt more acutely than at other times when every single member of the group has a specific duty that is integral to the ability of the group's completing particular tasks. When that is the case, the academic grade, even for the individuals doing what they are supposed to do, can suffer if the completion of a particular project has direct bearing on each individual's grade.

It is important that the teacher make it clear at the outset that this is the case so that if it is necessary for students to report to the teacher that a person with an important task within the overall task is failing to function, they can make such a report soon enough in order to get a team replacement, or in order for the teacher to intervene and impress upon the non-cooperative team member why he or she must do what they are supposed to do not only for the individual self but for the good of the team. And, part of impressing upon that individual the importance of their functioning within the team would be making it clear that should it be necessary for that individual to be removed from the team because of behavior, then that individual, without then affecting the entire team, will receive a flunking grade for their non-cooperation which translates into incompletion of the task which contains an academic evaluation.

It is my belief that academic and social growth in grouping is realized to its fullest when there are heterogeneous groups, and even random selection of students placed into heterogeneous groupings. And if it turns out that somehow the attempted random selection results in homogeneity wherein the brighter students somehow all chose the number three and became a part of the three group, or wherein the most talkative students all chose the number one, observing that, the teacher should change the grouping with an explanation. The changing of the grouping is necessary in order to achieve optimum academic and social growth results. The explanation is necessary so that the students do not feel that the teacher is cheating somehow.

Where there is heterogeneous grouping of students, there is opportunity for students who are more advanced, more gifted, if you will, to help those who are less advanced, less gifted, and all students get an opportunity to feel that they are as much a part of the class as any other student.

If the use of grouping should occur several times within the school year, it is a good idea to change the groups so that students learn to function with different group personalities. Even where a particular group seems to do well with each other and, consequently, would appear to benefit from staying together, since school is the laboratory for success in later life, it is important that students get a variety of experiences, even when it might appear that their confidence will be shaken by taking them out of a group that they have learned to effectively participate in because just as they gained confidence and learned how to participate well in one group, that experience is not a valuable experience unless it can be transformed into becoming an integral and successful part of another group.

To the degree that it is manageable, all group assignments should require maximum participation for all individuals in those groups. The reason for this is to create a climate that not only emphasizes the importance of every individual but also prevents certain individuals in the group from riding on the coattails of other individuals. In adult society, it appears that 90% of organizations, particularly volunteer organizations, have only 15% of the membership doing 90% of the work, and it is just possible that the habits of those who consider themselves members of organizations but do not make any contributions until it's time for the press release or the photos to be taken learned that behavior from the time that they were children and allowed to "lay back" while others did for them. In this grouping experience, because everybody will benefit from the collective grade, teachers need to take care that activities are developed that require maximum participation from all individuals within the groups in order that the group grade earned is, indeed, a reflection of group participation and not of one very zealous student taking on all of the responsibilities and the group grade for that particular group being reflective of a single person's effort.

We should not encourage one person who does all the work by awarding the entire group an excellent group grade and then suggesting that we know who did all the work, but that's all right if they wanted to do all the work, it still resulted in a great group grade. The purpose is not to simply have an excellent outcome by whatever means necessary. In this exercise the means in and of itself represents a desired outcome as all members of the group cooperate from the beginning until the grade is given. Just as we move about the classroom when students are involved in working as individuals not as a part of small groups, we should move about the classroom from group to group to make sure groups are functioning as groups.

The idea of the group grade is to reflect the degree to which individuals in the group make their contributions to the success of that particular group. But having different groups is not for the purpose of developing a competition. It is for the purpose of having manageable small groups function as teams rather than the entire classroom functioning as a group within itself. The team atmosphere in the classroom certainly needs to be maintained and in that regard, grouping should not be used all year long for every unit taught or for every subject area, but during particular units or during certain exercises. Grouping is a valuable approach toward helping students grow academically and socially.

SELF AND INSTRUCTION

Lesson 35
Require Students to Write and Recite
Beginning at an Early Age

Recently while visiting one of the cities on the East Coast, I heard a newscaster say "And now, news for those who fly by air." And it occurred to me that most of the people whom I know who fly, do, indeed, fly by air. I'm not altogether certain why it was necessary to add "by air." It was difficult for me to imagine how we might fly otherwise. In my home-town of Kansas City, Missouri, I heard a local sportscaster discussing George Brett of the Royals baseball team. Because Brett was being used as right fielder rather than a first baseman or designated hitter, the sportscaster made the statement that Brett's playing right field "may be temporarily permanent for a while." And I thought that was an interesting turn on a phrase. How something can be "temporarily permanent" escapes me, especially if it's "temporarily permanent" only for a while, but it lets me know that even in the professional ranks of broadcast journalism there is a need for citizens to learn how to use the English language.

I often hear people utter such redundancies as "We are going to have regular monthly meetings once a month," or "Would you please repeat that again?" It is clear that many of us are not concerned about the way we speak or are unaware of our failure to speak properly. As in so many things, we learn to speak properly by practicing proper speaking habits and we learn how to speak properly more efficiently as children than as adults. It is important that students from a very young age matriculate in a climate where examples of proper speaking abound and where opportunities to speak properly are offered.

Those opportunities can come from students being required to recite in front of the class, being required to read aloud, being required to participate in class discussions, and in being required to be a part of mock interviews that might be conducted when students begin to apply for work. The only way that speaking properly will become a regular habit for adults will be for students to have regular opportunities to practice good speaking habits. In the lesson "Always Grade English" (Lesson 12), I suggested that educators often make a distinction between content and grammar. I suggested that content suffers for lack of grammatical correctness. We are too complacent and too permissive when we allow students to give us single-word answers or sentence fragments that theoretically represent the correct answer to the questions that we offer. And, we do, indeed, find that there are adults in professional fields, and not only professional fields but professional fields which depend upon their ability to speak, who have grown accustomed to speaking improperly because they have never been held accountable where proper speaking is concerned. The accountability begins at home, it continues in school, and goes on to the workplace. But there are some homes where parents do not emphasize the use of proper English and there are some jobs where the perception is that the use of English has no impact one way or another on productivity.

However, in our schools we are paid to take particular care in presenting lessons designed to help every student realize their greatest and fullest potential. The foundation for realizing one's fullest potential is laid as one learns how to communicate. Parents must communicate with their children, usually through the spoken word, in order to guide them in the direction that children ought to go. Teachers must communicate with the students in order to insure that students understand lessons presented, and students must communicate with teachers in order to insure that the teacher knows that students understand lessons presented. Prospective employees must communicate well at job interviews in order to get the job applied for. Employers must communicate effectively with employees in order to insure that the desired work is done and done well.

Success in school, careers, and relationships depends upon clear communication and since so much of communication relies upon speaking, it is extremely important that the educational experience is largely a speaking experience, and that it is a speaking experience wherein those speaking are corrected when they are incorrect and encouraged when they are correct.

Suggesting that we always grade English is to suggest that whatever the subject area, whatever the assignment, it is imperative that students be required to indicate their mastery of subject matter through clear and concise oral and written practices. I suggest going beyond simply always grading English to requiring extensive speaking and writing exercises. Where many math problems can be solved simply through the use of numbers, occasionally students should be required to explain math problems using their verbal skills. Where various science formulae can be printed on a computer or written on a chalkboard, I am suggesting that from time to time students be required to verbalize those formulae without access to the computer or the chalkboard and to paint such a vivid picture in their verbalization that the entire class can understand the statement of the problem and the solution to that problem.

While there are some students who are complimented for having a tremendous musical ear or for being able to play by ear, or composing without knowing how to write out the configuration of notes, I suggest that from time to time those students be required to explain the chromatic scale, the number of beats in a measure, and the difference between half-steps, whole-steps, minor chords and major chords, and to verbally express what it is that they are doing, what it is that they are feeling, and why they are writing particular types of songs. This will not stifle their creativity but might enhance their ability to be even more creative as the verbalization of what they are feeling helps them to understand how to reproduce something that they may think they have stumbled upon.

Students who are gifted athletes should be required to discuss their athletic prowess and their practice regimen. It will help others to appreciate their discipline and their focus and it will help them to develop communications that can be used in places other than on the field or in the classroom in later life. And, indeed, if those with athletic prowess should become successful professional athletes, the ability to communicate well can translate into enhanced earnings as they are asked to endorse products or become sportscasters on major networks.

Students who run for classroom or school offices must be required to make campaign speeches and explain platforms. There are some institutions where this is done extremely well and there are some institutions where students are so popular or have such tremendous senses of humor that they are allowed to get away with sloganizing and trivializing the campaign in which they are involved. But for later life as well as current experiences, it is important that they be required to recite and to recite well, and the rest of the school, the voting population, ought to be taught to listen to the candidates so that their vote would not be reduced to trivialization.

In cases where students get into trouble they should be required to explain themselves and explain themselves articulately. Sometimes students who are in trouble, who have the ability to articulate what the issues really are, what a particular case really is, can find themselves quickly out of trouble because they have the ability to clear up what was previously misunderstood by a principal or a teacher. We must insist that students explain themselves at the elementary and secondary educational level not only to solve the immediate issue but also to help them practice for what life has before them—the skills in clearing the air through proper communication.

Teachers should correct students every time they make grammatical errors in the classroom and even in the halls or on the school playground so that students, in order to avoid the nuisance of constant corrections, will employ their better speaking skills. Of course, the quality of the "teacher nuisance" factor is impacted upon by teachers being exemplars of using proper grammar. Construction workers are required to wear hard hats all the time that they are at a site where a mistake being made could result in an injury for life. Part of the paraphernalia that teachers need to wear all day is the use of proper grammar in order that a slip might not result in an intellectual injury for life.

It is important that we as educators realize that terminology peculiar to the practice of our profession is the terminology embodied in the proper use of the English language. Insurance and automobile sales people seize upon every opportunity during and after their work day to discuss with us their current offerings that will enhance our lifestyles to the point where we actually tire of sales people bothering us about their products. Educators must seize upon every opportunity to discuss with our students the offerings that we have that will enhance their lives and lifestyles to the point where they might, indeed, get tired of teachers bothering them about their potential for success. Certainly part of "bothering" is to correct their speech when it is wrong and to give endless opportunities for them to speak correctly.

The same is true for writing. Americans are generally not a writing people. There are Americans who write letters to the editor, usually when they are upset about something and, occasionally, when they are delighted with something. There are those who write papers and books, as authors, for profit and/or when there is some burning issue that we want to relate to a particular audience. But as a rule, our society is quite lazy about communicating through the written word.

We do not write often enough to our political representatives to let them know in no uncertain terms what we expect of them and how we feel about certain campaigns and issues that confront us. We do not write often enough to the Better Business Bureau when we are offended by practices that are anywhere from unprofessional to illegal. We do not write the local business manager when we are very pleased with the service given us by one of that business manager's employees. We do not write to our children's schools when we have concerns or compliments in regards to the way our children are being taught. We do not write to the sponsors of TV programs that offend us—programs which we feel should not be aired and particularly during hours when children are likely to be awake and watching.

And one of the reasons that we are not a writing public is because we did not get practice not only in the skill of writing but in the habit of writing at an early age. And it is not a practice that we take to very naturally. It is a habit that must be imposed upon us by our teachers, and we as teachers must require our students to write and to write different kinds of letters or papers with different kinds of treatment. And I think that this requirement to write must not be confined to English or language arts classes, but must include math, science, physical education, music, and art classes.

We do not like writing assignments because lengthy essays become tiresome when grading them. The tendency is that if we must grade 120 essays, we read every word of the first 32 and then begin to skim over the next 28 and then begin to run our fingers across the next 60 attempting to gain some appreciation for what the students have written through some form of physiological osmosis. But it may very well be that we could satisfy our alertness in grading and the requirement for our students to write by staggering the writing assignments and not giving the same due date on essays for 120 students from 5 or 6 different classes.

It is shameful enough that we as Americans are largely mono-lingual and must suffer the embarrassment of having to have translators almost everywhere we go outside of the U.S., but it is even worse when many of us need translators in our own native land because of our inability to articulate well or to understand those who articulate well. There are times when we compliment students for coming up with the correct solution to a problem even though it is not the solution that we had in mind, and I think that it's fine to compliment the student provided that the student can explain the process used to come up with what we consider the correct solution. We will not know that the students deliberately arrived at the same conclusions as we unless the students can articulate the process used to get the results.

Unfair at it may be, I know people who have received foot-in-the-door opportunities before others who were more qualified simply based upon their ability to speak well in interviews and in other situations that impact upon getting certain jobs. I've heard numerous stories of friends being able to avoid traffic tickets just because of their ability to converse with the policeman who is favorably impressed, not only by their attitude but also impressed with their articulation.

Many students are not intimidated on the dance floor because they dance well and they dance well because they dance often. Many young student athletes are confident because they are competent on the playing field and the playing field is where they are comfortable. In fact, in some cases, they are giants on the playing field. They define themselves by what they do on the playing field and the definition is accurate because they get so much practice at what they do on the playing field. School must be the dance floor of academia and the playing field of articulation. It must be where students do a lot of reciting and a lot of writing in an arena where they will be corrected in order that they become so competent that they grow confident and comfortable using language, both orally and on paper.

Show me someone who is outstanding in any field and I will show you someone who works at whatever that field represents constantly and intently. In our efforts to make school enjoyable as well as productive for young people we might neglect to do some things that may be a bother to them. But inasmuch as we are preparing them for the greater part of their lives, if, indeed, we live to be seventy-plus years and we only attend school for 16 years and for some, 16 to 20 years, the greater part of our lives will be spent after we leave school. If it is necessary to make our students a little bit uncomfortable for a small part of their lives in order that they can be far more comfortable the greater part of their lives, then we are charged with the responsibility to do exactly that.

When students get tired of the requirement to write and recite properly, we can indicate to them that we will lighten up our demands when they tighten up their skills. The more proficient they become, the less likely we are to bother them about doing more writing and reciting.

SELF AND COMMUNITY

Lesson 36
Know Your Competition

Considering that there are a number of entities competing with each other for our children's minds, it is imperative that those of us in education whose job it is to work with shape, and mold the minds of our children be very familiar with those competing elements. It is important for us to recognize that while we are generally idealistic in our approach toward preparing young people for the future, that there are those who are devious. There are those who are criminal. There are those, indeed, who would use the manipulation of children's minds, in order to use the bodies and the purses of children.

When we talk about competition, we need to recognize that the competition for our children's minds is formidable. Sometimes it is disgraceful, but unfortunately, far too often, it is successful. When I talk about the disgraceful competition, I'm talking about those who would engage children in devious and/or criminal activity. All too often we hear about child pornography, sexual abuse, incest, children who are drug-runners, and far too often, drug-abusers, and in recognizing that there are so many people who are on the deviant end of the human scale, we must be aware and we must fortify ourselves with skills that would help us to defeat such enemies in this competition for our children's minds.

But when I talk about being familiar with and interacting in the community and understanding who our competitors are, I am not talking about the obvious, devious competition. When I talk about the competition that deals with criminal activity and/or sexual abuse, it is not difficult to get a listening ear and to have any number of people join in the struggle to insure that no child is molested and no child is misused in criminal activity. Even the molesters and the criminals join such efforts in order to improve upon their image. They understand that most people in this society—I would suspect most people in the world—do not approve of misusing children, and consequently they will hide their misdeeds behind an image and persona of being upright citizens. If there is a march against criminal activity, particularly as it pertains to children, if there are petitions to be signed as it pertains to pornographic activities with children, many of the people who might, indeed, be devious would be among the first to sign the petition and join the march, because the image that they would like to project would be one that is in keeping with at least their perceptions of what is acceptable in our society.

The competition that I am talking about, however, is competition that is considered to be certainly legal, but even popular—the competition of today's music, of movies our children attend, of endless hours of television that does many things in the guise of entertainment, of peer pressure within the community, of the socioeconomic level of the various communities: the obvious competition of a low socioeconomic level that has children attempting to matriculate without the resources that they need and the more subtle competition of high socioeconomic levels within communities where it is taken for granted that children that have everything that they need will be good students. The competition that I'm talking about is whatever causes our children to focus on issues and/or activities that are the opposite of, or significantly different from, what they ought to be learning in school.

It is important to know what competition exists on the larger scale that is probably experienced in most every community—television, movies, peer pressure, and the like—and that it is important for us to know what competition exists within the particular community where we teach, and, in cases where children are bused from different areas, within the different communities from which our students come. As I explained in the 5-Ex Cycle, I suggested that it is important for teachers to learn as much as they can about the positive experiences that impact upon the lives of our children even before we meet them; suggesting, indeed, that every child has some body of experiences before coming to school that reflects positively on that child's sub-culture within the milieu of the large society.

As we investigate, we must also take into consideration and learn as much as we can about the negative experiences of our children prior to our meeting them. And if some of the experiences are considered to be positive but are not helpful in terms of children doing well in school, they are without a doubt things with which we ought to be familiar. This familiarity will not come from having young people fill out a survey. The familiarity will not come from intuition. The familiarity will not come from simply polling other teachers or asking the parents of children to assist us. The familiarity comes when we allow ourselves, indeed, require ourselves, to become a part of our students' experiences—when we decide to take a bus ride in the community where we teach or bus rides in the several communities from which our students come. It is a good idea for us to know where our children shop for their clothing. It is a good idea to survey the communities' (without jeopardizing our actual physical safety) recreational facilities—the places where our children or our students go—parties, skating rinks, parks, swimming pools, vacant lots, and fast food facilities.

We should take note of the amount of traffic at particular locations, in particular areas within the communities from which our students come, and the kind of traffic. For instance, do our students congregate in the parking lots of fast food facilities to socialize, to race vehicles, to show off their cycling skills, to flirt with one another? Does the frequency of traffic suggest that there might be some illicit activities? Is the kind of traffic that frequents a certain area the kind of traffic that you would not mind your own son or daughter being a part of? Inasmuch as we should survey the malls where our young people shop, we should also be aware of the library where they study. We should take note of the fact that there is less traffic in the area of the library than there is in the area of the skating rink.

It is important for us to look at the competition as it pertains to not only where our young people shop, but the items they purchase. Are there items that are designed to go against the grain in our school buildings? If you consider that there are young people who, for instance, purchase beepers recognizing that at one point those who were seen in schools with beepers were identified with drug trafficking, and that, then, became a popular symbol because it meant that you were daring, you were brave, you would do something that was risque in front of authority figures. Are there clothes that are designed to emphasize the sexuality of our young girls and our young men and, therefore, certain to be considered inappropriate at schools? We must ask ourselves whether or not the merchants have a responsibility to assist us in our attempt to help young people understand those things that are socially redeeming, and in understanding that responsibility, then making available to young people a preponderance of that which promotes positiveness and wholesomeness and de-emphasizes sexual clothing, beepers, drug paraphernalia, and the like.

It is important that we understand that the climate in which young people grow has a great deal to do with their self-perception. Their self-perception is not shaped in school. It is either enhanced because it is a positive self-perception or, hopefully, changed if it is a negative self-perception, but, certainly, those perceptions come from the homes in which the students live, the community in which the students live, and/or the interactions between students and their peers and the adults whom the young people emulate.

If we are going to know our competition, then we need to take a good look at that which young people encounter most frequently. One of the things that makes an impression upon all of us is repetition. There are those in marketing and advertising who suggest that a particular commercial must be seen and heard 7 times before people understand what it is that is being sold and what message is being delivered, and thus repetition is important to those who are in marketing. Well, lifestyles are being marketed as well as products, and if young people have before them the repetition of negative, apathetic, mediocre, or anti-social lifestyles, then what they will emulate, what they will take in, what they will see not only 7 times but 70 x 7 times, would be things that make negative impressions. But also because the impression is so repetitive, therefore, so dynamic, you can see how young people become that which they experience most.

If there are parents in the home who repeat in the presence of the children positive things about the schools our children attend, it is likely that young people will come to school with a positive perception of who we are and what we do. If there are merchants who continue in their back-to-school campaigns and their back-to-school sales to have positive slogans and positive campaigns that would include, for instance, A and B sales; that is, children who achieve 'A's and 'B's in school, then get discounts on clothing and recreational materials, then perhaps that would identify the merchants with something positive where the schools are concerned. If the recreational leaders in the Boys' and Girls' clubs, the YMCA, and local community and recreational centers on an on-going basis discuss the need for young people to do well in school, to behave in school in order to be eligible to participate in certain activities, perhaps our young people could see the entire community being involved with the positiveness of their educational institutions.

Unfortunately, one of our competitors is the negative image that many schools get. And by definition, image is something that is created in the eye of the beholder and not only of the beholder, but the communicator. If our news media make it a point to discuss more negative things about schools than positive things, then an image is created that suggests that our schools are negative. If parents, instead of repeating positive things about the schools their children attend on an on-going basis, make statements like "Those people don't know what they're doing", "As soon as I get a chance, I'm going take my child out of that school", "I visited that school and those teachers didn't know as much as I know,"—and such statements as that in the presence of their children, then the perception that the children get will be that school has no worth, has no value, and therefore, they do not have to pay attention in school because their inattentiveness is being validated by the statements their parents and other adults—authority figures in the community—make. If that is also reenforced by peers who may not be doing so well and, recognizing that misery loves company, continue to encourage our students to pay little attention to school, indeed, not even to attend school on a regular basis, then that negative image continues to grow within the minds of young people who might otherwise be attracted to what goes on in school. Consequently, the perception that schools have little to offer and the image that is projected that schools are negative at worst and of little value at best permeates not only the individual student but the society of students who would rather be associated with something that is popular than be associated with something that is considered to be a non-entity.

Our competition is formidable not because our competition is right but because it is commonly accepted. In the U.S., and perhaps in other societies as well, it is suggested that some terminology becomes acceptable terminology due to common usage.

If we repeat things enough in our society, then whether those things are right or wrong, they become fact based upon the repetition. If we say often enough that there is no chance for America's schools to be as great as schools in other developed nations around the world, then the repetition of that observation makes that observation in the minds of some a fact. It is competitive as far as we are concerned because part of what we must do in order to assist young people in buying into what we have to offer, is to project an air of optimism, an air of "Yes, we can," and, therefore, we are going against the grain.

When we are aware of the competition, we can engage the competition. Case in point: If young people were to find their way to recreational centers instead of going to school, we could go to those who run the recreational centers and request their cooperation in seeing to it that young people are not rewarded for misbehaving or being truant. Youngsters could not seek refuge in recreation in the Boys' and Girls' club during school hours because the officials and the recreational directors of a club would know that those youngsters belonged in school. If they sought refuge in a YMCA, that particular recreational facility would know that young people needed to be in school and would not allow them to come and play on the basketball court or direct the pre-school youngsters in some activity. The legitimate community recreational centers would not represent competition in this regard because they would not allow the youngsters to manipulate them in that direction.

But suppose there were a local pool. Suppose there was just a vacant lot basketball court. Suppose there were older adults who decided that if young people were going to be out of school, they might as well be engaged in something productive, and so they give them light tasks to do and paid them for those light tasks. In this case, I'm not even talking about illicit or illegal activities which is another competitor. I'm talking about people who honestly believe that they are helping the situation by engaging the youngsters in something positive "if they're going to be out of school anyway." If we were aware of who those people were and what those activities were, then we could go to them and ask their assistance in keeping youngsters in school by making sure that youngsters have no where to go when they're out of school.

I recognize that this is old-fashioned, but I hope not naive. I can remember a time when community schools received the cooperation of people in the community because they knew the youngsters, knew when they were supposed to be in school, and would not only refuse to allow the youngsters to hang around where they were, but in most instances would take the youngsters up to school themselves. There are too many abandoned houses and apartment buildings, too many opportunities for escape for young people, too many economic opportunities in the illegal drug trade rewarding their behavior somewhere other than in the school building.

If we decided as a body in a particular school and district, to actually go collectively to merchants inquiring of them about the merchandise that they sell and informing them of those things that students wear to school and bring to school that would be helpful rather than hindering, we might be able to get merchants on our side. And I believe that our school districts could write up proposals for our merchants in such a way that the merchants could actually see a profit in cooperating with the schools in what they sell and they way that they sell it.

In fact, while I am, indeed, discussing the kind of competition that is more subtle than the overt, illegal competition that openly defies authority and scoffs at what we attempt to do in schools, I honestly believe that properly, soberly engaged, there are some drug traffickers and gang leaders who would cooperate with school authorities if they could be confronted with the right platform in the appropriate arena. Again, I know that I'm talking about old-fashioned ideas but the fact of the matter is, it is time to reclaim some of the old-fashioned ideas. If those people who have the greatest influence on our young could be engaged in a serious conversation that was not confrontational but indicates that whatever the plight of the adults in the community, whether it be unfortunate, illegal, successful, we all have a responsibility to assist the children in developing lifestyle options. In some cases our illegal, defiant competitors will tell us where to go and how to get there, but in other cases, they may cooperate as no one ever reached out to them in this way before.

What we tend to do as competitors is write each other off. As an educator who does not drink and does not smoke and does not deal in drugs and who, indeed, abhors the idea of someone putting that stuff on children, I am not enthralled with the idea of conversing with those who exploit our children. As drug traffickers, gang-bangers, criminals, and people who want to get over, those involved probably have no enthusiasm whatsoever about talking with me just to give me an opportunity to put them down and tell them why they are no good. If this is the way we feel about each other, then battle lines having been drawn, we will fight against each other with our children in the middle suffering on both ends because they will not do well in school with that kind of competition outside of school and they will experience self-destruction outside of school because we have not been able to give them the tools for survival in the mean streets of the inner-city and suburbia and rural U.S. It may be time not only to know the competition but to confront the competition or, better, to engage the competition.

One of the attitudes that gives impetus to our competition is the attitude that is inappropriate for us to engage even in an informal way those who are competing with us for our children's minds. Unfortunately, what that does is suggest to children that we are not wise enough to discern who our competitors are or courageous enough to engage our competitors in their behalf. And I think that when the future is at stake and our children are so valuable, the very least we can do is explore ways to teach those who are keeping us from teaching our children at least two lessons. One, that we will be serious, even relentless, in reclaiming our children and giving them the tools to succeed. And the second lesson is that bright, healthy, optimistic students represent a productive future for all of us. They are as important to those who seem bent on destroying their chances and limiting their options as they are to those of us who are intent on seeing that they know how to think independently, have exposure to the greatest possible number of positive options, and have the skills to exercise those options most consistent with their aspirations.

For those who complain about the society having caused them to be disenfranchised and, therefore, in their bitterness have determined that they will turn young people away from school, they need to be helped to realize that their bitterness is caused by conditions that cannot be overcome by making their children bitter as well, or seeing that their children are just as disenfranchised as they. The only way that they can insure that their children's plight will not be the same and even that their own plight might be changed in their lifetime is to assist in efforts to teach our children about the injustices in life, and to give them the tools, intellectual as well as psychological and emotional, to make the necessary changes. To cause young people to buy into the deficit mode of thinking and acting is to insure that such deficits will continue to occur and to exist.

It does not make sense, on one hand, for those who consider themselves to be so far outside of the mainstream that they can justify illegal behavior to suggest on the other hand that their bitterness is based upon their desire to participate fully in a society that will not let them do so. As educators we need to teach that many of their observations are accurate and, indeed, there are those who are outside of the mainstream. We need to teach also that their frustration and yet their immense energy ought to be a part of changing our society, and that can only be done with clear minds and healthy bodies. In other words, we need to join forces in many cases with what is now considered to be the competition.

Because certain people do bad things, it is not necessarily a certainty that they are bad people. Those who work against us cannot state a clear case for what's wrong with schools if they never bother to come and see what it is that we are attempting to teach. It may be that what we are attempting with their children will help them a great deal more than it will hurt them. By the same token, we cannot effectively address that which works against us if we do not take the time to get to know those who work against us.

Among our greatest competitors is community apathy. One of the things that it is important for us to realize is that everyone does not share our enthusiasm and passion for helping young people learn. If we assume that simply stating a clear case will convince those who seem to be working against us, we need to take another look at that assumption. There are some people who are not convinced not because they have difficulty understanding, but simply because even understanding, they don't care. We must be prepared to do all we can to convince all whom we can to join us in an actual struggle to assist our students in preparing for a bright future. But after we've done all we can, we must also prepare for moving on without those who are not at all willing. Apathy has no particular socioeconomic level, no particular ethnicity, no particular geographic location. It can be found among all strata of society, unfortunately, including many of the parents of our students. On the other hand, concern and willingness to help have no particular ethnicity, socioeconomic, or geographic location either, and sometimes those most willing are among those whom we originally might have thought would be less enthusiastic about joining us in our efforts. The only way to accurately determine who's who and what's what as it pertains to competition versus allies, is to give the benefit of the doubt to the entire community surrounding the school.

Some students believe that the teacher's perception of where those students live is that the community is not an inviting place to visit. Therefore, the teacher's relationship with the student is immediately enhanced when the student feels that the teacher does not have a negative perception of were the student lives. One of the reasons that the students behavior improves when the teacher visits the home is because the unspoken message that is sent to the student is "If, indeed, something should go wrong in school, I now have direct access to the home, to your parents, to where you live, so you don't have refuge in a place away from the school because I now have access to that." It doesn't necessarily have to state itself in such negative terms, but it is a spin-off message that is sent to the students.

Needless to say, a great deal of benefit is derived from the trip to the student's home because that means getting into the community, seeing what the surroundings are like, seeing what kinds of activities go on, having an opportunity to speak to other young people who will certainly ask you where you're going and when they find out that you're going to one of the other students' homes, they realize that you are serious about coming to their homes and that they might be next and if not next, you will be visiting them very soon. The other thing is, you can begin to feel a part of each child's community.

When there is a situation where it is difficult to visit students or visit all of the students based upon their being bused from remote parts of the city, and in some cases suburbs to inner-city and inner-city to suburbs, at least the visits that you can make can help you develop a sense of community once returning to the school. It is important to have that sense of belonging, of team camaraderie, and it only enhances that sense of community when we seize upon every opportunity to see students outside of the regular activity and climate of the classroom. It is good when we attend extra-curricular activities so that we can see what the students do after school, and they feel good about our taking that extra time, and certainly visiting the homes is one of the most effective ways to get that feeling of community.

Certainly if a teacher is going to feel comfortable in having opportunities where students can visit the teacher at home, one of the ways to break the ice is for the teacher to initiate this home visit and it will help to establish the kind of relationship where both the student and teacher feel comfortable with a visit to the teacher's home.

One of the good things about establishing this new relationship is that once the formal visit has taken place, there are times when a longer, less formal, more cordial visit can take place.

In the cases where it is either not possible or not practical to visit students in their homes, and it is not possible or practical to visit a group of parents in a community center within a particular community, I would suggest that early in the school year that parents be invited to the school for an orientation conference in that part of the school building that is least threatening and most comfortable. I would suggest that this informal school visit be the last of the three choices—home, community center, then school—because it is important that on this particular visit that the parent feel good about the visit because the purpose of it is to establish rapport. At any rate, getting the opportunity to see the parents and students as people, and for them to get the opportunity to see the teacher as a person is not only a good idea but I would think that it is an imperative as we attempt to welcome the 21st century with modern approaches toward the student/parent/teacher relationship, and to give our students the best that we have as their instructional leaders.

I would also suggest that teachers who practice home visits share their discovery with their colleagues and encourage others to make home visits as well. It if becomes one of the things that teachers do in this school, it will be easier to arrange visits where two or three are going into the same community at the same time. Parents' receptivity will probably be at a higher level because they anticipate that this is going to occur, and others will receive the same kinds of benefits as the one who initiated the home visits project. I am in agreement with Jim Comer who speaks of the need for schools to be a community and I believe that it is important that those in the schools get into the several communities from which their students come in order to make it even more possible for the schools to be an extension of those several communities and, indeed, to become a community in and of itself.

Over time we discover who will be our greatest assets when we give opportunities for parents and others to come to the school as volunteers, tutors, teachers aides, members of school advisory committees and parent-teacher associations. We can make a determination as to who are our allies by the quality of that participation. If we make appeals to the community to join in campaigns to have students attend school regularly, we can make some determinations based upon those who joined the campaign, those who indicate that they would have liked to join but were not able to do so, those who do not join, and those who actively work against it. When we make classes available within the community, at community centers, churches, mosques, synagogues and other places of worship, in buildings where organizations meet, and other available locations in which we actually teach the ramifications of excellence in education and some people attend those classes and some people refuse to attend those classes and some people hamper the efforts for us to even give the classes, we can begin to know who our competitors are and who our allies are.

When we develop dress and acceptable behavior codes and observe those of influence in the community who adopt and adhere to those codes and also observe those who actively work against embracing those codes, we get some idea of who our competitors are. When we make appeals to media asking that they assist us in projecting certain images and we find that there are those who because what we project is not sensational enough, is not commercially appealing enough to become engaged and others who not only enthusiastically accept our proposals for media involvement but take the lead in assisting us in knowing how better to use media in order to get our message across, we get some idea of who our allies are versus those who represent our competition.

When we look at young people and the peer pressure that has a great deal of impact and encourage, even give, skills to young people to project positive rather than negative peer pressure and observe those of influence who insist upon projecting negative peer pressure, we can get a very clear idea as to who is competing with us rather than working with us. And as we make these observations, it will also give us some insights as to what we need to do to enhance our ability to resist the competition. We would get some ideas as to whether or not we need to shore up our communicative skills, whether or not we need to be better exemplars of what proper dress ought to look like, whether or not we need to enhance our skills in terms of becoming a part of the community where our schools sit, and whether or not we need to enhance our skills in debating the issues concerning the relevance of education to the lifestyles of our young people.

And as we discover what we need to do, we need to act on it. If we need to engage the business community to help us become astute as to how we can make an impact on the commercial establishments around our school, then we need to let them teach us. If we need to develop skills in gaining entry into the anti-social community that is a part of the larger community in order to gain an ear with some who want to state their case to us just like we want to state our case to them, then, indeed, let us shore up those skills by talking to colleagues and others who are more "street-smart" than we.

We have a great deal of competition within the communities where we teach; we have a need to know who and what that competition is; and we need to develop skills in engaging, confronting, and/or overcoming that competition.

SELF AND COMMUNITY

Lesson 37
Plan and Take "Feel Trips"

When I was in elementary school and even, on occasion, in high school, one of the days I looked forward to with great anticipation was the day on which our class would take a field trip. On this particular day we could get away from the regular classroom work. We could pack a brown bag lunch. We would take a bus to some sight that was determined by the teacher that would either enhance what we were learning or reward us because we had done well in terms of what we were learning and/or attendance or behavior.

The field trips that we took were great not only because it got us out of the regular classroom atmosphere but also because it gave us an opportunity to see the teacher a different way—to see a more human and sometimes humorous side of the teacher. It gave an opportunity for informal conversation with our classmates. It was pretty much a fun day all around. Our teachers also designed those field trips to insure that something would be brought back to the class that enhanced whatever it was that we were studying at the time. Even in cases where we were taken on picnics or to restaurants, we were to come back and talk about some of the social graces that must be emphasized in social settings.

I am suggesting that we remember the significance of those field trips in terms of what we learned as well as how we felt. The reason I used the term "feel trip" rather than field trip is I think that in the modern world where young people experience not only immediate gratification but any number of forms of entertainment media, it is important that the experiences that they have be experiences that they can relate to in an immediate and impactful way.

I mentioned earlier that I have met teachers who would seize upon any opportunity to take a field trip simply based upon the fact that a colleague was going on a field trip. And I am suggesting that unless the trip has some real relevance to what's going on in the classroom, the field trip is not advisable. Students usually know the difference between a purposeful activity and a whimsical activity. Not only that, students will grow accustomed to the kind of teaching style we present to them, and if our teaching style is to seize upon opportunities to relax or to take a break rather than seize upon every opportunity to teach a lesson, young people will become accustomed to that style and their expectations will be lowered. Consequently, they will not take us seriously as people and will not take what we are attempting to teach seriously.

As it relates to the community, the kinds of "feel trips" I am recommending are the kinds of field trips that would see us taking a bus ride or a subway ride, in some cases, a walk through certain parts of the community. Here the recommendation is that we take a good look at whether or not such a walking trip or a bus-riding trip would serve as an embarrassment to a student who might think that we're looking upon his particular neighborhood in a disrespectful or curious kind of way. Perhaps if we went into enough neighborhoods within the community, no students would see that as a personal affront because we are visiting all segments of a community in order to know the community better.

Another "feel trip" would be to plan for and engage in a police ride-along. This would give the teacher and the students an opportunity to see what kinds of things law enforcement confront on a regular basis, and such an arrangement can be made with local authorities and they will determine for the particular community whether or not there is an age requirement and what kinds of restrictions would be involved. Another advantage of such a "feel trip" would be to allow law enforcers to get to know students and teachers, and how they feel about the environment in which they live.

A "feel trip" is a trip to the local library where students may not leave the library without a library card. A "feel trip" for a senior student if they have reached the age of 18 is to go to a local registrar with the idea being that every student reaching the age of 18 then registers to be a voter. A trip to a plant would be considered a "feel trip" if that plant happens to be the place that has formed a partnership with one's school and has, for instance, determined that students who are not pursuing post-secondary degrees might be their first choices for entry-level positions or training positions at that plant, and the idea of the trip is to introduce them not only to what their partners do but also to introduce the young people to their first major full-time job opportunity.

One of the field trips that students seldom, if ever, take is a "feel trip" through their own school. A teacher might make a wish list of what the students feel the building ought to look like. A teacher might ask students whether or not they have a sense of pride in the washrooms and if their answer cannot be "Yes", engaging students in a conversation as to what can be done to make sure that washrooms are clean and deodorized and usable. When students get to certain corners of the building that are remote corners that appear not to be safe, ask what kinds of things might be done to brighten up those dark, remote corners and to make them as comfortable an environment as the rest of the school through use so that there is more traffic making it less remote.

When students begin to look at the school grounds and become engaged in conversations about the degree to which the school is a part of the surrounding community, perhaps they can make some determinations as to whether or not there are ways to enhance the relationship of the school to the community rather than the school being an island unto itself within a community that does not regard it as a part of the rest of those who reside therein. When students can take a look at such facilities as the cafeteria, gymnasium, and the auditorium and determine that those are places where large numbers of students gather and the degree to which those places are functional and kept clean and reflect the best that is in the students is more up to the students than anyone else in the school and when the students can declare some degree of ownership in the school and pride in themselves, perhaps the gymnasium, auditorium, and the cafeteria can be places to which they will be proud to bring their friends and parents and other visitors.

As students look into different classrooms while classes are in session without the teachers and the students knowing that another class from the very same school is observing, perhaps the students can get a very good look at what they look like when they are in their own classroom, and they ought to regard it either with a great deal of pride or with at least some degree of shame. And seeing what they look like might prompt them to look better when they go back to the classroom from which they have taken this particular field trip.

I think it's a good idea for the students to understand clearly what the responsibilities of the principal are, and to know clearly who the principal is, to know the responsibilities of the principal's assistants and who they are, to understand the job description of a teacher, understanding that the idea behind students and teacher interacting is not to develop an adversarial relationship but, indeed, to work together to enhance the overall climate and effectiveness of the school.

Other "feel trips" might include even going to a residence having particular students host the visit; and this, of course, would be totally voluntary. Now it might be called a field trip, but it would be a casual visit.

Similarly, it would not be a bad idea for the teacher to invite students to the home—again, so that students get to know a little more about the teacher. And for all kinds of good social reasons these particular kinds of home visit "feel trips" might take place somewhere near the end of the school year after proper rapport has been established between teacher and students, but in the case of the students it might involve more than just one home. And in the case of the teacher, it might even involve more than just one visit, obviously depending upon how the first visit goes.

"Feel trips" would be trips where students would go to a local computer center and get an opportunity to work with the computers. It would be where students might go to a local health center and prepare when they get there to actually work out. "Feel trips" are trips when the experience of the trip is in-depth rather than just visiting a site and looking at the site.

Because of the need for teachers to gain a greater understanding of the community in which they teach, it would be a good idea for one or more of the field trips during a particular year to be planned by the students who are residents of that community so that if teachers wanted to understand better how certain recreational facilities function or how young people function within their own comfortable domain, it could be facilitated through the active planning of the residents who happen to be students in a particular class. This would cause the young people to get a great deal more out of it because they would be involved in the planning as well as taking an active role in serving as "tour guides". However, they might plan it, the outcomes would certainly be positive in terms of learning for the teacher and participation for the students.

A "feel trip" might involve a class rehearsing an original song or poem or work that the entire class would do and taking it to a local studio to record and make that a part of their year's experience. The same would be true of going into a local cable television studio and taping a skit and making that a part of their video yearbook or some other appropriate record. A "feel trip" might be to take a trip to a local hospital, not only to understand the job descriptions and the duties of the different people who make up the medical profession but also to gain greater appreciation for the need to keep our bodies in the best of health. Sometimes one of the greatest ways to assist people, for instance in never smoking, is to let them see graphic slide presentations of what happens to the lungs when people smoke over a period of time. If you look at trauma units and find out that the street life is, indeed, not so glamorous when you find out what happens when people have to come into the emergency room. Here, again, in terms of an age requirement, certain young people would not be exposed to all that goes on, for instance in surgery or in an emergency room or the lung cross-section that would be shown on slides, but where appropriate, if the age is right, it is a good idea to expose young people who might be prevented from adopting a lifestyle of poor health rather than waiting until later to try to get adults to change their lifestyles of poor health.

In suggesting that field trips ought be to "feel trips" that have relevance to what is going on in the classroom does not in any way suggest that field trips cannot be fun. There can be a great deal of fun in academic pursuits when planned right. Inasmuch as these are trips being planned in an educational institution, it ought to be quite clear that the outcome ought to have educational value, and the more geographic, the more personal the trip can be for the students in a given classroom, the more the students will get out of that particular trip. When students can participate in the planning, chances are they will get more out of it. If it turns out that it's the kind of trip that needs planning from the instructor, the instructor ought to make sure that part of that planning includes students having an experience that would cause them to learn based upon the experience and cause them to be able to relate those experiences to what's going on in the classroom and subsequently, life.

SELF AND COMMUNITY

Lesson 38
Visit Students' Homes

Visiting students' homes often prevents many discipline problems that might otherwise arise because when students are visited at home, parents often feel closer to the teacher and, consequently, adamant about their students behaving "in that teacher's" classroom. I am not suggesting that is fair or proper on the part of the parents. What I am suggesting is that being human, we tend to be more compassionate toward people whom we know than toward people we don't know. Obviously every parent ought to send their children to school in a mind-set toward cooperating with every teacher. The fact is, that does not happen. The fact is also that parents and teachers who know each other are more cooperative than parents and teachers who do not know each other. One of the simple ways to bridge the gap is to simply arrange for a home visit.

Now in terms of the kinds of home visits I am discussing here, I am suggesting that the visit be early in the school year, be congenial in nature, and not as a result of a child doing something wrong. Be brief and be informational. The reason I suggest that it be a congenial visit is because the receptivity on the part of the parents is a lot greater when a teacher informs them that they would like to come over to discuss what is expected of the child and to ask what is expected of the teachers than if the teacher says, "I need to come and see you because your child is disrupting the class." The reason that I suggest that the visit be brief is because (1) many people do not have a lot of time to discuss informational kinds of things, and (2) the likelihood that a teacher will be welcomed back into the home may, indeed, be enhanced by teachers realizing that they should not stay too long on the first visit.

The parent needs to understand that there is a purpose for this visit. The information that needs to be shared, for instance, would be the mission of the school, the school rules, the kinds of supplies that the student needs to bring to school on a daily basis, what is expected of the parents in case of emergency, and how the parent can get in touch with the teacher in case the parents need to do that.

It would also be informational from the standpoint of the teacher when the teacher says, "Now you know what I expect of your child. I'd be interested in finding out from you what you expect of me as your child's teacher." After exchanging those bits of information, the visit really, from the standpoint of a formal visit, should be over. It should not take more than about 15 minutes. Now, in some cases, parents will engage the teacher in more informal conversation which might be all right depending upon the teacher's visit schedule, because it is important to be on time to the next home. But certainly, that informal conversation should come after the information has been shared.

To prepare for home visits, I would begin the school year by writing a letter to parents that reads something like this: "Dear Parent: Your son/daughter is a student in Room 214. As the teacher in Room 214, I am interested in letting you know what I expect of your child. I am also interested in finding out from you what you expect of me as your child's teacher. In that regard, I am requesting that you allow me to visit you at your home at your convenience after 4:00 p.m. on weekdays, anytime on Saturday, and anytime after 2:00 p.m. on Sunday. The visit will take approximately 15 minutes and I am very interested in our meeting face to face. If this meets with your approval, please indicate three choices, with the first choice being first listed, of days and times when I might be allowed to come to your home."

This letter is sent home to the parent by the students. If parents were not heard from within two weeks, a similar letter would be mailed to the home. And what I found out was that the rate of cooperation was about 85-90%. Parents were not only willing to have me visit their homes, but they were delighted to have the teacher actually come to them with good news rather than bad news. I can say that in the cases where parents allowed me to visit their homes, especially when I visited more than once, the incidents involving discipline where their children were concerned were almost eliminated.

The rapport established with a simple visit is immeasurable. More often than not parents and students feel that it is a privilege to have the teacher come to their home. The teacher benefits immediately because seeing how the child functions in the environment of the home gives great insight into why a child functions the way they do in a classroom. In some instances where I shared with colleagues what I learned in my home visits, and especially when I shared with colleagues who had also visited homes, the conclusion drawn was that it is admirable that students make it to school under the conditions of the home. So where we previously have criticized children for their behavior, we are now applauding them because of their ability to cope with what we discovered in the home. Those were rare occasions. The great majority of the time, the homes visited were well-kept, positive, and socially inviting environments, and, therefore, once getting into the home, the teacher could say to the child that there is no excuse for not excelling based upon the concern that their parents have shown and based upon the kind of home from which they come.

In many instances you will find that children are quite well-behaved in front of their parents. When you see that to be the case, then that gives you a clue as to how to help the child behave well in school. If they behave well in front of their parents, there's a reason for that and you know that you can go to the parent when there is need to check the child's behavior. In cases where it would appear that children seem to have a free rein at home, it gives a clue as to the need to tighten up when they come to the classroom because they are in an environment where nobody seems to be doing that at home.

Not only is it a good idea from the standpoint of gaining insight and establishing rapport, but beyond rapport, there can be established an actual friendship. Friends go to each other's homes. Parents feel closer and yet not familiar because assuming a professional air is something the teacher can do even in the informal atmosphere of a child's home. Now, I recognize that in some cases it is impractical for teachers to visit the homes of children. In this day of busing to achieve desegregation sometimes the children live so far away from the local school and in so many different directions that it becomes difficult to make two and three visits an evening which I was able to do because I taught in neighborhood schools. It is also, in some cases, not just a matter of practicality but a matter of personal safety. I admit that being a man and being familiar with the area where I visited homes, I had some advantage over a female who might not be familiar with the surroundings into which she is invited. I think that it would make sense to take note of where one might be going, and in cases where there might be some reasons for reluctance or fear, it would be a good idea to travel in pairs.

Now in some urban areas and, I am sure, in some suburban areas as well, and in some rural areas it is absolutely prohibitive to go into the community. Where we are teaching youngsters who live in a climate of criminal behavior, gang drive-by shootings, in communities where one's physical safety is certainly at jeopardy, to achieve the personal kind of visit might mean visiting more than one parent at a time at a local community center or gathering place within the community. It does not give the same feeling nor promote the same degree of comfort as going into one's home, but it still gives a feel for the community and allows for a less formal exchange than in the school classroom.

Establishing this "friendly" relationship by visiting parents at home also helps parents feel comfortable—even volunteering—in the classroom.

SELF AND COMMUNITY

Lesson 39
Become Involved in the Community
Where You Teach

Lesson 39 is a logical extension of Lesson 38. It suggests that not only should we visit the homes of students but as we survey the communities from which our students come, we should also survey the possibilities for becoming directly involved in what's going on, and then after exploring those possibilities, become involved. In order to explain fully Lesson 39 I need to address some of my personal philosophy as it pertains to the relationship between the school and the community.

I am a proponent of neighborhood schools. As a matter of fact, I may be the foremost proponent of neighborhood schools. I believe that they are good for a number of reasons: (1) it provides an opportunity for children to matriculate in an environment that is perceived to be a less hostile environment; (2) I think that the close proximity of the school to the parents of children who attend the school affords easy access and results in more parent participation; and (3) neighborhood schooling is more cost effective than requiring students to go outside of their communities in order to achieve something that we have referred to as desegregation for 36 years.

Personally, I believe that America has put the onus on children to do what the larger society refuses to do, and that is to desegregate; even, eventually, integrate. I think that the civil rights emphasis should have been placed on open housing. If people could live without fear, and without social recriminations anywhere that they want to live, then children could attend the local schools that reflect the "quality" of the local communities. The fact of the matter is, in the U.S. even as we approach the 21st century, people cannot live anywhere they want to live. There are social, economic, racial, and ethnic barriers; and there is outright hostility projected and practiced to see that those barriers continue to exist. But in 1954 a Supreme Court decision ruled that it is illegal for schools to remain segregated. So for 36 years, now, we've been attempting to overcome the social and educational barriers by desegregating schools.

I am not at all convinced that on any significant scale desegregation has resulted in the benefits we anticipated when the court case was decided. Many felt that children having the experience of going to school with children of other communities and other races would result in better human understanding across racial lines and a more peaceful society in which to live. It is now the 1990s and we are experiencing what appears to be a higher degree of racism, a resurgence of race-oriented organizations, a greater degree of violence and domestic violence than ever in our history; and a significant degree of deterioration in neighborhoods where it appears that the children of the neighborhoods, and the adults who live therein, do not feel a sense of belonging or camaraderie.

Personally, I think that schools can and should play a significant role in the development and sustenance of a community based upon being the neighborhood anchor, the place where traditions are born and kept, the place where role models within the actual community are reachable, touchable, and accessible. To continue in the cross-city and city to suburb busing patterns that take young people out of their own communities for a significant part of their day, and continue to limit the access of parents, is to perpetuate a failing desegregation effort, and to keep our schools from being the positive force in the communities they ostensibly serve.

I recall with fondness and a deep sense of pride the neighborhood school I attended when I grew up in Ida B. Wells housing projects in Chicago, Illinois and attended Wendell Phillips Elementary School. My parents knew just about every teacher at the school, and some of my friends' parents had gone to school under the same teachers who were now teaching us. The activities in the community were focused around the high school and Madden Park which is the park where Phillips' track and football teams practiced. Auxiliary staff at the schools often came from the recreational centers surrounding the school. What I'm getting at is the fact that people knew each other. Not only did we know each other but we were all involved in activities whose success depended upon our assisting one another. If the activities were recreational or athletic, our community would point with pride at the number of medals and trophies won by Madden Park or Wendell Phillips. When there were local rivalries, even the rivals wished each other well when not playing against each other.

The community merchants knew where the young people attended school and, therefore, could find parttime workers by going to the school. When local business owners recruited from, and made contributions to, the school, they were supporting the very people who supported them. When students achieved in the community—though not in the school—teachers considered it, and made it, a school achievement. If a young person sang a solo or made a speech in church, it was noted by teachers in school the next day. The young person achieving meritoriously in park district events was considered a credit to the local school. Social and recreational centers in need of space to conduct awards programs often called upon the school in the neighborhood. Because the school was a part of the community and the community felt like a part of the school, the school building was often opened for athletic and social events at night without fear of vandalism or violence. Those kinds of fears came about in the 1960s and 1970s, perhaps coincidentally after we determined that attending schools outside of the neighborhood (to achieve desegregation) was better—or more important—than improving neighborhood schools. This has always bothered me because I believe that when you suggest to students that attending a school outside of one's neighborhood will serve one better, the underlying message is that the school(s) where you live are inferior—thus, your neighborhood is inferior—thus, you are inferior. The reason there was a Brown vs. The (Topeka) Board of Education was because Linda Brown and her friends were required to pass up her neighborhood school which was an all white school to attend a school that was all black. If we had interpreted the case to suggest that a child is better served attending his/her neighborhood school—and that neighborhoods should be desegregated "with all deliberate speed"—rather than interpreting the case that minority children suffer a deficit when not allowed to attend school with white children, the implementation of desegregation might have focused on quality neighborhoods as foundations for quality schools, with adults leading the way, rather than trying it (not very successfully, I might add) the other way around. We have attempted for more than 36 years to desegregate schools; but have made no comparable attempt to desegregate neighborhoods. It is 1991. We remain separate and unequal.

Desegregating schools without desegregating curricula is, both, superficial and hypocritical. Not only should we rethink where students are taught, we must take another look at what, and how, students are taught.

As an African American privileged to travel to school districts throughout the nation, I see a serious need for a major increase in the number of African American teachers, not only as "touchable" role models for increasing numbers of black students in previously all, or predominantly, white schools, but also as models for all students and teachers who have not been exposed to us as authority figures. If I feel that way as a black educator, I suspect that my Hispanic American, Native American, Asian American and "other" American counterparts certainly feel the same as it regards their own cultural-ethnic backgrounds.

Now, given that backdrop on my personal philosophy on neighborhood versus "desegregated" schools, let me indicate why I think teachers should become involved in the communities where they teach. Our direct involvement in the community surrounding our schools promotes a sense of community within the school. When I suggest that visiting the homes of students enhances our personal relationships with students, I am suggesting, in a like manner, that becoming involved in agencies, businesses and institutions in the school community will enhance our school relationship with those agencies, businesses and institutions.

The reciprocity of benefits will be realized quickly and continuously when the school is a part of the community and the community is encouraged, by the school, to become a part of the school. Jobs for students at local business establishments, in-kind contributions and human resources (see Lesson 40), scholarships, school organization participation, and positive publicity are but a few offerings that might emanate from the community. I'm talking about doing things like volunteering time with neighborhood youth organizations and recreational centers. Teachers might offer one hour per week as tutors at a local Boys' and Girls' club, YMCA, YWCA, church, mosque, synagogue or learning center. If you are a teacher who feels that working all day is enough time to spend with youth (and, that is a legitimate attitude), you might become involved with community adults, facilitating support groups or teaching parents how to interact, effectively, with their children's teachers.

Teachers can develop a Who's Who In The "X" High School community, showing which young people are doing well in various categories, including students who attend schools other than "X" in the community. Teachers might run a local tournament (softball, baseball, basketball or bowling) featuring young people in the neighborhood, even (again) if the young people do not attend the local school. Running the tournament, and awarding the prizes gives an opportunity to teachers to meet youngsters in the community under some very positive circumstances. You can sponsor, or participate in, walk-a-thons or other such activities in behalf of charitable efforts in the community. Should the school sponsor the event, students, and neighborhood residents can be involved in the planning, and conducting, of the activity.

As educational experts, teachers can become involved in the community by lending their expertise to local businesses and agencies. Helping a community center fix up bulletin boards is fairly simple. If one teaches social studies, one might plan and conduct political science clinics much like professional athletes plan and conduct sports clinics. Such clinics would be, of course, non-partisan, but could be most informative and educational.

I would imagine that the obvious benefits from involvement in the community in positive ways would be apparent: acceptance of teachers by community residents; reduction in violence and vandalism; opportunities to establish or expand upon school-business partnerships; increased credibility for school personnel as community leaders; and, increased support for school efforts, from support for programs to votes for school bond issues.

Less obvious benefits might manifest themselves in the future. Smaller children, who learn more by example than instruction, may grow up following the cooperative example of their parents and older siblings who have been involved, qualitatively, with school personnel. Former students may return to offer some volunteer time and support in the schools they recall as having been so much a part of the community. To become involved in the community where one teaches is not only to perform a service but it is also to make a positive statement concerning how we feel about where we teach. Young people develop self-perceptions based upon how others treat them. The behavior of others toward young people is a major factor in young people's view of who they are; and teachers—regardless of reports discussing our mediocrity—are still highly respected by youth, and they value what we project as an attitude toward them. And, when we go into a community, we must show that we like being a part of that community. We must show that we enjoy working with parents, recreational center directors, clergy and others whom our students respect. The more young people see respected adults working together toward the common purpose of providing a positive future for them, the more likely they are to cooperate with us because they realize that there is nowhere in the community to (i.e., no one in the community with whom they can) get away with misbehaving or underachieving.

In those cases where the students of the school do not live in the community, they have an opportunity to "adopt" a common community near the schools they attend. Sharing a sense of community around the school can foster a sense of community within the school. When there is involvement in the community on the part of a school, it is important that many members of the staff share in that involvement and not just a few. If only one teacher makes the effort to become involved that one teacher stands to be perceived as the "rare exception" against a backdrop of those other folks "up there" who don't care.

(One reason that it is often difficult for teachers to intervene in an altercation near the school—aside from the apparent danger—is the lack of any relationship with, therefore absence of recognition of, those involved in the altercation. We're not enough a part of the community to call out by name, or later identify, perpetrators. We simply refer to them—to preserve reputation, but also because we don't know them—as "outsiders". That reference is unfortunate on two counts:

1. It is unfortunate that people living within proximity to a school are seen as "outsiders" when the school can make them "insiders"; and,

2. We should know more people in the school community than only those enrolled in the school.)

Today's world sees young people with "multiple-involvements." They can choose to be involved in recreational centers, parttime work, religious organizations, special social and civic programs, informal social activities, and more. If this sounds like things are the same as when you were young, please consider that for past generations many of those activities were coordinated jointly among the (far fewer) organizations to which we were exposed. Due to a relaxing, if you will, of parent monitoring and coordinated adult guidance, our youngsters are doing a lot of "free-lancing" nowadays. We need more cooperation and coordination among adults to bring structure and continuity to the lives of our children. To spearhead that structure and continuity, I recommend that those who are professional at it lead the movement. Our society needs teachers to become involved in the communities where they teach.

SELF AND COMMUNITY

Lesson 40
Cultivate and Use Community Resources

A natural extension of Lesson 39, Lesson 40 emphasizes the importance of utilizing the human and material resources available in every community. Certainly if we get involved in our communities, we are in good positions to cultivate, and use, resources, therein. It makes sense to deal with human resources, first, because the availability of material resources often depends upon how well we relate to the people who control those resources. Human resources also come to us without materials, as speakers, tutors, discussion leaders, volunteers and consultants. While there are some obvious resources we should cultivate, such as the human resources like preachers, lawyers, media personalities, and such, to lead discussions and address assemblies; and such material resources as computers from major companies or refreshments for special programs from local bottlers or grocers; there are some less conspicuous resources we might discover if we would but look around. Rather than having a single-day career conference once a year, we might invite a speaker per week—for 40 weeks—to address those students whose grade level most appropriately fits the need and/or those students most interested in particular careers. The exchange between students and guests would be in-depth and the agenda more focused than when several guests are seated near "flashy" displays around gymnasium floors. Closer relationships leading to jobs and/or technical assistance may be the result.

Senior citizens often look forward to interacting with younger folks in the community. Not only do many of these seniors have expertise in a variety of categories, from the streets to the suites, but they are also often good story tellers. Those older citizens who have been in a particular community for a while can give us an appreciation for local history; and, in a very practical way, can offer information of a kind that gives insight into the behavior of some of our students based upon what we learn about their backgrounds. The reciprocity in benefits gained from developing and cultivating relationships with local senior citizens is realized in how they teach and "touch" our students (and us) and in how our students give them purpose and continuous contact with others more active than themselves.

One of the reasons that I believe teachers need to earn more than they do is because many of us spend a lot of our own pocket money to get things done. Perhaps tapping local resources can include encouraging merchants to offer teachers discounts on our purchases (this was done in Chicago when I began my teaching career in 1964—and, not only at teachers' supplies stores). Merchants may be more willing to offer discounts than we know. And we won't know if we don't reach out and ask. Our schools need to go back to "holding chapel." That is, students need periodic inspirational assemblies. Within the context that I am using the term, chapel, here, does not refer to a religious program, or sermon, but it certainly does pertain to a focus on morality. I mentioned that one kind of "feel trip" students should take is a police ride-a-long; a trip that involves using local law enforcement as a resource. Well, as strange as it may seem, another resource can be the local criminal element. Needless to say, every school community does not have a criminal problem, but in too many school communities across the nation there is not only a problem, but a significant criminal problem. Recovering addicts and ex-convicts (even some with awful records); and, in some cases even the current gang leadership, would be willing to be called upon as resources to speak to young people about the hazards of adopting a criminal lifestyle. There is an advantage to having those who have experienced the darker side talking to young people about avoiding that lifestyle, but there is a necessary precaution.

As we call upon the criminal element as human resources to assist us in encouraging young people to do right, we must be careful not to glorify the lifestyle or the criminal element when we invite them in as our guests. Those who come to speak should be interviewed extensively before the invitation is set forth to make sure that they do not bring with them some distortions about the glamor of the lifestyle and the peculiarity of their just having been caught. Unfortunately, some ex-convicts, gang members, and others inadvertently give that message, and we need to be careful that that is not the message given. But when the ex-criminal element or current criminal element attempting to change is accepted as creditable in terms of their current direction, they can be valuable human resources when our students seem bent on going in a self-destructive direction.

In the same vein, there are cases when recovering alcoholics, former drunk drivers, and previously unscrupulous business people can be called upon to demonstrate why it is important for students to never become involved in self-destructive habits and to adopt the mentality of a sound work ethic.

The degree to which these human resources within a local community ought to be used must not only be tempered with, but there should be a preponderance of, positive role models rather than a preponderance of the "recovering, ex-previously, formerly, or anti-social" type of guest appearing before our students. This preponderance of positive role models does not suggest that one type of human resource is necessarily better than another type of human resource, but we do not want to project to our students the idea that one is only authentic and credible when one has gone through some great negative experience and now has emerged successful. The reason that we don't want to send that message is because, unfortunately, there are many who have such experiences who do not get through those experiences and who do not emerge successful. The reason, indeed, that they are not here to tell about it is because that experience that they had was not just life-threatening but life-ending.

The cultivation of human resources within the community suggests work on the part of the teacher. In order to cultivate a resource, there needs to be the development of a relationship. In cultivating the resource it means that we should allow ourselves to be called upon even as we are calling upon others. There must be reciprocity in this relationship. However, the cultivation of human resources does not suggest the manipulation of human resources. When parents, professionals, and merchants know where it is we are coming from, they will probably be more disposed toward assisting us in taking our students to where they need to go.

The use of community resources may often manifest itself in the development of a local community speakers' pool or calling upon individuals within the community for their particular areas of expertise and/or, indeed, calling upon business people and merchants within the community to assist us in getting materials, supplies and equipment that we need to help us in teaching certain units and conducting certain activities at the school. But the use of buildings within the community, or equipment that some businesses have available to them—either temporary usage with that equipment being brought to the school or temporary usage on site where students may come into the local business and use their computers to enhance their capability and understanding of today's technology should result in a similar offer from us to businesses.

Sometimes we are concerned about the fact that children who come to us are obviously not eating on a regular basis or obviously are absent oftentimes because they don't have clothing that they can be proud of and, consequently, stay away from school so as not to be ridiculed for what they are wearing or, indeed, what they are not wearing. In many communities surrounding our schools, there are agencies that not only provide for feeding those who are without food but also can provide for clothing, and who are professional enough at what they do to insure that those children are not pointed out for purposes of ridicule because of their need. And it behooves us to survey and find out what resources might be available, even in anticipation of such problems and not as a reaction to it so that students do not lose any time at school or suffer any malnutrition because we had not anticipated that such a problem might arise.

In addition to individual resources within our community, there are organizations within the school community which can be called upon to assist in particular projects or to assist over the period of a school year in helping our students. Local sororities-fraternities, business and civic organizations, as well as others can be called upon to conduct career clinics, college scholarship clinics, develop and conduct tutorial assistance programs, sponsor certain kinds of field trips where some students may not be able to afford to go, conduct a school year-end awards banquet for students who do well, or assign one member from their group per month to come as volunteers into the school.

One of the ways to gain entry into some of the organizations, businesses, religious institutions, and others surrounding our local school is to find out from our students what kinds of things they are involved in and where they work part-time and whom they look up to within the community as being sensitive to their needs and being involved with their activities. Having a mutual friend, that is, the student, it is easy to introduce ourselves to those who might assist in making the possibilities for that mutual friendship to be successful. The number of students in attendance at a particular school suggests that most every organization or business is somehow touched by someone in our schools. In fact, it is doubtful that the business could exist or the organizations could remain intact without this direct involvement; that is, a membership from or employment of the students, or indirectly, membership of their parents or some part of their family in those organizations. Therefore, getting information from students as to who and what they are involved in gives us an introduction and an opportunity to state our case and needs, and when people see themselves as being needed, they are often willing to be called upon.

If we survey the materials or the human resources that are needed within our school buildings, we might just find by also surveying what is available within the community that all of our needs can be met without adding to our operational budgets and, indeed, without adding any significant time to our already overloaded schedule of teaching activities. One thing is for certain: **If we investigate and inquire about the use of community resources, we may get an affirmative response; if we do not investigate nor inquire, we certainly shall not get any response.** There are people within our communities who long for the opportunity to be called upon to perform services that they feel comfortable in performing or provide goods that they have in great supply.

Senior citizens did not become senior without being exposed to a great deal of information and phenomena. One of the reasons that we seem to be losing a sense of our history in society is because we do not listen enough to those who made our history. Our young people are being deprived of a very significant learning opportunity when they live in homes that do not have great-grandparents and grandparents, and when there is not one in their community that reflects more than one or two most recent generations. To call upon senior citizens really represents not only wisdom on our part but a sensitivity to their need to be considered useful. When senior citizens begin to talk about the mores and customs that were peculiar to the society in which they grew up, it might give our students an opportunity to see themselves in today's society in another light. This experience can be particularly meaningful if young people are exposed to senior citizens of various cultures, ethnic groups and backgrounds, because students can begin to understand that they are products of more than the generation just before them, and that their friends in school are the products of more than what they are displaying on a day-to-day basis in terms of their peculiar personalities and habits and, in fact, our students may find out that what they are doing and/or what their friends are doing are the exact opposite of what their cultural heritage projects and stands for. There's a great deal of information omitted from our history books, and even if accuracy were reflected in all of our history books, the hearing of history directly from those involved should have a great deal more impact than simply reading about it.

A school should not, indeed, must not, function as an island unto itself within the midst of any community because the school needs to reflect what a local community ought to be, and the only way we will be able to determine what a community ought to be is to have knowledge of what that community is. And, if local school communities work toward making purposeful, peaceful, and productive local areas, then perhaps the various areas with that similarity of purpose will come together using their local community models to shape a larger, purposeful, peaceful, and productive community.

School is not a time frame that is measured between the years from kindergarten through twelfth grade. It is a life-long process. All segments of the community ought to be involved, not only in learning more but also in giving of what they have learned to the young people who will make life better for us all. We have a need and a responsibility to cultivate and use all of our community resources.

SELF AND COMMUNITY

Lesson 41
Encourage Visits to Your School;
Write up Procedures and Guidelines

One of the interesting things that began to take place, I suspect, in the '60s and more so in the '70s, was the locking of doors in our schools and even putting chains and locks on all but one or two entrances. The idea here was, and is, to keep out the undesirable elements. Signs of welcome to our schools were replaced by signs of "No Trespassing." Hall guards were replaced by security guards. There is currently a call for having metal detectors placed at the entrances of school across our nation in order to insure that students who are in attendance and visitors do not bring weapons into the school building. In some cases administrators and faculty members simply by our body language make visitors to the school feel unwelcome. It appears that it is a chore for us to visit with those who come to see us, and those whom we request to come and see us seem to view the trip to the school as a burden. Because of actual acts of vandalism or the image of young people who "hang around" our schools, we see a need to protect ourselves, and so, in many instances, around the nation schools are more like fortresses than extensions of the educational needs of our local and larger communities. That being the case, those who would like to visit for legitimate reasons stay home and those who are vandals, criminals, or anti-social, see it as a formidable challenge that they cannot resist and, therefore, they come to school with greater intent to wreak havoc than their original intent to just "hang around."

We should encourage school visits at times of the day deemed appropriate by the staff and under conditions that are conducive to enhancing relationships rather than hindering relationships. I believe that parents have every right to come to our schools any time of the day, and day of the week, as long as the intent of the visit it to observe or to assist, and where it has been prearranged, to engage in a conference with the administrator or teachers. The school belongs to the community and it only makes sense that members of that community, especially if we become involved with our communities and cultivate human resources, should feel comfortable in visiting the school with no loftier purpose than, indeed, to see what's going on.

As we establish guidelines for school visits those guidelines need to deal with informal and formal visits. In terms of the informal visit, visitors need to understand what is observation and what is disruption. Observation means simply to take a look and be as unobtrusive as possible. Observation does not mean going into a classroom and asking questions or requiring the teacher's attention. Outside observers can enhance the climate in a school when they come in with positive attitudes and with positive exchanges with the students.

Guidelines would include first appearing in the principal's office and signing in and indicating where one is going. That would be for personal safety in case of an emergency drill or some other happenstance and for organizational purposes in the school and even in terms of record keeping.

As far as formal visits are concerned, a brief pamphlet ought to be made available to parents, community members, and former students of the school outlining the guidelines for a formal visit. Among those items that ought to be included in such a pamphlet would be: contacting the administrator of the school when one intends to make a formal visit; and contacting the particular teacher or teachers whom one desires to visit, not only with a choice of times when one would like to come, but also with information regarding the nature of the proposed visit. In order to help those visitors determine a choice of desired times to visit, the pamphlet must include the available times that the administrator and faculty members have to conduct formal interviews with those who would like to confer. In that pamphlet also there might be a section that deals with alumni visit days. There may be two times a year that students who have graduated from the elementary school and are now in high school may return to visit with their teachers. And on those two days, declared Alumni Day, the students may be allowed to come back, talk with teachers, and if it is a day during which the elementary school students are in session, also to talk with the elementary school students about high school and their experiences.

There also might be designated two alumni days on the high school level where students who have graduated and gone on to college or post-secondary careers would return and visit with their teachers, and if classes are in session, would also visit with their former school mates and talk about their college or work experiences. The reason for setting up alumni visit days would be to discourage drop-in visits where students do not just want to be observational guests but would, indeed, like to talk to the teachers about their success after their experiences with us. Most, if not all of us, enjoy these visits and would like very much to talk to the students who are before us rather than to teach the classes we are supposed to be teaching. And while it is a pleasant disruption, it is still a disruption. But if students are made aware that there are alumni visit days and if these visits can be coordinated with the local high school in the case of the elementary school alumni visit days, it might be a pleasant, enjoyable, almost festive, occasion.

But the idea is to create an image within the local school that suggests that inasmuch as we are a part of the community, we encourage the community coming to us and feeling comfortable in doing so rather than discouraging visits because of the vandalism of a few. We need to encourage visits because of the need to cultivate relationships with the many. As we are using local resources, some of those resources may very well be influential people in the community whose visits could be coordinated or volunteer services could be coordinated to coincide with the warmer weather or times where there is the suspicion that someone may be coming to the school for purposes other than observation or good rapport.

It may even be necessary to ask local law enforcers to increase their patrols around the school. It may be necessary to ask volunteers within the community to set up a quasi-security-type of function that would have parents monitor the halls and even the area surrounding the school, but, hopefully, this measure of increased security patrolling would be a stop-gap measure that would be temporary, not because the patrols would scare vandals away, but because, over time, the would-be vandals might eventually see the school as part of the community and find not only a vested interest in, but no desire to mar that which is such an important part of their community.

I don't think anyone should take a naive approach, and I'm certain that no one will. If a school exists within a truly dangerous community where the incidence of criminal behavior and violence is high, then certainly buildings should not be open on an on-going basis for observers who would take advantage of that access in order to perpetuate gang fights or the like. But I would hope that such situations are the rare exception rather than the rule. I would also hope that we realize that by our actions we can play a part in the perpetuation of a negative image by anticipating bad behavior and, therefore, closing ourselves in and away from the community.

We need to encourage visits to our school so that there could be enough traffic in the school so that any act of theft or vandalism would be totally inconvenienced by the volume of positive traffic in and around our schools. From a philosophical standpoint, I'm talking about the school projecting an image of inclusion rather than exclusion; that is, to look like and act like a part of the community rather than to be or become apart from the community.

While I don't know the status of the Roosevelt Neighborhood School Board in Louisville, Kentucky, at this point, I do recall that one of the things with which I was impressed upon my visit in 1976 was the parents' lounge. This was a gathering place for visiting parents who were either a part of the school board, the neighborhood school board, or, perhaps, were volunteers or visitors to the school. I think that perhaps as we are constructing new school buildings, that one of the major rooms would be something akin to a community lounge or gathering place where visitors to the school could meet each other, congregate in an informal kind of way, and feel that the school is, indeed, a part of the community and even manifest itself in the fact that the community has a lounge that belongs to them within the school building.

One of the things that I did not mention when I was talking about guidelines was consequences if, indeed, the visiting privileges are abused. I don't want to mention it because I would hope that the abuse of privileges would be a rare occurrence, but, certainly in that rare occurrence, a school must reserve the right to modify its policies in order to make sure that the main goal of the school—preparing our young for productive lives and lifestyle and preparing your young to improve the society in which we live—is met. And that can only be met within an atmosphere that is totally conducive to learning. Anytime a school visit or school visits hinder our attempts to do the absolute best job of giving a quality education to every child, we must reserve and exercise the right and the responsibility to modify our policy.

I believe that allowing visits, indeed, encouraging visits, will enhance the educational climate as our children recognize that they are part of a total community rather than a single classroom at a time. And because I believe this, I think that visits ought to be encouraged and facilitated by the local school.

SELF AND COMMUNITY

Lesson 42
Use Local Media to Publicize Good Things

In our schools if a riot breaks out, we do not have to call upon media. It will be on the local news. If, in our schools, it is discovered that our reading and math scores have plummeted and now the district in which we teach is at the bottom of national scores, it is likely to appear in our local print and electronic media. If a teacher is accused of racism or abuse, if local school board members are warring with each other because of factions on the school board, if the school superintendent has a poor report card from the board that hired him or her, if students decide to walk out of school to protest something that a teacher did or that the principal did, it is certain that without calling a press conference, there will be attention paid on the part of the media.

Many things that are negative are reported in newspapers and magazines, on television, and radio. Unfortunately, we have a need to report the good things ourselves because many of the good things are not picked up as readily as the bad things that occur in our schools. Does that necessarily make the media our enemy? Does that mean that the media is insensitive? Does that mean that the media functions to insure that our schools have a negative image? I would suggest that the nature of all media in America is to reflect sensationalism—to reflect things that hit our emotions, And the reason for reflecting these things is not only because it is important that the community be aware but also because Pulitzer prizes are not given for in-depth reports on a child breakthrough in discovering that he or she could, indeed, read or calculate or get along well with the person who sits next to them. Our society courts the sensational which is more often sensationally bad than sensationally good. That does not make representatives of the media bad people. It makes them competitors. It makes them survivors in a field that suggests that while you would like to be very nice, you would also like to keep your job, and keeping your job means to follow the flow of sensationalism and emotionalism.

Media representatives are human beings and sometimes do not print the good things that occur in schools because we don't give them the good news. We have a responsibility as we cultivate local resources to make sure that on our list of those to be cultivated are media representatives. We need to use local media in positive ways. How do we use local media? One, to ask that media representatives attend press conferences that are called specifically to announce some new, positive campaign or some breakthrough or some announcement dealing with the fact that we have achieved beyond the standards that we had set and that needs to be known. Aside from the formal press conference, we need to send out announcements and press kits on activities that are occurring in and around our schools that reflect positively on the achievements of our students, and the efforts we are making toward giving our students a quality education.

We need to ask media representatives to teach us how to use media effectively in getting our story out even in the midst of a society that thinks that we are mediocre or worse. As media representatives teach us how to use the various media, not only are our skills enhanced but they become more a part of who we are and what we do. We need to go into local studios and learn how not only to use media effectively as it pertains to getting the word out that we want to get out, but we need to be trained in how to use equipment so that we can tell our own story in various ways, especially in those communities that have community access to cable channels. We need to use local media in positive ways by inundating our media with photographs and slide/tape presentations and representative works from our students' classes, where, indeed, visual representations can be produced that can be shown on television and photographed for the papers, to the point where, while our reports do not represent sensationalism, there are so many reports of the good things that occasionally media will feel compelled to report some of the good things that we do.

We can use local media by having our students request internships and other kinds of work experiences in studios and stations, and a part of the terms of the internship will be that the student be responsible for positive school news. It might be a good idea to ask the major newspapers in our towns to allow a column to be written on what's going on in education with those columns focusing on the breakthroughs in educational reform.

We can use local media by inviting the media representatives into our schools, as was mentioned in an earlier lesson, to hold chapel and to talk about ethics in media, explaining to our young people and, for that matter, to us why there is so much negativism portrayed in media and the kinds of things that we can do as a society and the school as a local society to protect more positive issues and activities in the media. We ought to make it a point to become familiar not only with the major media throughout the city but local newsletters and newspapers that reflect the ethnic make-up of our different communities, and attempt to get them to focus on what the students are doing to enhance multiculturalism and positive social relationships.

Because we see a preponderance of negative publicity as it pertains to young people and our schools, we must not make the assumption that media representatives will not listen to anything that is good. We need to assume that the reason they are not reporting the good things is because we are not giving them information on the good things or the information that we give them pertaining to the good things is not made newsworthy because we present it in a very dull and matter-of-fact way. Our responsibility to ourselves is to seek out media and to state our case in such a fashion that it cannot be ignored.

The reason each chapter embodying 7 lessons in the 49 lessons toward positive teaching begins with the word "Self" is because my belief is: The responsibility for changing things that are bad to good rests with the person who realizes that things are bad—not with the perpetrators of the bad. The reason I speak of "Self" is because for us to simply complain about the fact that there is no good news is not a solution to the problem, and if we want good news to be reported, we need to be makers of good news, doing things that are creditable in our schools that they are worthy of good report, and then assuming the responsibility ourselves of getting that word out rather than waiting for an enterprising investigative reporter to come to us.

Our media can be used for public service announcements that inform the community as to meetings that we are holding and things that we are doing, activities that are being conducted that should involve members of the school community. Because of the high visibility of media representatives, we can conduct activities that include them. If we have benefit bowling, basketball or golf tournaments, the media representatives can be hosts of the tournaments and/or participants therein. Not only should administrators and faculty members develop a knowledge of how to prepare a press kit and call press conferences, we ought to pass on that knowledge to our students so that when students originate positive activities, they can call press conferences themselves.

One of the positive spin-offs from looking for good things to send to media representatives is our need to promote our colleagues and our need for students to adopt a school spirit/team-type mind set. Individually, one may not have enough good news to inundate media sources but, if we look at what our colleagues and students are doing, we may encourage our colleagues and students to send those reports to media representatives or we may, indeed, do it in their behalf.

Realizing that we are inexplicably tied together when an image is projected of who we are and what we do ought to prompt us to promote positiveness in all those with whom we work and for whom we work—that being the students—so that we can gather enough solid, good information that media representatives will, indeed, feel obligated to report on a periodic basis the good news that emanates from schools working in effective ways to give our students what they need.

Educators and excellent students should make themselves available for interviews on radio and TV talk programs. We ought to practice writing letters to editors in order to get viewpoints across, and we ought to make part of our school visits policy an open door to media so that they, like other observers, can come in and see the positive things that are going on within our schools. With our increased technology and an increased number of media outlets, particularly electronic media outlets, we ought to be able to find an ear for the good things that we are doing somewhere within the mix of media personalities and capabilities available to us. Let us look for and seize upon every opportunity to use our media to focus on the good things happening in our schools.

* * *   * * *

Lessons 43 through 49 are simply "General Tips". These are things that we need to do ourselves to make an impact on what our students do because of the things that we do. There are certain things over which we have no control, but these lessons, 1 through 49, deal with things over which we can exercise some control. Therefore, Lessons 43 through 49, in keeping with Lessons 1 through 42, could very easily have said "Self/General Tips" because we have control over such things as...

GENERAL TIPS

Lesson 43
Pass Students the Old Fashioned Way—
Make Them Earn It

I hope that for your school district I didn't write too fast when I said, "This is something over which we have some control." I am hearing more and more about the "waiver" proposition wherein if a student is marked for retention, the parent has the right of waiver and can suggest that the student, indeed, should not be retained but passed on even if, in the teacher's assessment, the student has not mastered enough of the subject matter to warrant going on to the next grade. In this regard then, perhaps what the teacher has control over is the education and not the passing or the failing. But in exercising control over not only one's authority to evaluate but also one's ability to evaluate, a teacher has an obligation to see to it that the evaluation accurately reflects the student's academic abilities. In doing that, it is important for us to realize that what we want to do is not only help the student understand his capacity to work with the material presented, but we also want to prepare him for the real world. Whatever the desires and/or options of the parent, the child must eventually face a world that is not concerned about the fact that he is the tallest person on the assembly line and therefore ought to be promoted because he will feel insecure about being so tall among his shorter work mates. This child must matriculate in a world that is, unfortunately, not concerned about her social development, but is, indeed, concerned about her productivity. This student is about to graduate into a world where the parent will not always be there to intervene and exercise the right of waiver when promotions or even firings are being considered. And our recognition of the kind of world our students are getting ready to face ought to prompt us to be fair with them even if that being fair is to make them repeat the lessons that they fail to comprehend. To repeat particular lessons does not make one a failure, so when we assist the child in learning, we need to adopt the mastery learning orientation that says "Every child can learn as much as any child, but because children are different, they learn at different paces, and they have different learning styles." Our responsibility is not to simply "pass them anyway." Our responsibility is to find out how they best learn the material we think is important for them to understand.

There are some students who feel that to give them an undeserved grade is to give them a break. Worse, there are some students who feel that teachers who give them an undeserved grade have allowed them to get by. Well, it is not giving them a break, and one of the things they need to learn early in life is to get something that is not deserved, indeed, is not to get by but it is to be instilled with a false sense of security and to be faced with a very rude awakening later in life when those skills not learned are needed in some important endeavor that might mean loss of a job or even someone's loss of life.

The teacher should be more familiar than anyone with the students ability to deal with subject matter. The teacher should be more familiar with the student's ability based upon our professional training and our personal everyday observation of the student's work. In that regard, a parent ought to accept the advice of the teacher. The likelihood of the parent's acceptance is greater if the teacher and the parent have had a meaningful relationship from the beginning of the school year to that time that the child is subject to being retained. If there is no meaningful relationship between the teacher and the parent, and if the parent has not been kept abreast of the child's progress or lack of progress, it is more likely that the parent will refuse the teacher's advice.

A similar statement can be made as it pertains to the relationship between the teacher and the student. It is unfair for a student to find out that he is failing 40 weeks into the school year. Now, not only is that unlikely but it sounds almost impossible. But unfortunately, something akin to that can occur when the teacher has encouraged a student even though the student hasn't been doing well, with "We know that you can make it—all you have to do is try a little harder," and then drop the bomb on the student when all of his friends or her friends are passing and he or she is being retained. Students and their parents need to know early on in the school year when problems exist, whether they are behavioral or academic. The proper school/home relationship will not only help the child and the parent to monitor progress (or the lack thereof) but could, indeed, prevent the situation where a child might need to be retained.

But whatever the school/home relationship might happen to be, if one had to make a choice dealing with developing good relationships versus an honest evaluation of a child's abilities at this point, the honest evaluation must be given even if it temporarily jeopardizes the good relationship. The relationship will improve later if the child is given an honest evaluation because then that child will be given the necessary skills to carry him or her forward in later life. The relationship will not be a good one later in life if a child is allowed to simply pass without skills, and it shows up when perhaps the child wanted to be on the basketball team but could not make grades or the child was allowed to pass through elementary school and then found out at a more devastating time in life that he or she would not graduate with their classmates from senior high school or if this child determined that life would continue to give things "unearned" and found out even after sliding through high school in a work-related situation that when the bottom line is involved, society does not give away good grades.

We need to insure that our students understand that school is the preparatory ground for subsequent life, and our obligation to them is to see to it that they are proficient and efficient in what they do. This is the laboratory. We work on things until we get them right, and our responsibility in helping students to get things right is to let them know when they have gotten them wrong.

I wouldn't call my students failures. I believe that students don't fail—teachers fail when students do not learn. What I want is to enlist the help of the student to make me a success by showing me that they have learned what I have attempted to teach, and if they have not learned well, my assessment of myself is that I have not taught well. Therefore, I will attempt to teach it better, but, just to make myself feel good, I must not pass students if they have not earned the right to pass. On the other hand, in making an assessment of those things that they have done wrong, I must not characterize them as failures. I must determine and help them to agree with the determination that "We need to look at some new ways to help you to pass, and you will only pass if that passing reflects the amount of knowledge that you have."

In this time of the media taking so much note of test scores, there are educators being accused of teaching the test. There are educators who are allegedly so concerned about students looking good on test results that they are actually cheating on behalf of the students. I am suggesting that helping students look good now will make society look terrible later, and that is a luxury we cannot afford. So whatever it takes to help them learn and learn well, particularly at the elementary school level and certainly at the secondary level, those are things that we must do so that when they pass they have mastered the material that they can use comfortably in later life.

I do not want to be on an interstate traveling at 65 miles per hour along side of or facing someone who was allowed to slide by on their driver's test. I don't want to go an emergency room and need surgery and be operated upon by someone who was allowed to slide by in medical school. I don't want to be represented in court by someone whose oratory skills got them through law school though they have no idea of the letter or spirit of the law. I don't want my children to be taught by a teacher who was taught by me if I allowed that teacher to slide by.

We are guiding when our students aren't sliding.
We are teaching when both students, and we, keep reaching.
The only way their successes will last is
If we make them earn it when they pass.

GENERAL TIPS

Lesson 44
Be Not Guilty of Substance Abuse;
i.e., Style Over Substance

Students are very perceptive even at a very young age, and if not immediately, over time they will recognize when we are using our style to entertain them or to mesmerize them while the substance of the lesson goes begging. It is important for us to emphasize substance even as that emphasis is complemented by our style. I think that style is important; that is, I think that one's teaching style ought to be consistent with one's personality. We should not try to imitate somebody else's style and I think that it is important that even as we find our own style, that it should not become a substitute for getting into the deeper matters of substance.

When I speak in terms of substance abuse, I am speaking in terms of one's ability to make students laugh, feel good, to create a wonderful, happy, positive climate in the classroom without imparting the skills that students will need when they go to a teacher next year who has a different, more formal, less relaxed style. When one can marry the conducive style to the discovery of substance, that is the essence of effective instruction, and for some teachers, that is a marriage that takes place over time. There are some who have an effective style just based upon a charismatic personality when they first enter our ranks as a teacher. And the marriage of that style with the substance of the lessons presented takes place early and lasts for a long time.

And that is magnificent when one can come in and start with that style and substance, but for some among us, the style versus substance represents a wedding but not the marriage. And while students will buy into it immediately; i.e., during the wedding and the honeymoon of initial introductions to each other, over time students will begin to discern that the style outweighs the substance and consequently the marriage does not last even though the wedding was exciting. It is important for us, if we must decide between the two, to understand that both are important but the importance of the substance outweighs the importance of the style. Sometimes it takes a while for us to develop a teaching personality and that's all right, but in the quest to learn who we are within the context of that classroom and interacting with our students, we must not sacrifice substance in favor of "finding ourselves."

In the 1960s it seemed to me that there was a need in our schools to allow students to "do their own thing," to make school centers of unusual excitement and entertainment as opposed to centers of deeper learning and critical thinking. And because that was so, it appeared that many of us in the classroom were more bent on appealing to the visual and entertainment needs of our students than the academic and disciplinary needs of our students. Many of the schools visited during that time were magnificently splendored with hall and classroom displays on an on-going basis which had merit then and still has merit provided that the displays were representations of the essence and substance of lessons being taught. But I fear that the display lent itself more to style than substance.

For some among us, that has become characteristic of the way they attempt to teach, and when one adopts that style of teaching and is rewarded and awarded for it because it "looks so good", then one might convince himself or herself that this is, indeed, teaching when, in fact, it is entertaining. This is not to say that teaching cannot be entertaining but students should not be led to expect to be entertained above being helped to think, analyze, be disciplined, and to prepare for a world that is sometimes entertaining but also sometimes boring, dangerous, confusing, and always in need of intellectual and moral leadership.

If the classroom is a microcosm of a larger society, then we will only sometimes be entertaining and, yes, sometimes we will be boring, but the important thing is that we are always focused on what students need to learn. And inasmuch as we teach so much by example, we ought to be exemplars of serious educators even when we entertain.

When my fifth grade teacher at Wendell Phillips Elementary School, Mr. Isaac Clark, played the piano, he was quite entertaining. When Mr. Clark discussed mathematics, he was almost boring, but Mr. Clark was always serious about things that we needed to learn even when he played the piano and taught us how to listen, sing, and to get into entertainment when it was time to entertain, and to get into mathematics when it was time to learn to think. My eighth grade teacher, Mrs. Lucille H. Montgomery, had a totally different style easily distinguished from Isaac Clark's but there was no question about the fact that Mrs. Montgomery was serious about what she taught and about the profession of teaching itself.

Discover your own strength as it pertains to who you are and what you might do to be an effective instructor, but please understand that if that strength is to be the teacher equivalent of the class clown while you might perceive it as a strength, it will be perceived by the student as a weakness and exploited as such. We have the responsibility as teachers to be mature enough to choose substance over style.

The emphasizing of one's own strength might find some classes very quiet and others loud; even, almost, noisy at times. But, a quiet classroom—representing a certain style—is not necessarily a dynamic one.

Let us find our niche without carving a rut, and use style only to complement important substance.

GENERAL TIPS

Lesson 45
Distinguish Between a Niche and a Rut

You have probably heard the statement that by now is a cliché, "Some teachers teach for 25 years; others teach one year 25 times." The idea behind Lesson 45 is to suggest that it is easy to fall into a rut and not quite so easy to carve one's niche. The reason that it is easy to fall into a rut is because we are creatures of habit. When we discover our comfort index, we are likely to remain in that index because it is comfortable. Also, in times of stress or heavy emotion, it is a psychological mechanism within all of us to resort to that which is most comfortable—that arena wherein we feel best.

It is difficult to carve a niche because sometimes in so carving we don't recognize what truly is our niche. Because dealing with human beings is so dynamic, it seems that as soon as one believes that the niches has been carved, some set of circumstances or some peculiar human phenomenon arises within the class that causes us to rethink our definition of what a niche is. For example, if one is a professional educator who has taught seventh grade for four years, finally by the end of the fourth year one feels very strongly that he or she has mastered those teaching skills required to be effective at that level. Then in the fifth year this same teacher is asked now to teach on the fourth grade level or the ninth grade level and suddenly is thrust into a situation where many of the things done at the seventh grade level will not work. Consequently, it's necessary to find new approaches toward being effective at the fourth grade level or the ninth grade level that are peculiar to those grades and have little to do with the seventh grade level. Another example of one thinking that a niche has been carved might be working at the same grade level for several years and having pretty much the same kind of student. The danger, of course, is to make a generalization that would suggest that all students are the same and certainly they are not. But let us suppose that for those four years that I discussed, that the students come primarily from one particular neighborhood and their parents approximate the same socioeconomic level and set of social values, and, now, because of our efforts to desegregate or because of a housing development that has come up in the community, a group of students are in attendance in the fifth year whose demography is significantly different from those who were in attendance in the first four years. The niche one thought had been carved was really a comfort index and now one needs to be more creative in order to address the individual needs of students whose backgrounds are dissimilar from those to whom one has grown accustomed.

There are situations where one would feel that they have carved their niche as it pertains to a teaching style, and something may happen that would cause them to move out of the community in which they live and take up a teaching job in an entirely new city or a new area of the city. And similar to the situation where students from different backgrounds present different challenges, now one's own change presents a new set of challenges. When one considers those human kinds of things that impact upon one's ability to carve a niche in teaching, it is important to understand that the term "niche" as here applied refers to one's ability to adjust to different teaching situations and still use skills gained over time, study, conferences and conversation with colleagues to remain effective as an instructional leader at the classroom level. The niche would see one being able to make efficient use of time and in that efficient use of time, being task-oriented in achieving objectives set and desirable outcomes and, at the same time, not being so task-oriented that one does not enjoy within the context of that niche flexible structure.

A niche has been carved when an educator by direction of the school principal or by force of demographic changes has to confront a totally different educational situation than one has grown accustomed to, and yet can continue to be competent, confident, caring, and consistent.

A rut expresses itself when one confronts a different situation and reverts to entertaining or style over substance. Among the differences between a niche and a rut are when one carves a competent and effective instructional niche, one seeks new materials, approaches, and innovations that one can use complementary to their teaching substance with style. A rut is when one refuses to seek out new materials and innovations out of fear that it might disturb one's style absence of substance. A niche is carved when one greets new students of different backgrounds with delight and anticipation of gaining more experience, insights, and opportunities to learn from those students who are coming in with a new set of experiences. A rut is recognized when one determines that it doesn't matter how different the backgrounds of the new students are, everyone will conform to the rules and standards and guidelines already present and should not even think that they are going to be a part of some new dynamic. They are going to have to make the adjustments, not the teacher.

A niche is recognized when the professionalism of the classroom teacher manifests itself in working as a part of the team of
which one is currently a member, or even the new team that one
meets when one transfers in ways that assist in the cohesiveness
and productivity of that team even if there are personalities
among other team members that one does not particularly like.
A rut is recognized when one determines that their role on the
team is that of a particular role and it doesn't matter what the
rest of the team says. And if, indeed, the rest of the team dis-
agrees, then one will simply not be a part of the team but will
function apart from the team. That kind of rut might, for instance, be one who perceives himself or herself to be the team
leader, and if they are not, then there's no other role that they
are willing to play. Another role of that person who is in a rut as
it pertains to relating to the team might be that "I will not
assume an active participatory role, but I will support what
others do. Beyond that, I will not function as member of this
team." Whatever that obstinacy projects, whether it is unreasonable attempts at being a leader or apathetic attitudes and
refusal to participate at any high level, it is rut rather than a
niche.

A niche is recognized when a teacher does not understand
the ways and values of today's children, but is still sensitive to
their needs and attempts to teach them from where they are. A
rut is recognized when a teacher refuses to teach today's
children until they change their ways and values to suit the
teacher. A niche manifests itself not only in a teacher recognizing the dynamic that causes society to change in significant ways
from decade to decade, perhaps as things are going now, from
half-decade to half-decade or year to year, but also is a part of the
dynamic that brings about positive change. A rut manifests itself
in a teacher's inability to understand the dynamic of change
enough to be a part of it, and even if given the understanding of
the change, would not be willing to be a part or even to recognize
the change as being significant or valuable.

A professional teacher's niche invites advice. A rut is when
one thinks that his or hers is the only approach toward effective
instruction and rather maintains an attitude that "I know how
to do this. This is how it's been since I started teaching and this

is the way I'm going to do it. I don't need to go to an in-service
or a conference or read what is new in educational reform. I will
just stick to what worked for me in 1947."

I would certainly agree that there are certain principles that
even in a dynamic society do not change as it pertains to human
behavior and human needs. Students need reward. They need
approval. They need care and understanding. They need discipline. They need proper examples set before them in order for
them to know the kind of behavior they should emulate. There
are certainly many things that need to be done on a continuous
basis as it pertains to respecting the experiences of children
related to their own sub-culture, but in observing those con-
stants as it pertains to respect and care and understanding and
discipline and sensitivity to children's sub-culture, the way that
such respect and care manifests itself is being able to adjust to
the times in which we live without eroding sound values in the
process. And that adjustment can be made when one carves such
a professional niche that not only are they able to continue to be
effective in a variety of settings but also they are able to distinguish between a niche and a rut.

GENERAL TIPS

Lesson 46
Push Hard, But Not Constantly

In today's world of "winning is the only thing" it is unfortunate that from a very young age children are taught that there
is no worth in simply exerting effort and only worth in emerging
at the top of the heap. I think that it is certainly good to instill
within young people an appreciation for the value of persistence.
I think that young people need to be motivated toward rising to
the level of their potential. I certainly belive that where there are
young people who show an extraordinary capacity to be effective
in one or a number of realms, that they should not be allowed
within our presence to de-emphasize those skills or play down
that talent. We should certainly push them in the direction of

being the best that they can be. But pushing should not manifest itself in making children and ourselves uncomfortable.

It is important that there be times in the experience of our students that those who are children be allowed at points to be children. I'm not just suggesting that they be allowed to play from time to time. I'm also suggesting that they be allowed to falter, to miss the perfect score, indeed, to just "mess up" sometimes because that is the nature of being a child and having the need to reach maturity.

I know it will surprise some people, but children are not perfect, and I would imagine that it will surprise even more people but teachers are not perfect either. To treat our teaching situations as though the assumption is that all things ought to be perfect is to stifle the possibility of learning and critical thinking. We need to fail sometimes so that we can figure out how to overcome failure and end up doing things right. Again, to fail is not to be a failure. In fact, when one fails well and dares to fail often, one is likely to be a greater winner than one who seldom or never fails. I think I've heard a statement to the effect that one who never fails is one who never tries. In our attempts to help youngsters develop a pattern of succeeding, sometimes the best push is no push at all. This gives an opportunity for young people to discover their own initiative and their creative ways of figuring solutions to problems with which they were confronted, or that they might have created in the process of failing.

When we do push our students toward success, I certainly think we ought to push hard. But I also think that there are times when we need to lighten up. When a class takes on a character that seems bent on fulfilling the prophecy that they are a bad class or a slow class, it is time to push them and to push hard. When a student has determined, based upon the inability to master a particular subject area, a particular skill, that they are therefore failures and will never master that area of skill or anything else, it is time to push and to push hard. When particular students have shown glimpses of outright genius or particular aptitudes that they have decided for some peculiar reason to hide, to de-emphasize, it is time to push them and to push them hard. When it appears that mediocrity has been an acceptable standard among students up to the point where they have met you, it is time to push and to push hard. There is certainly nothing wrong with pushing hard and, in fact, there are many times when pushing hard is altogether desirable.

The point here is that because the definition of pushing hard is to exert extra effort toward achieving a desirable result, it is not a good idea to push hard constantly or exert effort that would be considered extra constantly. If it is constant, then it is no longer extra. That means that it would either become a mediocre push or one would burn out one's self and the students in all of the extra effort. Students need to regard us as sensitive and human. After a hard push, and that hard push may be a hard push for a few weeks, they need to see us come down and offer them some relaxation, some recreation, so that they will not only get some enjoyment but also can gear up for the next time that they are pushed to exceed what they perceive to be their reach.

Just as one needs relaxation periods in a heavy physical exercise program, one needs relaxation periods in a heavy mental exercise program. This is medically and physiologically sound as well as educationally sound. I believe that we should not be hard on students constantly because after a while they will turn off and I also believe that we should not be hard on ourselves constantly because we too need periods of relaxation and humanness. We are not perfect and it's good that we aren't because those imperfect mortals around us wouldn't be able to stand us. But as it turns out, none of us is perfect so all of us can understand human failures.

Because we understand it, we ought to be able at some point to say to our students, and for that matter to ourselves, "On this particular test in this particular situation, you did not do so well and that's all right because I'm sure that you will do much better the next time." Certainly there are instances when we would say to a student, "I am very disappointed in you. I don't expect ever to see grades or performance like this again. If you should ever show me a performance like this again, you and I are going to spend several hours together on Saturday to insure that your practice of this particular concept is what I know it can be with your intellect, talents, and capabilities."

There are ways we can really get on students for not rising to the level of their potential because we know or suspect that the reason they did not rise to that potential is because they were in a playful mood or were temporarily lazy. There may be some very important times to push hard when particular exams are coming up or as a result of something that we know should not have been done by the students as a class or as individuals and we have reason to push them hard in order to make them realize what they can do and certainly what they ought to do and what they ought to have done.

But in terms of the constant relationship that ought to exist between teacher and student, it is unrealistic for us to project an image that our expectation is "everything will be done perfectly all the time." This is not realistic. Young people know it and they know that we know it. We will not be taken seriously unless we understand that we should not push hard constantly and we will be taken even more seriously when it is known that not only do we understand that but we also understand when we should push hard and when we should be more relaxed.

Even in the intense structure of the military service there are days for rest and relaxation. Even as athletes prepare for the Olympic games or major boxing matches, there are times when they can relax and converse about things other than what they are preparing for in order to trigger the psychological mechanism within them that provides for, and signals the need for, a change of pace and focus. As we push hard and relax the pushing, we must be consistent in our educational styles so that the relaxation after the push does not look like we're being wishy-washy or inconsistent, but actually looks like, as professional educators, we recognize the need to relax for a while before getting back on that particular task. As a matter of fact, we should not consider the periods of relaxation as being periods when we're not on-task. We should consider those periods as being consistent with accomplishing the task by helping students to regain energy and enthusiasm while temporarily concentrating on other things.

Teachers need not confuse being dedicated with being unreasonably strict, either on self or on students. I can remember
when I didn't think that teachers went to the washroom or to
the grocery store. I certainly could not imagine a teacher being
romantic or participating in recreational sports. I came through
school at a time when men teachers wore coats and ties every
day and female teachers wore dresses, and I can recall being
surprised when I saw one of my teachers at the local grocery
store actually shopping for groceries in casual clothing and
saying "Hi, Carl!" instead of "Mr. Boyd, stand up and answer
this question." Now, as a teacher, I can see how foolish my thinking was. But it is equally foolish as a teacher to think that
students should not be given an opportunity to go to the washroom and to be romantic in their own ways, or to daydream from
time to time about the upcoming sports event in the neighborhood or after school.

I think that it is good for us to push our students when we
recognize the great potential that they have. But I am reminded
of a passage in Khalil Gibran's *The Prophet* when he speaks of
love where it suggests that there be spaces in our love. I think
that we ought to push our students and push hard, but we need
to let there be spaces in our pushing so that as we do, the pushing will be effective.

GENERAL TIPS

Lesson 47
Compare Students to Themselves —
Not Siblings or Classmates

Any number of teachers reading this particular lesson can
recall how upset you were when your classroom teachers asked
you why you couldn't be more like your older brother or sister.

There are those who recall how upset you were when your
parents suggested that you be more like your older brother or
sister, and even though you can recall how upset you were you
still insist that certain students ought to be much better students

because they come from such a "smart" family. It is important for us to understand and to emphasize that every student is an individual, and being that every student is an individual, each student has an individual personality, aptitude, and needs. For us to suggest that because a four-child family has two children whom we have met who are absolutely superb, that means that the third child is somehow abnormal because that child now coming before us in our classrooms does not have the same aptitude is ludicrous. It is unfair and unprofessional for us to require of that child to make the same grades and project the same personality that the two previous children from the same family projected when they were in our classrooms some years ago. In fact, it is unfair when two children are matriculating at the same time in the classroom for us to require the one or the other sibling to be like the sister or the brother because the behavior of the sister or the brother is more to our liking.

We need to make sure that our students are compared to their accomplishments during perhaps a previous year or previous grading period and are encouraged to do better in the future in light of what their apparent aptitude happens to be. We should not suggest that because there are certain young people in our classroom who happen to be friends of others, that the other ought to be just as nice, bright, or attentive. Each child has the need to develop in ways that are compatible with their own personalities and lifestyles, and what we ought to do is to help students realize that there is one person with whom they will live for the rest of their natural lives, and that is themselves. And inasmuch as we cannot depend upon them being a part of particular friendships forever, the measuring stick that we give them ought not be the comparison between them and their current set of friends. Since dynamics occur within a family that cause differences in a family structure over time, we should not measure students by current members of the household because that household may not be made up of the same siblings forever.

But if we can instill within young people a need to reach to the limits of their capabilities because we have instilled within them a desire to be the best that they can be, then we are doing what we ought to do as teachers. When young people recognize that there are some in their class who have a great aptitude in some direction but that happens not to be where their skills exist, we can help them to refrain from being jealous of other students by helping them to recognize the differences. But also we have an obligation to them to show them where their talents exist, and in most cases every child has some talents that other children do not have. And because that is the case, we should lift every voice and help them to sing.

As we interpret team building within the classroom, we should help our students to see that to function as a team member is not to function like other team members and that, in fact, what makes up a team is the individual differences working in harmony with each other in order to create a team that has members who pick up each other based upon the strengths and weaknesses of the members on the team. If the athletic analogy could be used in terms of volleyball, there are some members of a volleyball team who have height and reach and are great in serving, and there are others who have energy and jumping ability who are fantastic on the net, and there are others who can see and have quick reflexes who can be found on the floor diving to save a spike. If everybody was outstanding at the serve but nobody was willing to dive for the ball on the floor, you would have a very poor volleyball team. In the case of the classroom, some students have a personality that causes them to want to read 6 books a month. Other students have a personality that causes them to want to speak out and recite in class because they like being up front. Other students in the class may have an aptitude for writing. Therefore, when the class project must be done, it is important that those individual differences be appreciated. That will help us to instill within an appreciation for their own personal talents and one of the ways that we can exemplify our appreciation for the individual differences is never to compare the students with their siblings or with each other, but always to help students understand that they can do a little more themselves, they can do a little better than they did the previous year, and they can emphasize different aspects of their character and their personality. And as we do this, they will understand that we respect them as individuals and don't expect them to act as robots or clones of other members of the class or of their family.

GENERAL TIPS

Lesson 48
Cultivate a Sense of Humor

Students appreciate a teacher who has a sense of humor. Students do not appreciate a teacher who tries to be funny all the time. There are teachers who can cause students to feel good and laugh with them. There are other teachers who can cause students to laugh at them. As mentioned before, our profession should see us instructing rather than entertaining, so our sensitivity to the need to have a sense of humor does not suggest that every day all class period our students should be laughing at some situation at the teacher or at each other. It is simply to suggest that every situation in the class need not be taken seriously and many situations which might be viewed as a crisis situation could be used to reduce tension in the classroom and to heighten the human factor.

It would not be prudent for me to attempt to list the various situations that might be considered amusing versus situations that might be considered silly. I think that it will suffice to simply indicate that when one finds things that are amusing but not insulting, it ought to be all right to laugh an honest laugh. It is important that our students know that it's all right to find humor in the classroom, and it's okay to laugh. But when I talk about cultivating a sense of humor, I'm talking about the need to help students recognize the difference between something that is amusing because it is an unexpected circumstance that has elements of amusement in it and premeditated practical jokes that may be amusing to the joker but should not be amusing to anyone else. Spontaneous laughter, because of the unexpected, is psychologically healthy and can create a healthy classroom climate. Laughter that is not spontaneous but effected in order to attempt to create a certain classroom atmosphere is usually detected by the students and, consequently, rather than reducing tension can heighten tension as students laugh at the teacher who tried to put one over on them.

Now, there are some obvious exceptions to the "trying to be funny" rule. We have all probably encountered teachers at some level—elementary, secondary, or college—who purposely project an image of trying to be funny in order to break the ice because those teachers were intelligent enough to know that we, as their students, would recognize that what they said was not really funny but their attempt at humor would be found funny. We used to call it when I was growing up "corny." Then later there were those who would call it "being square." At the point when I began to teach, students would call such efforts "dead." But whatever term would describe those "corny" efforts, they were still acceptable because it was consistent with the personality of the teacher and would be all right because we would laugh not at the teacher but with the teacher at the same time because we recognize that the teacher set it up that way.

In cultivating a sense of humor, if it is not consistent with one's personality, it is not a good idea to just try to be funny or if one attempts to use humor as a reprimand—for instance, to embarrass a student—or if a student does something to make the class laugh and the teacher attempts to top the student in order to get over with the class, it may fail miserably and cause the student to dislike the teacher rather than to respect the teacher's attempt at discipline, and may cause the teacher to become bitter because the young people did not go along with the attempt to embarrass one of the other students.

As the exemplar in the class, a teacher's ability to distinguish that which is legitimately amusing and that which might be insulting or degrading helps young people learn appropriate responses to different situations. Displaying a sense of humor also helps young people learn through the teacher's example how long the laughter should last and how loud and how pronounced. Some students, seeing the teacher finding something amusing and smiling or laughing appropriately, will then show that loud student who goes overboard that is inappropriate and it will not be necessary for the teacher to do so because classmates will begin to make comments such as, "It's not that funny," or "All of that is not necessary."

It is good to cultivate and display a sense of humor because it is human, it is natural, and young people ought to understand that being human is all right. By the very same token, it is all right for teachers to help students to understand when they are upset, and helping students to understand that they are upset because they recognize that the students are not doing as much as they know they can, and in that way the students will learn that the teacher is not upset at the students as individual personalities, but they are upset because those students in whom they have so much confidence are not displaying the skills that they know those students have, and, consequently, they become upset.

In cultivating a sense of humor it is also a good idea for teachers to help their colleagues cultivate a sense of humor, or to look for some humor in situations that might otherwise be taken too seriously. As in anything else, cultivating a sense of humor takes practice. What that means is that if it is going to be a human tool, as it were, in the classroom, sometimes even manifesting itself as a teaching tool, then it will be a behavior that needs to be practiced outside of the classroom, and therefore one will begin to take stock of all life around one and begin to find humor in everyday kinds of things in order to be prepared for humorous events as they occur in the classroom.

If one of my lessons suggests that we push hard but not constantly, this lesson would certainly suggest that we look for humor but not always. Some things, while they might amuse us, might, indeed, hurt someone. So as we cultivate a sense of humor, we must also be sensitive to the fact that even if 99% of the class finds it funny, if there's one student in the class, if there's one person in the situation, who would be hurt by it or ultra-sensitive to it, we must help the students understand that it is not an amusing situation to everyone. Or if we inadvertently laugh and then discover that there is someone hurt by our laughter, we owe that person an apology and an explanation. And if we can do it and do it convincingly, then that person may even find the humor in it or at least will not feel bad about laughing on the next occasion when they find something to be amusing.

Humor ought to be a part of the classroom because, once again as has been repeated several times, the classroom is a microcosm of the larger world. If that is so, then there ought to be humor in the larger world and the classroom ought to reflect that. A comfortable and enjoyable classroom climate promotes learning and part of that comfort and enjoyment can be found in a teacher's having and projecting an appropriate sense of humor.

GENERAL TIPS

Lesson 49
Be a Teacher—Not a God

When many of us came into the teaching profession, we determined that we were going to be the best educator who ever lived. We determined that whatever else had gone before us, we were going to do things so special that every child was going to learn more than they had ever learned up to the point where they met us, every teacher who had the privilege of teaching on the same faculty as we would gain the benefits of our enthusiasm and professionalism, every administrator would thank their lucky stars for having met us and having us on their faculties, and every parent would come to us at the end of every year thanking us for being their child's or their children's teacher.

We came in with an attitude that if we saw children who needed clothing, we would make sure that they would be clothed. If there were children whom we met who needed food, we would make sure that they would be fed. We had determined that if there were children who need psychological assistance, that either we ourselves would become their psychologists or make sure that they received immediate referrals and would return to us full of health, verve, enthusiasm and, indeed, intelligence.

When we decided that we would become teachers, we knew that we were not likely to get rich but we looked forward to becoming wealthy in terms of the human returns on our intellectual investment. Somehow we figured that our entry into the profession would make such a difference that the profession itself would never be the same after encountering our efforts to make every child a bright and shining star and the instruments for world peace and productivity. I think that those are goals that we should always keep, but I think that it is important to be realistic—that our charge is to do the best we can to prepare young people for a successful, productive and happy life after they pass our way.

There are some things that other agencies and institutions must deal with. We are not asking journalists to teach journalism. We are not asking that parents come into our classroom and discipline their children in our classrooms for us. And by the same token, it is unfair for the larger society to ask us to be all things to all people. If everyone of us simply did an effective job of teaching, then many of the societal ills that we are concerned about would be eradicated because our children would be prepared to earn the kinds of living that would keep their children from going hungry and naked, and many of the physicians that we would produce would stamp out certain kinds of illness, and being the exemplars that we ought to be would produce the kinds of citizens who would make of this society what this society ought to be in order that everyone receive equitable fruits for their labors.

If we could just teach and teach well, we will have fulfilled our responsibilities to our profession and to our society. If we can, in addition to doing a great job of teaching, even an effective job of teaching, feed a few, clothe a few, and assist a few in developing sound minds, that is fantastic but it is not a requirement of the profession. And if we must choose between being providers of social services and being classroom teachers, by virtue of the fact that we have chosen this profession, we must choose to teach first. We adopt Robert Kennedy's quote, "Some see things as they are and ask, 'Why?' I dream things that never were and ask, 'Why not?'" We project into the future, based upon something that we impart to our students, a much better society than we have now. But if that dreaming should take us so far into the future that we forget to do those things required of us as classroom teachers today, then we have neglected our responsibilities as professionals.

Right now the one thing that we must concentrate on is being the best teacher we can be. After we have carved our niche, it might be possible to then be creative and stretch out into other arenas that might be complementary to, but are more than, those things that we do in the classroom. But that must come only after we have made sure that we're taking care of the business at hand, and that is to be excellent at teaching.

It disappoints us and, in some cases, moves us to tears when we see other social agencies that are supposed to be functioning around us falling down on the job. And as much as we want to be effective as teachers, we realize how difficult that can be when young people come to us who are ill-prepared to pay attention in class when their physiological and social needs have not been met outside of the classroom. But even though we are moved to tears, the best thing we can do for those young people is to exemplify what excellence is and to treat them as best we can within the context of why they are coming to us, and that is to be excellent teachers. Our youngsters are more resilient than we know. They are stronger than we suspect, and we ought to maintain high expectations for their abilities to succeed, even in spite of some of the things that they encounter in their young lives. And with those expectations, we need to go about the business of teaching as though every young person who comes our way might, indeed, be that savior that we are looking for to take us out of the mire of mediocrity as a society and into a world of peace and productivity. And we need to teach every young person with that in mind. Our knowledge of community resources should help us to identify where needy students can find help, and we can exert efforts to match students with appropriate resources. But, it is important for us to recognize that not only should we not attempt to be gods, but to recognize that even if we were absolutely outstanding already, we have not the capacity to be gods.

It is better for us to hone our skills as teachers, and just as we should compare young people not to siblings and others but to themselves so that they may continue to grow as they matriculate not only through school but through life, we must compare ourselves to the teachers we were last year and determine that we're going to be better teachers this year and in the future. If we make a decision to move out of the ranks of class-room teachers and decide to become administrators, then we ought to determine that we're going to be excellent administrators. If we determine that we have decided to move out of the classroom into another field of endeavor altogether, then we ought to determine that whatever we attempt to do, we're going to do it as well as anybody has ever done it before—then strive toward being ever better than anyone else has ever been. But as long as we are in the classroom, our responsibility is to be the absolute best teacher we can be. And if we do that, we may not be gods but we will be carrying out that which our god had called us to do. We can then realize that above all else, because we have this great opportunity to work with young people who definitely represent our future, it is time to get down to, or to get up with, plain teaching. And we must recognize that plain teaching is not common teaching—it is excellent teaching, plainly projected, so that all students can get the most out of the learning experience.

Epigrams

A teacher is one who realizes that it's not the method in the class but the class in the method.

A teacher knows that students don't fail. Teachers fail when students don't learn.

A teacher reaches out to students, reaches up with students, reaches for all students to maybe reach one student.

Teachers care for those with whom they work and work with those for whom they care. To work without caring or care without working is dead.

A teacher is professional enough to hear the covert messages from students regarding their needs, and sensitive enough to give them overt responses.

A teacher never makes a threat that cannot be carried out and never carries out a threat that has not been made.

A teacher always strives to win over students but never tries to triumph over them.

A teacher teaches by example, learns from example, cites experiences as examples, and serves as the example.

A teacher can become upset and show it without displaying anger, can be amused and reveal it without losing authority, and can make a mistake and acknowledge it without appearing unintelligent.

Teachers can raise their voices without raising anxiety and can lower their voices without losing command.

A teacher asks questions that students need to answer and answers questions that students want answered.

Teachers put life in their students' classes and class in their students' lives.

A teacher often finds opportunities to laugh at self but never seeks opportunities to laugh at students.

A teacher cannot help children by passing them on but would not hinder children by holding them back.

Inspirational Messages
One For Every Day Of The
School Year

Day 1   The one thing that you and I are going to remember today, is that nobody rises to low expectations.

Today, everybody's going to learn something, even if it's only that I believe that everybody can learn something.

Day 2   Please keep in mind the fact that confidence breeds confidence: teacher to self; teacher to student; student to self; student to classmate.

Day 3   Check this out. Find a student—I mean look for him or her, until you find him or her (I mean really look)—who has low esteem; who is convinced that failure is inevitable, and show that student how great he/she is and/or can be. Don't worry about finding two, or three. Today, find and convince just one.

Day 4   I am a teacher. I am someone special; not because of my name, my looks, my clothing, my family or my friends.

I am special because I'm a teacher; and I couldn't be a teacher without being someone special. This being so, I shall act accordingly. I shall treat those whom I serve—my students— as very special people because I realize that without them, I wouldn't be, I couldn't be, someone special.

Day 5   Thanks for understanding that nobody's perfect. Because of that understanding, I can apologize to students when I'm wrong, and not lose face; I can be corrected by students and not feel "put down" or lose authority. In fact, my presence is enhanced when I admit and correct my errors. And I can do this, candidly and immediately, because you helped me to know and understand that nobody's perfect.

Day 6 Consider this a "seed-planting day." If students seem inattentive, just keep on planting, maybe they will recall later what I felt was important today. If the best and the brightest don't seem to care, today just keep on planting—they are no less bright; they are still the best. And if you [If I] feel a little discouraged, keep planting, lest my attitude discourages someone whose future growth depends upon my planting.

Day 7 There is something I've wanted to say to you for a long time; but, out of fear that it might smack of conceit and sound self-serving, I've been reluctant.

But, since this conversation should be shared only between the three of us: Me, myself, and I. I shall trust that you won't take this message any further or the wrong way. Self—you're good!

Day 8 You have the very future of the world in your hands. What you do with the world's future is entirely up to you. Criminologists and law enforcers say that criminals act when there is a victim, an opportunity, a motive, and a weapon. They don't have to act when those things are present, but when they choose to act, a crime is committed.

Well, you have students, opportunities to teach them, intrinsic motivation, and teaching tools. The significant difference between the criminal and me is, when I choose not to act, a crime is committed.

Day 9 You finally did it. I'm glad you didn't do it, finally. You believed.

Day 10 Teach. Teach people, not subjects. Do not teach people as though they are subjects. Teach with love and compassion. Teach today about yesterday with deep concern for tomorrow. Teach with a personal need to learn all there is to know about what you are teaching as that will help you to make things clear. And, thank you for teaching.

Day 11   I don't know that this is true, but, because so many come our way, it's just possible that last night a young one had a dream that today I'd say something encouraging. Since I can't be sure who might have had that dream, today I'm going to encourage everyone.

Day 12   Take a moment today to recall something really pleasant about a teacher you had when you were the age your students are now. Do not require of yourself anymore than the recollection as the rest will take care of itself.

Day 13   Taking life seriously is essential. Taking me seriously is not. Please let me marry the seriousness of life with the insignificance of my brief existence that I might show students how to laugh at ourselves, cry for others, work toward peace and joy, and love limitlessly within the time limitations of mortality.

Day 14   Take a walk, today, if only through your mind. [An actual, physical, walk is better.] Look at things as if seeing them for the first time. Listen for things you've never heard. Smell only that which is fresh and sweet. Touch nature but feel her only on the inside. Taste the meal that was your favorite when you were 12 years old. Then, tomorrow, teach the same way.

Day 15   CATCH UP!

Day 16   Even in the midst of the mundane, inane, inhumane, overstrain, emotional drain, profane, cocaine, physical strain, insane, and migraine, I chose to teach and teach I must.

Day 17   Please know that you are going to lose some. But, be of good courage; someone currently lost will be found.

Day 18 Disappointment is a reality of life. The beautiful young scholar who followed a madman, bent on self (and others') destruction, to the crack house is, unfortunately, one of many. Try your best to win her back. She is worth it. But please do not forget those not so beautiful and far less scholarly who follow you, everyday, to the school house.

Day 19 Come on out! Say all of those wise, candid things today that you told me last night when preparation for sleep seemed to bring out the profound. Are you afraid that your candor will make me less popular? Do you fear that your wisdom will sound "out of touch"?

   Well, take a chance. These people know me. And they long to know you. And they know you're in there, somewhere. They, more than I, need to hear from you.

Day 20 Eat lunch with the students. You will feed far more than your hunger.

Day 21 "What's-her-name" (or is it, "what's-his-name?") wants you to remember his/her name, today.

   Thank you.

Day 22 Guess who's going to make your day for you, today?

Day 23 It is far better to practice one virtuous habit than it is to teach 1,000 virtuous sayings.

Day 24 Fragile. This End Up. Handle With Care. Keep In Cool Place. Perishable Goods. Must Be Delivered Within Three Days. Do Not Fold, Bend Or Mutilate. Net Weight, 133 lbs....

   Isn't it interesting that we receive more instructions on how to deliver packages than pupils? I think I'll select a student, today, and write a list of safe-delivery (to academic success) instructions.

Day 25   Don't worry. Be busy.

Day 26   Take undue criticism with a grain of salt. Turn life's lemons into lemonade.

Stir up classroom conversation with interesting topics. Pepper your lessons with thought-provoking questions.

Refuse to sugar-coat reports of students' lack of effort, and do not allow them to butter you up.

Don't be chicken.

Hold students' feet to the fire for the full course.

Check on them, periodically, as they rise to the top, and lettuce pray.

I'm not sure what kind of meal this is, but I'm cookin'.

Day 27   Take a deep breath before responding or reacting to Ralph, today. [In my case Ralph is _____.]

Day 28   I apologize for allowing myself to act like a student in front of the students. I can't believe that I, not only revealed that I had a "button" to be pushed but I revealed which button could be pushed to set me off.

I am appreciative that the students accepted my apology and felt that I had cause to show my anger. Even so, I know I must be in control. It is as important to me that you accept my apology as well as the students, for you must realize that I am not perfect, and should not act as though I expect me to be.

Should I falter again even as I work, conscientiously, to prevent it—I shall apologize again, and keep on stepping.

I shall strive for perfection, always; while always realizing my fallibility.

Dear Self, thanks for understanding.

| Day 29 | Look for the good that is in each one; understand the bad that is in everyone, assume responsibility for "number one."

| Day 30 | If your students knew everything you want them to know, they wouldn't be students, they'd be teachers.

Treat them as though they can learn everything. Teach them as though they know nothing. Lead them only where you have been. Inspire them to go much further.

| Day 31 | Someone will learn something, today, because I'm going to teach it. Someone will see their potential, today, because I shall help them reach it.

Someone will hear a message, this day, because I'm going to preach it.

There is promise of a teacher's love, today, and I won't breach it. This is truly a wonderful day.

| Day 32 | A student cried last night because they went to bed hungry. A student suffered the abuse of confused and angry parents. A student was introduced to a self-destructive substance and lifestyle. A student went "home" to an abandoned automobile or, yet, another relative's house. A student mourned the premature passing of a loved one who died too soon after living too fast. A student is wearing what an older sibling refused to wear. A student will come to me, today, in despair.

I pray that this will not be the one to whom I say, "Shut up and sit down."

| Day 33 | I think I'll start today using a new word for each new day. The word is: please.

| Day 34 | Did I ever tell you that I like the way you treat me? And, did I ever tell you that it's O.K. to like the way you treat me? Well, keep on treating me like that, and I'll keep on treating

others the same way, because I know how good it feels to be treated in a nice way.

Day 35 As usual, I arrived at school early. The building looked so peaceful with hardly anyone in it. I thought about the near-chaos that was going to erupt when the students arrived.

Wouldn't it be tranquil if they decided not to come? Think of the peace in this building if the students just stayed home. Do you know how much I could get done without the students? Quite a bit!

But, why?

Day 36 Experts through time, and spanning the globe, have confirmed that there are two things without which it is impossible for a school to be a school: students and teachers. Now, ain't I special?

Day 37 I continue to grapple with the issue of self-esteem vs. standards. Will I hurt a student's self-esteem by imposing standards too high to be met? Will I damage the school's image by lowering standards in order to enhance students' chances for success, thus building their esteem?

What mus' I do?

What mus' I do?

Well, Self, do you want your principal to lower standards so you can succeed as a teacher? What does that say about you? What does that say about your principal's confidence in you? School prepares students for post-secondary life. Do employers lower standards to make employees "feel good?"

Do you want to fly with a pilot with high self-esteem or with one who can keep the plane high off the ground?

Do you want a physician who feels good or one who can help you feel good? Where possible, let's do both: maintain— even continually raise—standards while enhancing esteem. But, if a choice must be made, let us trust the resiliency of youth and hold them to high standards for 1/4 of their lifetime so they can enjoy high esteem 3/4 of their lifetime.

Day 38 Your pride is showing. Be careful that your boasting about your successful student does not take credit away from the teacher who planted the seed years ago.

Be proud, not of self, but of the student and the many, before you, who planted, watered, nurtured, and kept watch over that which [who] decided to blossom in your presence but not necessarily due to your presence.

If, and when, you are due credit, let others bestow it upon you.

Day 39 Is it a bad sign when you rush out of the house in a hurry because you awakened late, and you see dimly lit headlights on the car you left in a no parking zone overnight?

Is it a bad sign when you rush back to the house to phone for assistance only to discover that you left your keys in the house and the door is locked? Is it a bad sign when this happens on the day you promised students "bodily harm" if they were late because this was their last chance to rehearse for this afternoon's program?

Self, those are bad signs. But, you know what? Those signs are not as bad as me. That's right, I'm bad. I'm so bad that I'm gonna MAKE this a great day, anyway—starting with laughing at this awful beginning.

(Self, I'm glad you're with me.)

Day 40 There are four teachers, a custodian, and two cafeteria workers at my school whom I do not know. I shall not write this same letter, tomorrow.

Day 41 Newsbrief: Students across the nation are involved in voluntary community service projects and programs. The overwhelming majority of female students do not get pregnant while in high school. Such organizations as Boy Scouts of

America, Girl Scouts of the U.S.A., Boys' and Girls' clubs, YMCA, YWCA, NAACP Youth Council, Black United Front Youth, Indian Youth of America, American Sokol Organization, The Aspian Association, Inc., Maids of Athena, Youth Circles (Polish National Alliance), B'nai B'rith Youth Organization, and hundreds more still outnumber youth gangs. Even the disenfranchised students stand when we sing "The Star Spangled Banner." And, a student in my school will befriend someone today. I only give you this newsbrief because things like this are seldom featured on the six o'clock news.

| Day 42 | Formula for success: NEVER QUIT!

| Day 43 | I found your lost property. I know you've been missing it for several years. I don't know how you've lasted without it. You knew it was gone, but kept trying to find it in all the wrong places: in the students' eyes, in the parents' attitudes, in the principal's leadership, in the community's support, in the media's accuracy, and in the board's policies. Though your search seemed logical, it is impossible to find your valuable property in those logical places. You have to find it where you lost it: inside of yourself. Since I am the only one who can return it to you, please accept, from me today, the property you lost: your faith.

| Day 44 | Today is the day to take the weight off. Leave yesterday's disappointments behind.

| Day 45 | Two students will have a dispute, today. They will depend on you to resolve the issue, and you are dependable. However, although ego might suggest otherwise, make them resolve the dispute, themselves.

| Day 46 | Dig this. A young brother was walking down the hall yesterday, hat on his head, earring in his ear, cutting a corner like one leg was shorter than the other and leaning to the

side like he was driving a "pimp-mo-bile". When I caught up with him—which wasn't difficult in as much as he was bent on walking slowly enough to be seen—I asked if I might have a word.

He viewed me suspiciously as if he wondered what a teacher could possibly want with him—in school.

I told him I liked his outfit (and without any sarcasm). "But," I said, "You remind me of about 87 fellows I grew up with, most of whom are still unemployed. Those who are employed—and sending children, like you, through school—no longer lean when they walk or joke when they talk. They don't wear hats inside their offices and they left their 'attitudes' back in their childhood." Hey, I ran it on down to lil brother.

It didn't work.

Finally, I said, "In this school, it is against the rules to wear your hat." He understood. He removed his hat and kept leaning. Tomorrow, I'll tell him about our "leaning" rule. Maybe, he'll straighten up.

| Day 47 | Did you know that the shortest distance between two jokes is a straight line.

Never try to outwit your students. When you do, you lose. Always try to OUT-WITH your students. When you do everybody wins.

| Day 48 | You will not become rich teaching; but ours is the only profession where we become interdependently wealthy.

| Day 49 | Today would be a great day to start exercising:

Exercising patience;

Exercising restraint;

Exercising good judgment;

Exercising persistence;

Exercising fairness.

A steady diet, like this, should create a very healthy student body.

Day 50 For a change, take a chance. Choose to follow your "first mind". Trust your professional instincts. Be intuitive. Feel. A teacher has very special sense(s). Use them, but don't take credit for them. We are blessed to be what, and who, we are. Others must benefit from our blessings. However, we musn't let our uncommon senses override our common sense.

Day 51 A driver cut in front of me this morning, nearly crashing into my front fender, then took off at breakneck speed, weaving in and out of traffic as he drove. But, I didn't let him get away with it. I took off after him at "breakerneck" speed, weaving in and out until I was in a position to return the favor of cutting him off. I came so close, I could see the terror in his eyes and in his wife's eyes. I thought it was because of me—until I saw the inside of her—just about ready to come out (she was pregnant), if jerks like me would just allow them to make it to the hospital. (There must be an object lesson, in this, that I can relate to my students).

Day 52 Whew!

Day 53 Roses are red
Violets are blue...
Or– ah– Roses are kinda burgundy,
Violets are purple.
Actually, check it out,
Roses are rose,
Violets are violet,
How come we don't just say
What we mean?

A rose is not a rose, by any other name. If it were named something else, that's what it'd be, understand what I'm sayin'?

Well, let me get back to what I was going to say in the first place. (Hey, I wonder if I sometimes take my students on "trips" like this. I'll watch it, today.)

Day 54 If I do not take the first step, right now, toward reaching my goal—however far away the proposed date of completion—one moment from now I will have missed my first deadline.

Day 55 Wisdom is not wasted on the young. Idealism is not visited upon the old. Aren't we blessed that God lets us teach while we're somewhere in between.

Day 56 The fruits of our labor sour if we do not pick them at just the "ripe time." Pick one, today, who is bursting to reveal that your labor has not been in vain. Then require of that fruit the planting of his/her seed by helping one who is younger that others shall grow from their example.

Day 57 Remember the good things from yesterday and do not let today go by without giving at least one child hope for tomorrow.

Day 58 It is better to be a great teacher than a great leader. A great leader is successful who causes others to follow. A great teacher is successful who causes others to surpass.

Day 59 Can you believe these kids, today? Yes. And you should.

Day 60 In the interest of time, I'll be brief.

Day 61   Lemme "ax" you sumpin', do you really look your best, today? Tell the truf. Do you look as good as when you go out to eat? I mean, are you as well dressed as when you go to the- er- theatah? Would you wear what you are wearing to your class reunion activities? Well, I understand how important the res- taurant folks, whom you do not know, the theater people you cannot see, and your classmates you haven't seen for 102 years must be; but, how important are the students who follow your examples everyday? Now, one mo' time: Lemme "ax" you sumpin'....

Day 62   Today is a day of sheer determination. No student's boredom will defeat my enthusiasm. No colleague's frustration will lower my expectations. No parent's wrath will harden my empathy. No community apathy will weaken my resolve. I am strong. I am convinced. I am unstoppable. I am a teacher.

Day 63   Use this day to create an opportunity for a student to excel. Ask a question that caters to her academic strengths. Assign a task that requires him to use his talents. Pair a team of two compatible personalities. Find a way, or make a way, to cause someone to shine. Their brilliance will only illuminate you all the more. Do not demand excellence, allow excellence.

Day 64   You did not cause today's sunshine; but if you take the credit, it will not shine any less. You were not responsible for yesterday's life-sustaining rain, but if you boast, it won't stop raining and sustaining. You did not give birth to the trees that shade us or provide the substance and soul that made us; it wasn't you who made grass grow, or caused the streams and rivers to flow. But, if you believe you did, and say you did, the growing and flowing will not stop to correct you, even though truth and history understands that you were blessed to be able to witness—not cause—these wonders. Some students who passed your way have risen to greatness in various fields. And, while they may tolerate your boasting, isn't it just possible that the cause for their greatness is the same as the cause for the sunshine and rain, the growing and the flowing? They will not stop to correct you, but rather than taking credit for our success stories, let us be thankful that we were allowed to witness them.

| Day 65 | You are where you are, at this time, for a reason. In the divine scheme of existence and time, you are not a coincidence but an integral part of what is, what has been, and what is to be.

You are independently unique and interdependently essential. Let not the importance of your role blind you to the significance of others. Let not the brevity and smallness of your presence—within the expanse of time and among the matter in the universe—quell your expectation. You, and those you teach, existed before you appeared and shall remain after your transition. Hope anticipated you. History shall remember you. The least you can do is the best you can do. Otherwise purpose is defeated and potential denied.

| Day 66 | There are scientists who suggest that we use but 1/10 of our brain as we travel through life. I have often wondered, if we only use 1/10 of our brain, how would we know? That is to say, if we began to use 2/5 of our brain we might discover that we had been using only 1/17 of our brain, rather than 1/10, see? Let's use today to see how good we can be by using 9/10 of our teaching ability rather than the 2/3 we usually use (nothing scientific here, just a guess). I'll bet we can really be something.

| Day 67 | Take a tour around your school, today. Observe the grounds, the surrounding community, the restrooms the auditorium, the cafeteria, gym, and media center.

Feel the school spirit—or the absence of spirit. Look at the lighting, the cleanliness, the bulletin boards and trophy cases. Observe the attitudes of colleagues, the enthusiasm of support staff and paraprofessionals, the optimism, or pessimism of the administration. If you gave yourself the assignment (as we often do to students after a field trip) to write about your tour, what would you have to say? This might explain why you feel as you do about where you work. If something needs improving, you now have another assignment.

Day 68 Before school, today, or during school, today or after school, today, tell someone, sincerely—not sensually nor selfishly, but sincerely—"I love you." (Even if you say it to yourself!)

Day 69 Think of yourself as a mentor and you'll understand your importance; think of yourself as a servant and you'll demonstrate your students' importance.

Day 70 Never try to teach a lesson you do not believe. Never try to teach a student you do not believe in.

Day 71 Practice what you preach, believe in what you teach, rise above your reach.

Day 72 Why am I impressed with:

Nelson Mandela? His consistency.
Martina Navratilova? Her work ethic.
Haki Mahubuti? His honesty.
Oprah Winfrey? Her perseverance.
Mikhail Gorbachev? His P.R.
Jimmy Carter? His commitment.
George McKenna? His expectations.
Shirley Ceasar? Her convictions.
My students? Their trust.

Day 73 As students come to us with stories, testimonies, situations, needs, let's keep in mind that most are honest. Even with our vast experience and deep understanding, let us be careful not to read into situations more than is there. Although we like being supersleuths, most things are just surface-deep.

Day 74 As long as the earth rotates on its axis and revolves around the sun, to stand still is to travel backwards. If we are to keep up, we must travel with the world. If we are to make a difference, we must stay ahead of the world. If we are to teach, we must understand where we have been, know where we're going and how to get there, and be committed to seeing that others get there ahead of us.

Day 75 I have a confession to make. I have been teaching as though it is required of me to know everything. This causes me to be embarrassed when I cannot answer a question; or causes me to stifle students' creativity out of fear that I'll be taken out of my comfort zone of knowledge. I'm going to change, today, realizing that the most comfortable place for a teacher to be is where learning is taking place—especially when the teacher is learning.

Day 76 You remember all that stuff you learned at the conference? Remember the conference you attended three years ago? You remember that stuff, too? Are you using it? Well, how come you goin' to all them conferences?

Day 77 You can enrich a student's life, today. Say yes to something to which you'd ordinarily say, no.

Day 78 Befriend a guest teacher today.

Day 79 It is time to get organized like you promised a month and half ago.

Day 80 Someone is going to take credit—not some credit, but full credit for an idea you initiated. You will get upset, and with good reason. But, believe it or not, you have taken unwarranted credit yourself. Someone complimented you and you accepted the compliment, then later mused, "I wonder what that was about." An Administrator cited you in an auditorium full of people for someone else's contribution, and, because you felt awkward, did not want to embarrass the Administrator, were taken by surprise, weren't sure of what she/he was talking about until the citation was complete (or some other reason other than desiring to take someone else's credit), you accepted the citation.

It happens to us all—both ways. Do not hold grudges. Just be sure—awkward situation, or not—that the next time you are given undue credit that you set the record straight—even in an auditorium full of people. Never do to someone what you don't like done to you. (Sound familiar?)

| Day 81 | Tote that barge, lift that bale, get a little drunk and...you don't need to be teaching.

| Day 82 | Are my students motivated? Are they enthusiastic? Are my students thirsting for knowledge? Confident? Talented? Alert? Are they disciplined? Prepared? Creative thinkers? Energetic? Respectful? Neat? Come to think of it, AM I?

| Day 83 | Dreams are wonderful, but they require sleeping. Goals are attainable but, by definition, they're a part of the future. Plans are practical, but relegated to paper. Purpose is essential, but serves only as a catalyst. The question is; what am I doing right now?

| Day 84 | How do we know he won't cure cancer?

How do we know she won't bring peace?

How do we know if they have the answer?

We really don't know, but that's why we teach.

| Day 85 | Make your students sweat. Make them earn those good grades. Refuse to accept mediocrity. Teach them to regard

discipline as the key to accomplishment. Raise your standards, and after they meet them, raise them higher. Demand excellence. But, please remember, they are not your enemies.

Day 86 When all else fails....

You taught wrong.

Day 87 Make your class a laboratory of human potential. Use this teaching opportunity to show what possibilities exist for people to work together to increase understanding, to value knowledge and exchange it in the interest of peace and productivity. When the experiment works, share it with the world.

Day 88 Who will history record as having been the world's answer to our quest for universal peace?

A. M. L. King, Jr.?
B. John F. Kennedy?
C. Ghandi?
D. A student I may teach, today?

Day 89 A penny for your thoughts. (Man, I'll be glad when they raise teachers' salaries!)

Day 90 You have but one opportunity to teach today's classes under today's circumstances. Just one.

Day 91 By the authority vested in me, by virtue of the fact that I gave you your job, I now officially pronounce you teacher and student. Never attempt to teach without being a perpetual learner.

Day 92 It's more important to teach with class than to teach in class. It's more important to learn with students than to learn for students. One interpretation of cooperative learning is teachers cooperating with students.

| Day 93 | Today is "be good to yourself" day. On a diet? Cheat (a little). Writing your dissertation? Think about something else (for the moment). Grading papers? Take a break. Of course it can be "be GOODER to yourself" day. Drop the diet and adopt an overall healthy lifestyle. Finish your dissertation. Get through grading papers and other assignments. Then you have set the stage for being good to yourself tomorrow, and tomorrow....

| Day 94 | Every earnest question deserves an earnest response even if it doesn't warrant an answer. While it is fine to inform a student of the need to deal with a particular question at another time, it is important that the explanation be complete and courteous. Satisfy the student's needs before demanding that the student address yours.

| Day 95 | Today, be an excellent listener. Hear what students are asking and saying. Hear through their inarticulateness and figure out what they mean to say, then help them to say it better. Hear, even, what they don't say by observing body language, moods, and attitudes. This is the kind of thing that makes students love you.

| Day 96 | You will have an opportunity, today, to do something you've never done before.

| Day 97 | All of the knowledge in the world is moot without a kind spirit. It is very important to understand your subjects, but even more important to understand your students.

| Day 98 | If your life were required of you, tonight, would you be proud of how you treated your students, today?

| Day 99 | Let's go somewhere special, today. Let's delve into our students' minds, find our way into their hearts, try to see things through their eyes, walk a step (or two) in their shoes and

put ourselves in their ears to hear how we sound when we preach and teach. Such a journey may help us find ourselves.

Day 100   "Happy New Year!" No matter what the date, a new year begins every day. Any resolutions?

Day 101   Beginning today, the following measures must be taken whenever you have a bad day: Decide otherwise.

Day 102   If I told you once, I told you time and time, again. (But if I told you once, and meant it, I wouldn't have to tell you time and time, again. I must remember that when dealing with students).

Day 103   The debate will go on as to whether great teachers are born or made; but, such a debate could not be engaged without great students.

Day 104   There comes a time when students are so trying, colleagues so insensitive, and efforts so fruitless that all one can do is decide to laugh at it all—including self—and start over in better spirits.

Day 105   However profound your thoughts, eloquent your presentation, articulate your speech; to one who is hurting, a good listener is always better than a good speaker.

Day 106   Find the date of birth of a student who hardly knows you, and when that day comes, say "Happy Birthday!" (Donna Burch, Principal, of Bryant Elementary School in Kansas City, Missouri, does that all the time. The students know her. It'll be even more fun to say it to one who doesn't know you.)

Day 107   Thank you for thinking to return that borrowed item, today. Though it hasn't been mentioned, I'll bet it's really needed.

Day 108   It is better to risk being unpopular and giving directions to live by than it is to court popularity and making allowances to die by. Students need our strength and candor.

Day 109   Pray!

Sometimes you just need to pray!

Day 110   Of all the position, professions, occupations, jobs there are in the world, isn't it great to be part of the profession that launches all others? I am a teacher.

Day 111   Your mission, today, should you choose to accept it, is to analyze—and internalize—why you became a teacher. When you have figured it out your brain will self-destruct in 30 seconds.

Day 112   Reach for the stars, you might touch the moon. (I just threw that in 'cause folks usually say it backwards.)

Day 113   The sun is going to set today and rise tomorrow whether or not I achieve my objective. Let me make my effort as consistent as the sun.

Day 114   When a student arrives at school in a terrible mood, ready to lash out at everyone including you, please do not take it personally. Obviously something occurred before you entered the picture. To return the anger is to exacerbate the situation. Try a little tenderness.

Day 115   Make this the day that you begin to take your own advice.

Day 116   Are you sitting? Well, get up! Teaching is a walking around, looking over students' shoulders, helping, coaching, encouraging, interacting, "feedbacking", moving, approving, prodding, nodding, exciting, dynamic profession. Naw, you couldn't be sitting.

Day 117   Friday afternoon at 2 p.m. is not a "natural time" to wind down. Monday morning at 7 a.m. is not a "natural time" to gear up. Every moment holds the possibility for a bright beginning.

Approach Friday afternoon as though it were Monday morning. That just might turn out to be a previously uninspired student's special moment.

Day 118   It may not be your birthday or a gift-giving holiday, but students need to share your presence.

Day 119   Today is "independence day." Require your students to do something on their own from conception to completion. (If not today, soon).

Day 120   Can your students be the nation's best? If anyone can, they can. If the definition of an excellent student is one who learns excellently, then any student can be the best student, because any student can be an excellent learner. Indeed, we should be helping students learn how to learn rather than teaching them what, and how to know.

I.Q. testing should yield to L.Q. testing (with L.Q. standing for Learning Quotient) wherein instruments are developed to determine how well a person catches on, figures out, and applies stuff, not only based upon traditional subject matter but also based upon one's subculture (even "street culture"). I am convinced that my students can be the best in the nation, and I am determined to prove it.

Day 121   Don't we sometimes say things to students such as, "Get that expression off your face," But, where else should an expression be? The next time we tell a student, "hurry back" without saying how long to take going, we should realize that youngsters are not the only folks who talk funny.

| Day 122 | Acey was the "baddest dude" around Madden Park. If somebody was about to mess with you, and you said you knew Acey, not only would they leave you alone, they would run. My man, Ace, was too tough. Now, Acey Harris is one of the nicest gentlemen anywhere in the world. I cannot help but believe that Ace was nice when we were growing up around 37th Street, but no teacher saw in him what he could become. I wonder if I will encounter any Aceys, today; and if I do, will I see their toughness or their potential?

| Day 123 | It sure was a good idea to start dribbling a basketball for exercise. I used my arms, my legs, my reflexes and my stamina. Not only am I stimulating my cardiovascular system, I am also reminiscing about my younger days when I played (at) ball. This morning, I practiced dribbling right-handed, behind my back and between my legs. I had to concentrate and do many repetitions before I could go the length of the court under my left leg, then my right, then my left, and so on, without stopping.

I didn't shoot the ball at all. In fact, where I was practicing the basket had been torn down by some young Turks imitating Darryl Dawkins when he was a child (CHOCOLATE THUNDER)!

Just working up a sweat with the basketball helped me to recall that good ball players are:

☐ disciplined ☐ committed
☐ versatile ☐ bright
☐ healthy ☐ alert
☐ cooperative ☐ coachable
☐ focused ☐ motivated
☐ prepared ☐ cheerful
☐ students

Perhaps, if I employ my best teaching/coaching skills, they'll be all of that, and more, in the classroom.

| Day 124 | Open For Business: The Courtesy Store Sale Items

Manners—No charge

Respect—No charge

Understanding—No charge

Kindness—No charge

Courtesy—No charge

Love—No charge

Sensitivity—No charge

Attentiveness—No charge

Honesty—No charge

Sincerity—No charge

Total cost—No charge

Bottom Line: My students need, and appreciate, the same things I need and appreciate.

| Day 125 | A name is very important. Students tend to look for reasons to laugh at—to make fun of—each other. The less mature they are, the more fun they make. Names sound "funny" when they are different. The more different the name, the "funnier" it sounds.

Students will sometimes give each other nicknames that are cute. Too often, however, names given are derogatory—even vicious. Being sensitive to students' proper names does not necessarily mean that nicknames are always inappropriate. With the proper relationship, it is not only appropriate to address a student the way the student prefers, it can also be an esteem-builder. But we must be careful to pay attention to students' sensitivities where names are concerned; and if we must err, it is better to err by using a student's proper name when he or she prefers a nickname, rather than becoming too familiar and using a nickname instead of the proper name.

Our example is likely to be followed, so let us be sober and sensitive when we consider the question, "What's in a name?" (A rose may be a rose by any other name, but probably prefers being called a rose.)

Day 126   Did you know that it's all right to have fun teaching? Well, know it from now on.

Day 127   My students know so little. Nothing seems to be clear. They have not been given skills needed for livin'. But, I guess that's why they're here.

Day 128   Do not overlook the obvious. Sometimes a student will read poorly because of a need for glasses. Sometimes one will seem unresponsive due to a hearing impairment. There are students who refuse to come forward because they are ashamed of their clothing. There are students who sleep in class because they work after school and do homework late at night.

Yes, it's true, some of today's youth are learning disabled, inattentive, uncooperative, or lazy. That is, some are. But sometimes we fail to consider the obvious.

Day 129   If we know it, we must show it, lest we blow it. (A teacher's answers are not to be kept secret from students.)

Day 130   Khalil Gibran's *The Prophet* teaches us that, "your children are not your children, they come through you but not from you...." We cannot live the life we wish we had lived through our students. Recognizing their talents, aptitudes, even special interests in certain areas will prompt us to advise them—and rightly so—to pursue those interests. But, however certain we are that particular aptitude is their guaranteed path to fame and fortune, they are not obligated to take our advice.

Our vicarious needs must not interfere with our students' self-determination.

Day 131   You can lead a class to chatter but you can't make 'em think....

Day 132   "Yours is not to reason, why...."
But for students, it is.

Day 133   Today, I'm going to teach using the "Smokey Robinson Principle": no matter how difficult it seems, for every time I fail to get students to understand, "I'll Try Something New."

Day 134   We often take on more than we should when we attempt to do more teaching than students do learning. We must allow students to participate—at a high level—in their learning. We must help them to help us teach them.

Day 135   Because of the needs, sensitivities, and fragility of our students—whether we realize it, or not—we conduct the most delicate operations everyday that we teach.

Day 136   A trumpet has three valves. A guitar has five strings. A piano has 88 keys. Soloists do not create harmony. A well prepared, well presented lesson from a competent teacher can create beautiful music; but only multiple contributions—operating on different, but compatible, frequencies—can create harmony.

Day 137   Following is a list of the 10 most effective teaching techniques of modern times:

1.	by example	6.	by example
2.	by example	7.	by example
3.	by example	8.	by example
4.	by example	9.	by example
5.	by example	10.	by example

Day 138   When I began my career as a classroom teacher in 1964, I believed that I could teach anything to anybody, anytime. I was going to maximize effort, mesmerize students, and minimize failure. My students and I were going to conquer the universe. In this regard, I still feel like 1964.

Day 139   Remember when there were things grown folks did and things "not-grown-folks" did.

Like drinking? That was for grown folks. Never was a good habit; but it was mostly for adults, not kids. Now, lots of kids—our students—drink. Smoking cigarettes? Cool, hip, debonair—very adult. Fatal, but very adult. A "federal offense" if kids did it. Smoking cigarettes in the "bafroom" at school got you two weeks suspension and a real topic for conversation throughout the building.

Gladys Knight and the Pips used to sing "Papa Could Swear." When we were growing up, Papa was the only one who didn't get in big trouble for swearin-cussin'. Now, do students swear? Now do students swear! Hey, drinking, smoking and swearing weren't good, weren't nice; still aren't. But they used to be grown folks' stuff—like having babies, staying out all night, selecting children's clothing, setting the volume on the radio, determining what time the family would eat dinner together. Now, the youngsters—our students—do all of that. They are not grown. We must not act toward them as though they are. But, one thing is for sure; we cannot teach them the way we were taught.

Day 140   Things that endure take time to cultivate. Let's not feel slighted when teachers who have taught longer have a stronger rapport with our students than we. With care, confidence and consistency, our time will come.

Day 141   A teacher, today, is on the cutting edge of the world transformation—not the slashing edge of hope for tomorrow. We must teach each student as though hope exists only in his or her soul—for surely, it does.

Day 142   There are no unimportant lessons, just de-emphasized presentations.

Day 143   Never gamble with a child's life. With every interaction, they are betting we'll be correct (not necessarily right, but certainly, correct).

Day 144   The smell of chalk dust, the anticipation in an unfinished bulletin board, decorations for the Christmas Assembly, files, forms and fillers, the motto, the mascot, the meals complained about, yet eaten, in the cafeteria. Romantic? Poetic? Not a chance—not meant to be. School is about kids. Period.

Day 145   Here is the latest "whether report," Our students really need us whether they act like it, or not.

Day 146   When you test your students, you test yourself. Earn yourself an excellent evaluation. Teach well.

Day 147   Today is a good day to invest in the best insurance policy anywhere, for all times: encouraged and enlightened students. My investment: encouraging and enlightening them.

Day 148   To talk "down on our students level", to bring students "up to our standards", to "reach down" and "pick them up", to "save just one" sounds like we have a very high perception of self or low perception of students; perhaps both. Let's talk on a communicative level, reach out to fellow human beings who happen to be younger and seek opportunities to save teachable moments that contain lessons for life.

Day 149   Dear Number One Teacher:
                 So are your students!

Day 150   Who: Our Students
What: Need Us
Why: To Lead Them
Where: Beyond Tomorrow
When: Rat Now!
How: By Example

Day 151   TEACH the "3 Rs":
Readin', 'Ritin', and 'Rithmetic
Use the "3 Ms":
Mentoring, Manners, Morals.

Day 152   Are teachers born or made?
Students don't care.

Day 153   A well placed phrase embodying praise most certainly pays.

Day 154   Today I shall look for my best student—within every young person I encounter.

Day 155   No two students are alike. Every two students are "I-like!"

Day 156   Sore? Soar! And take your students with you.

Day 157   Make your students an offer they can't refuse; Get "offer" your seat and into their hearts.

Day 158   It's time for a break: break out the new lesson; break up the monopoly; break through the learning blocks; break in some new techniques; break a record for a level of interaction, learning, and retention.

Day 159   Be reasonable. Once you've stretched students to the absolute outer limits of their intellectual potential, give them some slack—so you can stretch some more.

Day 160   Our job is our saving Grace... and Nancy and Khareem and Oua and Raphael and Ted and....

Day 161   Will someone I teach

Be someone I reach

Because I have taught them so well?

Will a student of mine

Eventually shine

With stories of love to tell?

Will a child's needs be met

By examples I set?

Will the future be brighter for one?

Will someone's self-esteem

Help them realize their dream

Because of something I've done?

Will one from my class

Make happiness last

Using lessons I might teach, today?

Will we improve our world

Through some boy or girl

I've been blessed to have come by my way?

I hope so. Dear God, I hope so.

Day 162   There is always room for growth. Especially when that room is my classroom.

Day 163   My colleagues—my fellow teachers—are dedicated and competent. They face the same obstacles that I face: negative press, parent apathy, lack of community support, and uninterested students.

Yet, when we visit in the teachers' lounge or talk at conferences, the continuing conversation deals with how we can do a better job of teaching.

With our common plight and collective determination, it would seem that one place—above all other places—is that we should find solace and support would be in each others' hearts.

| Day 164 | Too many adults know all the answers without ever having heard a child's question.

| Day 165 | There are times when it is good to read for pleasure—and nothing else. Read a good book. Don't analyze it. Don't philosophize. Just enjoy. Visit an art museum. Do not consider period, style, or why the artist used a particular medium while in a particular state of mind. Do not contemplate the painting—just enjoy the "pictures."

Take in a movie. Do not Siskel/Ebert the movie. Don't look for one with deep underlying messages, sub-plots. Just allow yourself to be entertained. Sometimes the deeper meaning of life is as shallow as one's willingness to be pleased. And, as we teach, let us remind students that learning does not always require investigation—it often comes as a result of simply allowing it.

| Day 166 | All teachers are alike. Except for the fact that some are more dedicated than others. And, then, some try to respect students while others try to intimidate them.

Oh, and some teachers use praise before punishment. Some teachers exemplify cooperation while others exercise authority.

Some instill, others insist.
Some encourage, others belittle.
Some inspire, others assign.

Yep, all teachers are alike like all people are alike. Problem is all people are not responsible for shaping the future of the world.

Day 167   "It's time."

I need a bumper sticker that reads, simply, "It's time."

People should wear buttons and lapel pins—and hoist balloons—with the message, "It's time."

And for each one who wears the message, there may be a different connotation; but, whatever it means to whomever, "it's time." In one case the reference may be toward making a commitment to a local civic or charitable organization. Another situation might ask if you have been in touch with your family. Have you apologized for a wrong committed not so long ago?

Have you launched your total health/fitness program? Are you supporting at least one civic or charitable effort in your community? Are you the best teacher you know how to be? Have you decided to live?

IT'S TIME.

Day 168   Consider "Doors."

Doors will open, soon, for students now passing our way. We must give them the skills and confidence to walk through.

Opportunity will soon knock on our students' doors. We must prepare them to open those doors and welcome opportunity in full readiness. When doors close in the faces of our students, God will open a window. We must help them gain the wisdom to see the open window and the intelligence to forget the closed doors. We must help students realize that the only way one's life can continue to be a revolving door is if one continues to push in circles.

We must tell students that life should not be left to chance: the only real "door prizes" go to those who know which ones to walk through, and when (and win). Now those are some "swinging" doors.

Day 169 There's no such thing as a bad student... and "fat meat ain't greasy. Grits ain't groceries, eggs ain't poultry, and Mona Lisa was a man."

I'm sorry, Father Flanagan, there are bad boys, and bad girls. There are bad people. Perhaps it is due to the absence of bonding with parents in infancy. Perhaps the environment, causes it. Perhaps a combination of heredity, environment, and absence of bonding cause some children to be bad; but, whatever it is, let us not be "too cute" in our efforts to explain behavior or our need to see all children the same way.

Our professionalism compels us to refer some children to specialists in the mental health field.

It may damage my ego to have to admit that I cannot "save all children" or cannot penetrate the heart of one in particular, but some are bad, y'all; just bad.

Day 170 "The best things in life are free." That must be true because one of the best things one can be in life is a teacher.

Day 171 Everybody deserves a second chance. For the student who messed up, and acknowledged it, give a second chance. For the parent who missed the first conference, allow a second chance.

For the colleagues whose lack of support disappointed you, consider a second chance. Give a second chance. To the administrator who completely misunderstood—and, so, misinterpreted—your approach to teaching, offer an explanation and a second chance. But most of all, to yourself even while striving for perfection, remember that everybody—including self—deserves a second chance.

346

| Day 172 | Back up. Take a moment.

Breathe. Think. Thanks.

| Day 173 | Your life is richer than you think. Share it with your class. Students' lives are richer than they think. Encourage them to share. The more we know about each other, the richer will be our experience together.

| Day 174 | Why do I have to keep going over the same stuff time and again, over and over?

Because I'm a teacher and I realize that the definition of learning is finally knowing something after several exposures. The definition of teaching is improved repetitions. Now, should I say that again? Of course!

| Day 175 | I really opened up a can of worms. But, even though it's an old gag, I laughed with the student who caught me and those who witnessed it. I couldn't rest, though, until we caught someone else.

| Day 176 | The world will be changed because of me. Either because of my knack or because of my lack, the world will be the same no more. This would be true if I were a construction worker, a plumber, an astronaut or computer analyst. The ripple effect of the way I handle my job and my life will continue long after I have passed this way. Oh, but I am a teacher. The waters are deeper, the ripples are more plentiful, more impactful and farther-reaching. My singular influence affects 30, today; 300 tomorrow; 3,000 through the years, and depending upon what particular students get me, and do with what they get, perhaps 3 million over time. I have said the world will be changed by me. I have not said that the change will be good or bad (that may depend on the teaching I do this very day).

| Day 177 | Soon we will meet the "crack babies" in our classrooms. We can exert our energies condemning their parents or

teaching the children. Let us teach. We will encounter an AIDS-infected family. We can curse the scourge and gossip about the source. Or, we can teach—even teaching toward prevention and coping. Let us teach.

We will soon meet the children of a violence-prone, arrogant generation who will be parents on whom we cannot depend because of attitudes shaped today. We can ignore the signs, refuse to prepare or change, or seek to remove ourselves before things really get rough. Or, we can determine that few people in the world are equipped to do what we do, and we owe it to the rest of the world to teach and teach well. We must prepare for a tomorrow that may try every nerve within us.

But, even as we look to, and prepare for tomorrow let us not forget that much of what we anticipate is, unfortunately, already here. Let us teach, now, and teach well. So well, in fact, that we erase many of the signs that portend a bleak future. We can win. Let us teach.

| Day 178 | Remember sitting in a class that had you so confused that you didn't ask questions because you couldn't figure out which question(s) to ask? Wouldn't it have been great if the teacher had, somehow, known there was someone like that in the class, and decided to make things easier or sought out that student? Well, now you're the teacher. Find that student.

| Day 179 | The school where you teach is your professional clothing. How do you look? Your school image bears your signature. Are you proud to sign your name?

The building where you practice your profession is a book to be read by residents of the community it serves. Are you on the bestseller list? Do all you can do to appear excellent. The best way to do that is to be excellent.

| Day 180 | Have you ever wondered why students "bother" you so much between classes and before and after school?

Worrisome, ain't it? Now, how would you feel if no student ever bothered you? H-m-m-m-m-m-m-m-m.

Day 181 When the going gets tough—at least you're still going.

Day 182 There is a new teacher in your school—if not new, newer than you. Five years from now it would be nice to have that teacher thank you for being so kind and so helpful in the early years; especially if the kindness is extended because you remember your early years.

Day 183 Teachers who had tremendous influence on me are teachers whose names I remember: Lucille Montgomery, James Collins, Isaac Clark, Carol Bozeman, Virginia Lewis, James Price, Mrs. Woodley, Mrs. Huggins, Mrs. Scott....

Now, does anybody know your name?

Day 184 I have no personal relationships with professional basketball players, but I pay to see them play and cheer them on until I lose my voice. I am not close to world-recognized statesmen and stateswomen, but I quote them and give them credit for influencing my point of view. I don't know any game show hosts or situation comedy stars, but (almost) every evening I turn them on that they might turn me on. I know my students and see them everyday. I think it's time to cheer them, quote them credit and turn them on. This, too, should turn me on.

Day 185 It was great to see Finis Henderson III at Xanie's Comedy Club in Chicago. He is the closest entertainer to Sammy Davis, Jr. I've seen. He is a complete entertainer and should go a long way in the business: a L-o-o-o-o-o-o-n-n-n-g way.

I mention Finis because he was in my 7th grade class at Douglas Elementary School on 32nd and Calumet. He seems to have reached his potential, and he is still reaching for more. I am sure he had that potential even when he was in my class. Wish I had been kinder, then. Will I see another Finis in my class, today? Second chance.

Day 186   The God of all life sees the maze we are in as we seek to know what the end shall bring. The advantage God has is seeing the whole maze and knowing the end. I pray that I will receive clear directions. Our students are in a maze. The advantage we have over our students is seeing the entire maze and knowing the likely end, based upon our experiences and observing their habits. I pray that we will give clear directions.

Day 187   It is a sad reality—statistics reveal—that children and teens are losing their very lives everyday in, often, tragic ways. If we knew that one we shall encounter, this day, faced imminent tragedy how compassionate might we be?

If we knew such tragedy could be avoided, what counsel would we give? With what urgency would we guide?

That's if we knew they faced imminent danger.

Question: How do we know they don't?

Day 188   Ask your class to please observe a moment of silence.

Day 189   How many students in your class need/wear glasses? How many are hearing impaired? Who are the students needing "special" motivational attention? What percentage of students in your school come from homes below poverty level? Who, in your class, is especially sensitive or fragile? Who is helped by criticism? Who is hurt by too many compliments? Would you characterize your class (or classes in secondary situations) as "conversational," "traditional" (i.e., listen, discuss, test), quiet, or "demonstrative" in their collective learning style? How well do you know your students, the learners? How well do you know yourself, the teacher? It pays to know.

Day 190   To teach an object lesson does not mean throwing an object at a student's head. Let us be compassionate, not combative; convincing, not condemning; inviting, not indicting; personable, not personal; encouraging, not critical. The best object lesson is to object to fear—believe in my students and myself.

Day 191   The simple truth is always best.

Day 192   Mark my words.

Give them low grades when they are unclear, mean, too loud, or profane.

Mark them excellent when my words are words to live by; first, for me, then for my students.

Day 193   Have you heard of "expectaphobia?" That is a teachers fear of expecting too much from their "poor," "unprepared" students. After all, how can we expect students to learn coming from "those" backgrounds? Well, lemme "ax" you somethin'? Where did you come from? What did folks expect of YOU? What is YOUR background? Well, you made it, didn't you? Everybody can't be a teacher! Now, expect even more from your students. I mean that!

Day 194   Who will carry the torch of leadership into tomorrow? The student you light a fire under today.

Day 195   The school year is coming to an end. Perhaps, now, I can relax. But, for some student, life begins in my class, today. I'd better not relax, too much.

Day 196   Dum-dum-dum-dum-dumdodooby-dum/Dum-dum-dum-dum-dumbedooby dum/dum-dum-dum-dum-dumbedooby-dum-wah, wah, wah, wah-o-o-h-h.

["Come Go With Me"—Del Vikings/1950s]

boom

Lip dip dip dip dip dip dip dip boom boom boom

["Get A Job"—Silhouettes/1950s]
Uh-uh-uh! Good God! Hit me! Uhn-Uhn! Two
times! Watch Me! Nah! Maceo! Three Times!
["Anything"—James Brown/1960s]
Hey, ain't today's rap music crazy!?

| Day 197 | Do not weep for those you did not try to help.

| Day 198 | One of the country's greatest race car drivers
decided to take a "busman's holiday" and drive home to Indiana
from a triumphant tour on the West Coast. With trophies in the
trunk and his sleek, efficient, race car on a trailer, this driver
began his homebound journey in San Bernadino, California.

He seized opportunities to view the land, and
being wise, he stopped frequently for rest. He was a pro. He
observed, as he drove, drivers being ticketed in various states for
exceeding the speed limit and he could not help but wonder why
anyone would want to speed on the highway. Speeding was for
racetracks. His trailer and trophies were testimony to that. The
man was a pro.

On two occasions, one in Nevada and one in
Nebraska, he saw serious accidents. In brief conversations with
state patrol officers, he was told, in each instance that the accidents occurred due to driver negligence. He did not gloat. He
simply wished that we'd all be more careful. He was willing to
teach driver safety. After all, he was a pro.

Finally, he approached home. A "hero's welcome"
awaited. After having triumphed in competition, then seeing all
he saw on the way back home, he could finally relax. he was
three blocks away from his home where he grew up. And, for a
split second enjoyed taking in that age-old tree where he carved
the initials of his "first love" (he was too shy to carve his own

next to hers). In that split-second, just three blocks from home, as he relaxed his professional demeanor, a small child came out to wave. Not seeing the child, the driver hit him. The child died.

After being professionally triumphant and safe, a hero's brief let down at the end of his journey resulted in the loss of a child who idolized him.

Hey, don't start feeling sad as that was some stuff I made up.

But, with just three days left in this school year, will my professional "let down" result in the loss of a child who "idolizes" me?

| Day 199 | Today could be the last chance you have to tell your students you love them.

Will it feel kinda funny? Well, it won't seven years from now if you start the tradition today.

| Day 200 | CONGRATULATIONS!

About the Author

Carl R. Boyd began teaching in September of 1964, after graduating from Chicago Teachers' College in June of that year.

In his second year of teaching at Douglas Elementary School (7th and 8th grade science) he was awarded an outstanding service award by his peers. This was the first of several teaching awards received by Mr. Boyd, including Chicago's Citizens' Schools Committee Dedicated Teacher Of The Year (1973) Award, and, even an award from peers at J. S. Chick Elementary School in Kansas City, Missouri after only six weeks of service at that school in 1980.

Carl was the Chicago Director of Operation PUSH's PUSH-EXCEL Program from 1977 until 1979, and after substitute teaching in Kansas City he worked with the School Advisory Assistance Center at Kansas City's Learning Exchange.

While continuing to work in one of Kansas City's local high schools, Carl's consultant duties take him across the country where he addresses tens of thousands of educators: from Naples, Maine to San Bernadino, California; from Granger, Washington to Conway, South Carolina.

Mr. Boyd was the first recipient of the Brown (vs. Topeka) Foundation Excellence In Education Award in June, 1989.

Carl has served as a presenter for annual I/D/E/A Fellows Institutes for administrators, and presided over the 1991 At-Risk conference.

In addition to his work in the classroom, and with school district administrators, Carl Boyd serves as national consultant to the National Crime Prevention Council, Board Member of the Brown Foundation, Province Chairman of Kappa Alpha Psi Fraternity's Guide Right Program, and police academy panelist for the Kansas City, Missouri Police Department. Carl also hosts a weekly radio call-in talk show for teens, called "The Generation Rap", on KPRS-FM Radio (103.3), Kansas City.

ORDER DIRECT 1-800-347-BOOK

☐ YES, I want ___ copies of **PLAIN TEACHING** for $15.95 plus $3.50 shipping.

Method of payment

☐ Check for $_____ to:
Westport Publishers
4050 Pennsylvania Ave.
Kansas City, MO 64111

Ship to: _____
_____
_____
_____

☐ Charge my credit card

☐ Visa   ☐ MasterCard

Account # _____
Exp. Date _____
Signature _____
Phone # _____

ORDER DIRECT 1-800-347-BOOK

☐ YES, I want ___ copies of **PLAIN TEACHING** for $15.95 plus $3.50 shipping.

Method of payment

☐ Check for $_____ to:
Westport Publishers
4050 Pennsylvania Ave.
Kansas City, MO 64111

Ship to: _____
_____
_____
_____

☐ Charge my credit card

☐ Visa   ☐ MasterCard

Account # _____
Exp. Date _____
Signature _____
Phone # _____